THE WRITINGS OF
WILL ROGERS
II

SPONSORED BY

The Will Rogers Memorial Commission
and Oklahoma State University

THE WRITINGS OF WILL ROGERS

SERIES I: *Books of Will Rogers*
1 *Ether and Me, or "Just Relax"*
2 *There's Not a Bathing Suit in Russia & Other Bare Facts*
3 *The Illiterate Digest*
4 *The Cowboy Philosopher on The Peace Conference*
5 *The Cowboy Philosopher on Prohibition*
6 *Letters of a Self-Made Diplomat to His President*

SERIES II: Convention Articles of Will Rogers (in one volume)

SERIES III: *Daily Telegrams of Will Rogers*
Vol. 1 1926-1928
Vol. 2 1929-1932
Vol. 3 1933-1935 (Index Vols. 1, 2, 3)

SERIES IV: *Weekly Articles of Will Rogers* (in four volumes)

SERIES V: *The Worst Story I've Heard Today* (in one volume)

OTHER VOLUMES TO BE ANNOUNCED

WILL ROGERS MEMORIAL COMMISSION

Raymond W. Knight, *Chairman*
James C. Leake
Roy G. Cartwright
Edward L. Byrd
Irving Fisher
Harry Hoagland
Will Rogers, Jr.
Governor David Boren, *ex-officio*

MEMORIAL STAFF

Reba Neighbors Collins, Curator
Delmar Collins, Manager

SPECIAL CREDIT

The late Paula McSpadden Love
Curator, 1938-73

OSU ADVISORY COMMITTEE

Odie B. Faulk, *Chairman*
E. Moses Frye
Marvin T. Edmison
George A. Gries
John W. Hamilton
Howard R. Jarrell
Roscoe Rouse
President Robert B. Kamm, *ex-officio*

EDITORIAL CONSULTANTS

Ray B. Browne, *Bowling Green State University*
LeRoy H. Fischer, *Oklahoma State University*
Wilbur R. Jacobs, *University of California, Santa Barbara*
Howard R. Lamar, *Yale University*
Russel B. Nye, *Michigan State University*

WILL ROGERS and PATRICK J. HURLEY, U. S. secretary of war, discuss the national political scene, 1931. *(Courtesy Will Rogers Memorial, Claremore, Oklahoma)*

CONVENTION ARTICLES of Will Rogers

Joseph A. Stout, Jr., *Editor*

Peter C. Rollins, *Assistant Editor*

OKLAHOMA STATE UNIVERSITY PRESS
Stillwater, Oklahoma
1976

Note to scholars: The convention articles are reproduced here with permission of the Will Rogers Memorial Commission, Claremore, Oklahoma, and The Rogers Company, Beverly Hills, California. The scholarly apparatus and notes in this volume are copyrighted and the usual rules about the use of copyrighted material apply.

International Standard Book Number 0-914956-08-6

Library of Congress Catalog Card Number 76-5609

Printed in the United States of America

CONTENTS

INTRODUCTION

Will Rogers thoroughly enjoyed political conventions. He was paid to write incisive and humorous comments about the national conventions of 1920, 1924, 1928, and 1932, but his wife said he used his job as an excuse to attend. She once commented about the conventions saying that "nothing could have kept him away from one." Rogers actually attended only the last three conventions, for during both conventions of 1920 he was unable to be there in person. The tragedy of the death of his son Fred Stone Rogers and other obligations precluded his attendance that year.

The conventions included in this volume are arranged chronologically; historical and personal introductions precede each of Rogers' efforts, and end notes explain people or occurences no longer widely known. The introductory sections provide the necessary background for understanding why the humorist said many of the things he did.

All of these convention articles appeared as daily "telegrams" or "articles." However, newspapers did not print all releases. In addition, individual editors changed slightly each article. As only notes and no complete manuscripts exist for these releases, we have chosen the best available text as the basis for the article to be printed. We have attempted also to show one major textual difference. For the variation we have used the *Tulsa Daily World* or *Oklahoma News,* for both carried most articles. We have noted variations in cases only when an editor changed Rogers' intent. Occasionally we have shown a variation which has been made for stylistic or grammatical reasons. For the Conventions of 1920 we have used the News Enterprise Association "tear sheets" as the primary article. Variations are based upon the *Oklahoma News.*

This volume, Series II in the *Writings of Will Rogers,* has required considerable effort on the part of a number of people. Reba Neighbors Collins, Curator of the Will Rogers Memorial, actually discovered several of the articles when researching her doctoral dissertation. She also gave additional help with the introductions and notes. Elwyn Isaacs of Claremore Junior College, Colleen Coatman, Bonnie J. Slavens, and Teresa A. Mathews typed, researched, and read galleys. Glenn D. Shirley's design of all the Will Rogers books has enhanced the project.

Finally, special appreciation is expressed for the continued support of the Will Rogers Memorial Commission, the Oklahoma State University Regents, administration, and advisory committee, the Oklahoma Historical Society, and the Oklahoma Legislature. Earlier in the project Kerr-McGee foundation, Phillips Petroleum Corporation, Mr. and Mrs. Robert Love, and Mrs. T. S. Loffland provided assistance.

The Editors

PREFACE

Without challenge, Will Rogers is the most enduring humorist and most incisive political satirist of the past century. It is entirely appropriate in this bicentennial period for his writings to be resurrected and recirculated for the enlightenment and delight of those millions who feel that our present political world is hopelessly bent out of shape.

The insights inculcated in these columns are as pertinent to today's political scene as in the days before air-conditioned convention halls, jet travel, television commentators and legal liquor. The reader can easily superimpose present-day names and current issues and find that Will's political wisdom is timeless. For the foibles and failures, as well as the genius inherent in our political system, survive little change. Only the outward appearances have taken on more of an element of emergency.

Will's gift to our times is to provide a sense of perspective. His accounts of political events and political figures of half a century ago give us a benchmark against which to measure present-day performance. His insights into the conduct of nominating conventions, and the antics of presidential and vice-presidential candidates, as well as senators, governors and party functionaries, are perhaps the finest status reports available to the layman of politics, vintage 1920-32.

Currently when politics has deservedly reached a new low in public esteem, these "re-runs" of Will Rogers will furnish a welcome leavening in a political loaf which is rapidly becoming too heavy to be palatable or healthy for either the nation or our representative system.

Henry Bellmon
United States Senator
Oklahoma

CONVENTION ARTICLES OF WILL ROGERS

II

REPUBLICAN CONVENTION OF 1920

Theodore Roosevelt died during 1919 and nine months later President Woodrow Wilson suffered a serious stroke, leaving the country without obvious presidential candidates for the election of 1920. Isolationism was the prevalent mood of the people who were tired of war, international intrigue, and domestic unrest. Thus, when the Republican party analyzed its position, it discovered that there was no obvious or strong candidate for the presidency. Several potential candidates existed, for Roosevelt had said that, if he were not a candidate, he would support General Leonard Wood. Wood seemed the heir apparent to the Roosevelt prestige, and the general had enjoyed a well-publicized military career.

Wood campaigned in uniform, surrounded by military aids, and steadfastly supported continued military preparedness. He attacked "reds" and the League of Nations; the latter he accused of being too idealistic, for he insisted that no such organization could ever prevent war. When pressured by progressives in the party, Wood first refused to relate his beliefs on economics and welfare, but eventually he admitted that he favored the repeal of the excess profits tax, and protective tariffs, and he supported economy in government. Wood soon learned that he was out of step with the times; he forgot that women, whose sons had fought and died in the recent war, would be voting for the first time and they would not support a military candidate. Nevertheless, he stubbornly refused to change his position.

Wood had no real political experience. He chose John King, a Connecticut national committeeman, to manage his campaign, but refused to give King sufficient power. King quickly resigned, and thereafter Colonel William Proctor assumed direction of the campaign. He spent huge sums of money in a nationwide campaign that alienated Wood supporters in most of the states.

Other candidates existed within the party. Frank Lowden, Governor of Illinois, seemed a viable choice. In congress for two terms, his career had not been distinguished. Yet he was elected governor in 1916, and proved to be an excellent choice to lead the state. He was an apt organizer, worked well with party, business, and labor leaders, and acquired few enemies. Lowden said little about the League of Nations, and he astutely avoided the red hysteria sweeping the country. He did offend some of the "big city bosses," for he was an avowed "dry" on the prohibition issue.

There was only one real progressive candidate within the Republican party, and that was Senator Hiram Johnson of California. However, Johnson absolutely opposed the League of Nations, and this position cost him many of the liberal votes he would have gotten. During the campaign his position became increasingly nationalistic, bringing him more in line with the Wood forces; but those conservatives would have no part of him for fear of his apparent progressivism in domestic affairs.

For many years several myths about the Republican convention of 1920 have existed, but little truth surrounds most of these stories. Some people have assumed incorrectly that Warren G. Harding was a dark-horse candidate who unexpectedly won the nomination. Harding was fifty-four years old and was completing his first term as senator from Ohio. Harry M. Daugherty, an Ohio politician, had pushed Harding for the Senate in 1914, and he realized that the only way he could enjoy the fruits of political power was to place Harding in the presidency. In 1919 Harding entered several primaries and the party response was favorable. Boies Penrose, Pennsylvania senator and a party leader, wanted to use Harding's candidacy to stop Wood and Lowden from winning.

Daugherty started a myth about Harding's nomination in 1920, when he allegedly told a reporter for the *New York Times* that he did not expect that his candidate would be nominated on the first ballot, perhaps not even after the third ballot, but that around 2:00 a.m. on the morning of the convention about fifteen or twenty men would be sitting at a table and someone would ask who should be nominated. At that instant, according to the report of Daugherty's prediction, someone would say that the party should nominate Harding. This was the origin of the "smoke-filled room" story. Daugherty did not make the statement as the *New York Times* reporter stated, but he did say something similar while trying to get away from the ambitious reporter.

There were several favorite son and dark horse candidates. Calvin Coolidge, governor of Massachusetts who had broken up the Boston police strike thereby winning national acclaim, was one such hopeful. William Allen White supported Henry Allen, Governor of Kansas, and Boies Penrose supported Philander C. Knox; the rest of the Pennsylvania delegation supported Governor William C. Sproul. New York's favorite son was Dr. Nicholas M. Butler, while several other well-known senators in the country championed their own candidates. A true dark horse candidate was Herbert Hoover of California, the former United States food administrator. Eventually Hoover entered the California primary as a Republican, but lost to Hiram Johnson.

General Leonard Wood entered more primaries than any one, and he employed more money to acquire the nomination (about $1.5 million). Lowden's campaign was not as well financed, but he spent $400,000 out of his own pocket. He printed campaign literature, but forbade paid advertising as being an effort that degraded the presidency. When all the state primaries were completed, Wood seemed the winner. He had amassed 124 convention delegates to Johnson's 112, Lowden's 72, and Harding's 39. Johnson was the popular choice and Harding trailed so far that he seemed virtually eliminated. Complicating matters even more before the convention, the Republicans began fighting among themselves. Senator Johnson heard of Wood's enormous campaign expenditures and asked that Senator Borah begin investigations on campaign practices and expenditures. All of this party bickering resulted in Johnson's being politically ruined; Wood and Lowden's prospects were severely damaged. An ensuing Senate investigation revealed that Wood had spent $1,500,000—a sum large enough to indicate to some people that the candidate was trying to buy the election. In addition, some question arose about Lowden's contribution to two St. Louis men who mysteriously had become Lowden delegates. Although Lowden was never proven guilty of any illegal practices, his presidential chances were destroyed. In effect, Wood, Lowden, and Johnson all were discredited, and thus the party was forced to select a minor candidate. Harry Daugherty had waited patiently for the correct time to push his candidate; he had no doubt that Harding would be the beneficiary of the party squabble.

The Republican national convention began in Chicago on June 8, 1920. This was a convention in which business, industry, and finance were most influential and closely involved in the final choice of candidates. Edward L. Doheny, Jake Hamon, and Harry F. Sinclair supported the oil industry. Cornelius Vanderbilt was present as was Elbert M. Gary supporting the steel interests in the country. Publisher George Harvey and four Morgan partners also were present; they manipulated votes. Henry Cabot Lodge, who had opposed the Versailles Treaty, was appointed temporary chairman; William Hays became permanent leader during the convention. For the first two days the delegates heard speeches on matters of all types while committees drafted a noncommittal platform.

Nominations began on Friday morning when Governor Allen placed General Wood's name in nomination. Wood's speech was uninspiring, but his delegates put on a forty-two minute demonstration after he finished. Frank Lowden was next placed in nomination, and the resulting forty-five minute demonstration was equally noisy. Charles Stetson Wheeler of California nominated Hiram Johnson in a disastrous fashion, reopening many of the party's old wounds and exposing the divisiveness of Johnson's candidacy. The resulting thirty-seven minute demonstration did not offset the error.

Thereafter Nicholas Murray Butler, Herbert Hoover, Calvin Coolidge, and others were nominated. Frank B. Willis of Ohio nominated Harding with a folksy and humorous speech; the ten minute ovation was warm and friendly. The first ballot showed just how divided the convention really was, for no candidate received enough votes even to approach winning the nomination. Several delegates, trying to stop Wood, gave some of their votes to Lowden on the first ballot. Senatorial leaders who wanted to stop the General made deals to release votes on the second ballot. Yet through four ballots Wood slowly gained votes. Then through a bit of parliamentary chicanery old guard Senators—all opposing Wood—forced an adjournment of the convention without roll call votes. During the night of June 11-12 deals were made, and the smoke-filled room myth was born. Out of the night's dealings Harding emerged as the man to support. When the Convention assembled for a fifth ballot, the air was rife with rumors that the task was all but done—Harding was the party's man. Yet the balloting had to be manipulated. Harding gained through the seventh ballot, while Lowden and Wood remained tied. It was on the eighth ballot that Wood's chances for nomination disappeared. Some of his delegates along with a few of Lowden's suddenly switched to Harding.

The chicanery was not yet over, for just at this critical time some powerful Senators attempted to nominate Hays, the national committee chairman. Actually, these men had planned to do so all along when they thought that the two leading candidates were defeated. Their efforts failed, however, as they underestimated Harding's fast growing support. During the recess that followed, Wood and Lowden cooperated to try to turn the convention away from Harding, but they were not able to stop the landslide that was being manipulated behind the scenes. When the convention met for the ninth ballot, Kansas—whose delegates had caucused during the recess—changed its position and cast all twenty votes for Harding; thereafter the other necessary votes to win nomination fell in place. On the tenth ballot Harding swept to victory, and on the floor Calvin Coolidge was nominated for vice president and approved by a landslide vote.

Harding's presidency was ill fated, however, for in 1923, amid revelations of widespread corruption in his administration, he suddenly died. Calvin Coolidge succeeded him, and would seek to become president in his own right during the elections of 1924.

φ φ φ φ

Already recognized as a political commentator for his droll remarks on current events from the vaudeville stage and his performances with the Ziegfeld Follies—remarks that were frequently picked up by newspaper columnists or repeated by persons of such prestige as President Woodrow Wilson—it is not surprising that Will Rogers was asked to "cover" the political conventions of 1920. What is rather surprising is that he managed to write the daily articles without attending the conventions.

In June, 1919, Will Rogers with his family and his horses had moved from the rented home on Long Island to southern California where he would continue his fledgling career in motion pictures. He had been traveling with the Ziegfeld Follies, earning $750 a week for his fifteen minutes of rope twirling and humor amid the beautiful Follies girls; yet he was so unhappy at having to be away from his growing family for weeks at a time that when Samuel Goldwyn tendered an offer that would double his salary the first year and triple it the next, he could not refuse. Most attractive to him was the opportunity to live in California, remain at home more often, and establish a permanent home for the first time in his fast-moving career. He had made his first film, *Laughing Bill Hyde* in 1918 while he was still appearing in the Follies in New York. In California he quickly made three more silents before the end of 1919, and he was in the middle of filming his eighth one in June 1920 when the conventions began. In addition to the Goldwyn pictures, he was also writing and making weekly comments for Pathe Films in a short feature called "The Illiterate Digest."

Writing was not entirely new to Rogers, but covering the political conventions was a new venture, one he definitely enjoyed. The "Goldwyn Clip Sheet" for June 26, 1920, boasted that Will Rogers had the honor of being the first motion picture actor ever invited to report a political convention. But the article stated, "He hasn't been to Chicago at all. He has been at the Goldwyn studio in Culver City working away on *Cupid the Cowpuncher.* Rogers saw nothing strange about his absence, and he remarked:

> I've heard a lot about "absent treatments," and that is what I'm giving this convention. You don't have to hear somebody say a thing to know it. Why, I'll bet any typewriter—I'm referring to the machine and not the blonde who runs it—which had lived through a convention or two, could just automatically run off the speeches, including the "applause" and "wild cheering for twenty minutes." Whether anybody but the guy who makes the speech ever reads it is a matter I've thought about a lot. Probably his wife reads it and, of course, if he has a doting old maid aunt, she cuts it out and puts it in the family Bible.
>
> But why make a fuss about my not going to the convention? I've known a bunch of newspaper men in my time and I always noticed that the way they "covered" their assignments was to stand with one foot on a brass rail and then call up the office every now and then to say they'd not been able to get all the dope, but they'd have it soon. Of course the going out of fashion of the brass rail may account for the fact that I'm the only absentee reporter, anyway. If I was there, I might find out a fact now and then, and that would upset me terribly.
>
> Much better just to drool along by the law which says the red won't win always, but that the black also will have its innings. I'm bound to hit it right now and then. If I had too high a batting average, the real reporters might agitate for a closed shop.

From advanced promotional material which Newspaper Enterprise Association mailed on May 29, 1920, it was clear that Rogers had agreed to write the articles. In full newspaper-size advertising sheets, NEA promised subscribers to the syndicated articles at least ten jokes a day by the "FAMOUS OKLAHOMA COWBOY HUMORIST AND GOLDWYN MOTION PICTURE COMEDIAN" who was "THE MOST WITTY WRITER IN THE LAND." Will Rogers, the sheet promised, would "POKE FUN AT THE CONVENTION DOINGS DAY BY DAY." Heading for the syndicated articles was "WILL ROGERS SAYS"—the same one used by McNaught Syndicate when they began his daily articles in 1926. Whether or not he originally agreed to attend the convention in Chicago is not known. A later dispatch which NEA sent explained that Rogers would not be able to attend due to the death of his son; however, he would fulfill his agreement and furnish the articles as promised. This would indicate that NEA had expected him to be attending in person.

This was a tragic period in the life of the Rogers family. The three boys—Will, Jr., Jimmy and little Fred Stone Rogers—all contracted sore throats. Mrs. Rogers thought at first it was tonsilitis. Rogers was on location making a movie, and she hated to bother him. Then she suddenly learned the children had the dreaded diptheria; on June 17, young Freddie Rogers died. He was not quite two years old.

Stricken with grief, Rogers was unable to talk about the loss, and he probably was glad to use the production of a picture as an excuse for not going to the conventions. Nevertheless, he did write the articles, getting his information from the daily papers. These writings have an amazing on-the-scene ring, even though the emotionally distressed Rogers remained in California.

His style of reporting in 1920 closely resembled the collection of "gags" or jokes he used on stage, in the *Illiterate Digest* for Pathe, and in the first two books of "Rogersisms,"—*The Cowboy Philosopher on the Peace Conference* and *The Cowboy Philosopher on Prohibition.* Although his style of writing began to flow more smoothly only after he began his weekly columns in December of 1922, some of his devices for humor remain evident in these writings.

He presented himself as a confidant and jester to men in power, personalizing those who too often seemed beyond public reach. And there was some truth in this: he did know many of the men personally, and he had long called them by their first names or nicknames from the stage. He was merely shifting the scene of his humor from stage and screen to newsprint.

In order to appear to be in the midst of the action during the Republican convention in Chicago, without actually misleading his readers, Rogers pretended to be in Philadelphia with powerful Senator Boies Penrose, long known as the Republican boss of the Keystone state and a leader in the national party. The general public suspected that presidential nominations were actually made by leaders behind the scenes, and Rogers could play on that feeling by his pretense at being with Penrose.

Despite the fact that Penrose was seriously ill at this time, there were two "wires" into his bedroom in Philadelphia—one telephone and one telegraph line—and messages concerning events in Chicago were sent to him. Whether he received them or was able to influence the convention to any extent from his sickbed is a moot point. But by using this device, Rogers could be excused for not reporting certain facts that only a person at the convention would know, and still the Oklahoma humorist could give readers his comic reports. By addressing him as good old "Penny" or just "Pen," making up questions that the man-on-the-street might ask, and providing answers from "Penny," he gave his readers the "inside dope" on what was happening.

Using another term familiar to his readers in 1920, Rogers compared the entire Republican convention to "Chautauquas"—a type of summer program, sometimes held in large tents and lasting for days—that were made popular by such speakers as William Jennings Bryan. By comparing it to a form of entertainment, he was able to bring it down to the average reader's level. Yet his "gags" could unmask political rhetoric and reveal hypocrisy.

In his comic role, Rogers could clarify statements of party representatives. For example, instead of crediting Henry Cabot Lodge with giving an argument of merit, Rogers merely reported it as a form of empty Republican litany, reducing it to ideological differences on foreign policy between Wilson and Lodge. Through his imaginary dialogue with Penrose, Rogers made the astute point that the only viable issue the Republicans could exploit in 1920 was the sour feeling toward President Wilson which the settlement of World War I and Wilson's unpopular attempts to lead the United States into world alignment through the League of Nations had generated. Rogers realized that the anti-Wilson rhetoric employed by the Republicans was their best issue for gaining the White House, and he was able to show its comic excesses and partially deflate its rhetorical power.

(Texts for the following articles are from the News Enterprise Association "tear sheets." No consistent publication dates for the articles could be found. Variations are from the *Oklahoma News* OKN.—The Editors)

NEA, June, 1920

Article #1 Republican Convention

WILL ROGERS SAYS: "CHICAGO'S ONLY ONE OF TWO CITIES BIG ENOUGH TO HOLD ALL OF G. O. P. CANDIDATES"

By Will Rogers (Famous Oklahoma Cowboy Wit and Goldwyn Motion Picture Star.) [1]

I am being paid to write something funny about this Republican convention. That's funny.

* * *

All a fellow has to do to write something funny on a Republican convention is just write what happened.

* * *

Chauncey Depew[2] and I were about the last to decide to write. Chauncey has the advantage of me. He knows his jokes are good 'cause he has told them for years.

* * *

The convention is starting out with a big setback. A carload of champagne from California billed for Chicago for medicinal purposes was held up.[3]

* * *

In the first place the convention is to be held in Chicago. Chicago is located just north of the United States. I am well acquainted with the American consul there.

* * *

Chicago holds the record for murders and robberies and Republican conventions.

* * *

The Republicans had to hold their convention either in Chicago or New York this year as no other city was big enough to hold all their candidates.[4]

* * *

Mexico don't know how to get rid of Villa. Loan him to us for a Vice-President. That would get both nations rid of him.[5]

* * *

If the Republicans split as they did eight years ago everybody better start preparing to be kept out of another war.

* * *

They don't know whether to seat the colored delegates or not. If they do it will be far back near the door.

* * *

To show you true democracy will rule the convention, the first thing they did was to throw out two delegates the people had elected.

* * *

The Democrats are investigating the Republican slush funds and if they find where it's coming from they want theirs.[6]

NEA, published June, 1920

Article #2 Republican Convention

CONVENTION GAGS

By Will Rogers (Unbranded Oklahoma Cowboy Humorist and Famous Goldwyn Motion Picture Star)[7]

It looks like the way candidates are spending money it will finally be John D. Rockefeller who will be nominated.[8]

* * *

Lowden[9] offered every delegate in Missouri a Pullman car.[10]

* * *

Congress is investigating these slush funds. So that means nothing will be done about it.

* * *

Imagine a Congress that squanders $670,000,000 to make one airship,[11] trying to investigate where some candidate spent a few thousand.[12]

* * *

You know delegates are only elected every four years, and as very few of them do anything between times, you see they really are not charging too much.

* * *

In these times when our votes are seldom counted anyway, I think we should be allowed to get all we can for them.

* * *

Prohibition is to blame for the whole thing. Votes have not advanced. It is the commodity that we buy the votes with that caused so much money to be spent.

* * *

It took Johnson one whole wing of a cellar to land the California delegation.[13]

* * *

So many of Wood's[14] delegates have been thrown out, I guess he will get most of his money back.[15]

* * *

One quart of Old Crow in the National Committee room will seat more delegates than all the voters in the world.

* * *

A week ago the Republicans thought they could win with anybody. Now they can't find anybody they think they can win with.

* * *

Wood started in with two or three hundred delegates but by the time the convention starts he will be lucky if they do not take his army commission.[16]

* * *

De Valera says he wishes they could raise as money for presidential candidates in Ireland as they do here.[17]

NEA, June, 1920

Articles #3 and #4 Republican Convention

CONVENTION GAGS

By Will Rogers (Unbranded Oklahoma Cowboy Humorist and Famous Goldwyn Motion Picture Star)[18]

CHICAGO, June 6.—California's 26 delegates to the Chicago convention were accompanied by sixty bootleggers.

* * *

As these delegates were elected by the people the chances are they will be unseated before they reach Denver.

* * *

I see where they are cutting a lot of delegates down to half a vote. Guess they will let the half-a-vote delegates nominate the vice-president.

* * *

The South was going to send some white delegates but they didn't have any.[19]

* * *

To show they were real Republican strongholds two Southern States found delegates of both sides.[20]

* * *

There are several States in the South where the Negroes are allowed a vote but only one where it's ever counted.

* * *

As far as qualifications go, I think Knox[21] has the most suitable name for an American President, especially at this time.

* * *

Speaking of Knox, I see where the whole convention is getting superstitious and beginning to knock Wood.

* * *

They will mess around a week, and about next Thursday or Friday Penrose[22] will tell 'em who's nominated.

* * *

(NOTE: Some newspapers split this article here to make two articles)

The California delegation took a carload of California poppies to scatter in Chicago. They figure on catching the dope fiend vote which is very large this year.

* * *

Suppose the Kentucky delegation will bring some tobacco leaves and try and land the nicotine vote.

* * *

When Hiram Johnson arrived in Chicago he bowed and started to make a speech, when someone reminded him that the demonstration was for Babe Ruth.[23]

* * *

On Johnson's arrival he pulled the old gag which is always good; "Friends, if I am elected I will be for the common people." Yea, bo!

* * *

Penrose is for some guy named Sproul.[24] If he is nominated I hope Penrose introduces him to the crowd as no one there ever saw or heard of him.

* * *

De Valera, the president of our sister republic, Ireland, is a convention visitor. He is returning the visit President Wilson paid to Europe.[25]

* * *

If Penrose has a dark horse and he is from Pennsylvania he must be from Pittsburg.

* * *

Women delegates have been asked to remove their spring hats in the convention hall so their trip has been practically spoiled.

NEA, June, 1920

Article #5 Republican Convention

PENROSE TIPS WILL ROGERS WHO'LL BE NOMINEE AT CHI, BUT BILL WON'T TELL Y'SEE, HE DOESN'T WANT TO SPOIL THE SHOW AND MAKE THE HOTELS FEEL BAD.

By Will Rogers (Unbranded Oklahoma Cowboy Humorist and Famous Goldwyn Motion Picture Star) [26]

SOMEWHERE IN PENNSYLVANIA, June 7.—When I heard Boise Penrose was not going to Chicago, I decided to steal a march on the other eminent authors and go where the candidate would be nominated. So I came to see Penrose about it.

* * *

When I arrived off Hog Island I was met by that boat they built there. It's finished now.[27]

* * *

Why I came here was, I happened to be in Philadelphia the night of the last presidential election, and saw Penrose and Knox lead the parade for Hughes the one night he was President.[28]

* * *

Now Philadelphia was supposed to be slow, and there it was two days ahead of the facts.

* * *

So, I decided, there is the place to find out who is nominated before Penrose phones it to Chicago.

* * *

You see, I knew Boise Penrose on account of my being in Boise, Idaho, once, the town he was named after.

* * *

He said: "Why, hello, Will, I have heard of Idaho. That's the state Senator Borah is from."[29]

* * *

Now Penrose told me who was nominated, but he asked me not to tip it off, as the hotels and other crooks in Chicago wanted to keep the suckers there a few days till they were thoroughly renovated.

* * *

Boise told me, "You know, Will, your business and mine are alike. We have a few five reel features in politics, but most of them are one and two reel comedies."

* * *

Pen says to me, "For appearance sake, I am for Sproul." Then I asked him, "Who is Sproul?" and he said, "I don't know any more about him than you do, Will, but he was the darkest horse I could think of."

* * *

He has to stop now to phone Chicago what delegates to throw out, but he will give me some more dope on it maybe tomorrow.

NEA, June, 1920

Article #6 Republican Convention

WILL ROGERS SAYS:

By Will Rogers (Unbranded Oklahoma Cowboy Humorist and Famous Goldwyn Motion Picture Star)[30]

SOMEWHERE IN PHILADELPHIA, June 8—The Republican National Convention is being held right here in Philadelphia. Senator Penrose called himself to order this morning.

* * *

I am the only newspaper writer here as all the rest thought the Convention was going to Chicago, but I knew he wasn't.

* * *

I asked him this morning, "Well, Boies, what are you having them do out there today?"

* * *

"Oh, I will just let them pray today. That is the biggest novelty you can pull on a Republican."

* * *

I asked him, "What Republican can read a prayer?"

* * *

He said, "Oh, they will call in some Democrats. They are all praying this year."

* * *

I asked him, "Why did you make them think in Chicago that you were for Sproul?"

* * *

"Well, Will, I will tell you. The only way to keep a Governor from becoming Senator is to sidetrack him off into the Presidency."

* * *

"But," I asked him, "isn't the Presidency higher than Senator?"

* * *

He said, "Why, no; the Senate can make a sucker out of the President—and generally does."

* * *

I asked him, "In the old days didn't candidates stay at home till they were nominated?"

* * *

He said, "Yes, but these fellows know that all they will get out of it is the trip."

* * *

"Then, "I asked him, "what do you think of Johnson?"

* * *

He said, "Will, he would be good in the movies."

* * *

But I told him that talking pictures were not a success.

* * *

I then said: "How about Lowden?"

* * *

He said, "Well, Lowden can get the Pullman vote but what we want is a man that can land the daycoach vote."

* * *

Then I said, "How about Wood?"

* * *

He said, "Wood did all right managing Cuba, but Cuba was not organized and demanding time and a half for overtime."

NEA, June, 1920
Article #7 Republican Convention
WILL ROGERS SAYS:
By Will Rogers (Famous Oklahoma Cowboy Humorist and Goldwyn Motion Picture Star.) [31]

SOMEWHERE IN PHILADELPHIA, June 9. Senator Penrose and me sat here in Philadelphia with phones to our ears and he told them out in Chicago when to start the convention.

* * *

As none of the politicians present knew how to pray, they called in a professional.

* * *

Of course, Mr. Penrose had told them what to pray for.

* * *

Some leading Republicans were against having a prayer this year as they didn't think it necessary. But to add variety to an otherwise monotonous show—they decided to leave it in.

* * *

During that prayer as Pen and me sat in far-off Philly listening he said, "I'll bet that is the longest Johnson ever went without talking."

* * *

The senator seemed quite relieved at the finish when no one applauded as he said, "You never can tell what a Republican will do." And you can't, for they followed the prayer with Dardanella.[32]

* * *

In place of a raise in salary they gave Bill Hays[33] a nice new hammer gavel and told him every time he saw anything that looked like a Democrat to take a wallop at it.

* * *

The next thing we heard over the phone was another prayer. This time by Senator Lodge, who's text was, "Lord bless everybody but Wilson."[34]

* * *

I asked Boies why has he got it in so for Wilson. Boies said, "Lodge is sore because he took Mrs. Wilson to Europe instead of him."

* * *

Then I told Boies, "Why he took one Republican over there with him, didn't he?" Boies said, "Yes, he took one along so he would have someone along to argue with on the way over.[35]

* * *

I said, "But why do you suppose Lodge didn't pray for something to happen to Bryan,[36] too?" Boies said he didn't need to; something happened to him a long time ago.

* * *

I said, "Well, Mr. Penrose, what did you think of Lodge's speech?" He said, "I think it is the best speech I ever wrote."

NEA, June, 1920

Article #8 Republican Convention

CANDIDATES WHO DIDN'T PUT UP HAVEN'T ANY DELEGATES, PENROSE TELLS ROGERS THEY'D HAVE BRYAN ADDRESS THE CONVENTION BUT HE'S RAISED HIS PRICE

By Will Rogers (Unbranded Oklahoma Cowboy Humorist and Famous Goldwyn Motion Picture Star) [37]

"DATE LINE STILL IN PHILADELPHIA." June 10.—Senator Penrose and I didn't have long to listen over our phones today. That's one thing about a Republican Convention—if you happen to catch a day when Senator Lodge isn't speaking they generally turn out early.

* * *

I guess this is about the only chat-aqua[38] ever held in a big city. Lodge told jokes the first day and Chauncey Depew the next.

* * *

I asked Penrose who prayed today. He said: "The audience."[39]

* * *

I asked who will tell jokes tomorrow; he said: "We are trying to get Bryan, but he is trying to hold us up on the price."

* * *

I said: "Chauncey went pretty good with the audience." He said: "Yes, I believe those jokes went better this year than they have in years."

* * *

I asked Pen: "Why don't you run Depew for something?" Boies said: "Oh, he is like Bryan. People will laugh at him, but they won't vote for him."

* * *

I then asked him: "Do you think there will be anything said about nominating anybody for President?" Pen replied: "Well, not at least for the first two or three weeks." He told me he thought the whole thing was just a scheme to hold the people in Chicago till after the next census.

* * *

I asked Pen: "How can you tell who bought delegates? He said: "That's easy, the ones who didn't buy any are the ones who haven't got any."

* * *

I said: "This fellow Sproul you are for—nobody knows anything about him." Pen said: "That's just what makes it so hard to nominate those other Republican candidates; people know too much about them."

* * *

I asked him: "What do you think of Hearst[40] and Johnson?" He said: "They are a couple of Western boys come East with a new act trying to get along."

* * *

I asked Pen: "What do you think of Dr. Leonard Wood?" Boies said: "It will take more than a doctor to do this country any good the shape its in. What we need is a magician."

NEA, June, 1920

Article #9 Republican Convention

PENNY TELLS ROGERS SPEECHES WILL MAYBE BE OVER BY FOURTH OF JULY SO THEY'RE GOING TO FRISCO AND GET BACK TO CHI FOR THE WIND-UP

By Will Rogers (Unbranded Oklahoma Cowboy Humorist and Famous Goldwyn Motion Picture Star) [41]

SOMEWHERE IN PHILADELPHIA, June 11.—Well, Sen. Penrose and I went to sleep with the phones to our ears yesterday waiting for something to happen out at the chat-aqua in Chicago.

* * *

The Republicans sent clear back to Baltimore and brought on Cardinal Gibbons to pray for them.[42]

* * *

I said to Pen: "Why don't somebody tell some more jokes or talk about something?" Pen said: "I guess they have told all they know about Wilson."

* * *

Then I said to him, "Why, surely some of these Republicans must know of a case where he poisoned a well or dynamited an orphan asylum or something."

* * *

Then I asked Boies: "What do you think is responsible for all this delay out there in Chicago," and he said: "Why, Wilson is."

* * *

I asked him: "What do you think of the League of Nations platform they agreed on?" He said: "Oh, I just phoned that suggestion out there. It don't mean anything. I worded is so the delegates think it does. I will switch it all around before election."[43]

* * *

I said: "Do you think Johnson will start a third party?" Boies said: "If he does this will be the most successful convention the Democrats ever held."

* * *

I said to him: "If Johnson was elected it would be a good joke on all these other papers if Hearst turned out to be an American, wouldn't it?"

* * *

I asked Pen: "How does it come the New York delegates are practically uninstructed." Boies remarked to me: "You can't instruct a New Yorker, he knows it all."

* * *

Boies then said to me: "Will, you have just come from out in California. How do you think their delegates will vote?" So I told him: "I think they will vote for Johnson on the first ballot and for climate on all the rest."

* * *

I asked Boise, "Why don't you people nominate Admiral Sims for vice-president and get the Democrats to nominate Secretary Daniels?[44] Then we would hear no more of either one of them."[45]

* * *

I asked Pen: "How is it the Democrats require two-thirds to nominate and you Republicans only a majority?" Pen said: "We have to;

we couldn't get two-thirds of the Republicans to agree that Lincoln was dead."

* * *

I said: "Penny, what do you say we go out to the chat-aqua? You are feeling better." Penny said: "We will go but we will wait till after the Fourth of July. By that time most of the nominating speeches will be over."

* * *

So Penny and I finally agreed we would go to Frisco and watch the Democrats and stop off in Chicago on our way home and see the balloting.

NEA, June, 1920

Article #10 Republican Convention

WILL ROGERS SAYS:

By Will Rogers Unbranded Oklahoma Cowboy Humorist and Famous Goldwyn Motion Picture Star[46]

SOMEWHERE IN PHILADELPHIA, June 12,.–Sitting in Sen. Penrose's listening room yesterday he turned to me and said: "Bill, do you want to hear a little fun over the phone?" I said: "Why, yes, I ought to get something to repay me for this year I have been in Philadelphia this week."

* * *

So Pen. said: "All right, I will phone them out in the Chicago chat-aqua they can go ahead."

* * *

I said: "But ain't you going to listen over the phone, too, so you will know what's happening?" Pen. said: "Say, don't make me laugh, Bill. We rehearsed those ballots for weeks."

* * *

I said: "Why, Lowden is winning.[47] They cheered him for 52 minutes.[48] Pen. said: "Yes, but the American people are the only ones who cheer one way and vote another."

* * *

Governor Allen made the speech for Wood and said Wood started to the war and got as far as New York when Wilson told McAdoo not to sell him a ticket.[49]

* * *

Some bird named Wheeler nominated Johnson and it took him so long telling where California was and how you could reach there that the audience thought he was nominating the Golden Gate.[50]

* * *

I said: "Pen., there is a blind Congressman sure boosting Johnson." Pen said: "Yes, I could tell he was blind the things he said about Johnson."

* * *

I said: "Penny, that baby Sproul of yours ain't gettin' very far." Pen. said: "No, I forgot to give him a letter of introduction to anybody."

* * *

Boies said: "I might just as well sent Connie Mack out there. He couldn't a finished any further back."[51]

* * *

Wood led on the first ballot, showing that if he did spend money he got something for it.

* * *

I said: "What makes the delegates change? Don't they stay with their man?" Pen. said: "The delegates vote the way their people told them the first ballot. But after that they sell to the highest bidder."

* * *

I said: "But that's not honest, is it?"

* * *

Pen. said: "No, just politics."

DEMOCRATIC CONVENTION OF 1920

The Democratic Party in 1920 was greatly confused as its national convention began. President Woodrow Wilson had caused much of this by remaining silent about his plans for seeking a third term. In September 1919, he had suffered a physical collapse, and party leaders believed he was too ill to run again. Yet the President refused to disclose his plans or to eliminate himself as a candidate. When Wilson wrote a letter to be read before the Jackson Day dinners of January 8, 1920, that called for a campaign based on the issue of the League of Nations, it became obvious he wanted another term. Democratic leaders had hoped he would be more flexible on the League perhaps even announcing that he would not be a candidate for reelection.

William Gibbs McAdoo, the former secretary of the treasury, wanted the nomination, and Wilson's silence hurt McAdoo's chances. McAdoo believed he could not openly seek the job without hurting his father-in-law, but the former secretary had the support of administration liberals, the Anti-Saloon League, and even labor. During the preconvention period McAdoo remained silent about his intentions, but he allowed his friends to talk of his candidacy.

McAdoo indirectly may have been a candidate for the nomination, but Attorney General A. Mitchell Palmer directly and vocally sought the nomination. Palmer entered the Michigan primary as the only active candidate, but was beaten by Herbert Hoover who was not even a Democrat. Yet Palmer was the only candidate with any delegates, and therefore he was the leader. A third candidate to enter the race was Governor James M. Cox of Ohio, who had a progressive record while in office. Cox had some support from the moderates in the party and was apparently popular with labor. He was the type of person who would not offend too many people with his views, but neither did anyone feel strongly about his desirability.

The two dark-horse Democratic candidates were John W. Davis of West Virginia, supported by Under Secretary of the Navy Franklin D. Roosevelt, and Secretary of the Treasury Carter Glass of Virginia. Davis and Glass really had no chance for nomination because they came from states with little party organization, states that were not pivotal as far as votes were concerned. Favorite sons in the battle for nomination included Edwin T. Meredith of Iowa, Governor Alfred Smith of New York, and National Committee Chairman Homer Cummings of Connecticut. Vice-President Thomas R. Marshall also had some support; and, as usual, the perennial candidate from Nebraska, William J. Bryan, was ready and willing to lead the party.

However, President Wilson still seemed to be a viable candidate. He did nothing to dispel rumors of his wanting a third term. In fact, he did just the opposite when on June 15, 1920, he held a three-hour interview with a reporter from the *New York World,* allowing the writer to watch him signing bills and working a full schedule. On the same day the interview was published, McAdoo announced that he would not accept the nomination, but after a few days of political maneuvering he was "in" again when National Committeeman Love told the press that Texas had forty votes for McAdoo. Love also indicated that McAdoo had promised an interested North Carolina delegation that he would make no more withdrawal statements.

On June 28, 1920, the convention opened in San Francisco amid considerable political confusion. There were 1,092 delegates present and only 336 had any instructions about how to vote—most of these were to be cast on first ballot for favorite son candidates. Everything pointed to a deadlocked and long convention, for it was the first time such a meeting had been held on the coast in such pleasant surroundings. There were three main factions in San Francisco: one group supported Wilson and the administration; another segment supported Bryan and his policies, representing the drys, isolationists, and populist oriented agrarians; and finally a third group, each representing its own interests was present. Big city bosses including Charles Murphy of Tammany Hall, Thomas Taggart of Indiana and George Brennan of Illinois all wanted to block any attempt to nominate Wilson. These men wanted a candidate who would support legalization of alcoholic beverages, Irish independence, and other policies.

Homer Cummings became temporary chairman of the convention proceedings and opened the first day with a speech supporting the League of Nations—an act that set off a noisy pro-administration demonstration. The convention eventually settled on Senator Joseph T. Robinson of Arkansas as the best compromise choice. Wilson's moment of triumph arrived when a huge oil painting of the President was lowered from the ceiling of the convention hall while "Hail to the Chief" was played. Delegates enthusiastically stood up and paraded around the auditorium to salute their choice for the nomination. The outburst was more a gesture of gratification for war-time leadership than a call for a third term. Franklin D. Roosevelt suddenly took the New York standard, and struggled with his fellow delegates until he carried it off with the crowd cheering.

After the usual platform committee struggle, the nominating speeches were finally made. Senator Robert L. Owen of Oklahoma was nominated first, then James W. Gerard of New York, the former Ambassador to Germany, was named. Thereafter many favorite sons were nominated. Only the forty-three minute demonstration after McAdoo's nomination was as enthusiastic as each candidate had hoped.

As predicted, the first ballot proved that no one had sufficient delegates to win. It was late Friday night when the ballot was held and McAdoo led with 266 votes, but he needed 729 votes to win the nomination. Cox was third with 134 votes, Palmer was second with 256 in his corner. Roper and Baruch had taken McAdoo at his word about not wanting the nomination; therefore these masterful and influential manipulators were not at the Convention. This hurt McAdoo's chances mortally, and although he gained on the second ballot, he had no chance to win. The convention adjourned until Saturday morning after having been in session for thirteen consecutive hours. Significantly, President Wilson had not received even one vote during the first two ballots.

Bainbridge Colby watched the proceedings of the convention, but assumed that he could stampede delegates into nominating Wilson by acclamation whenever he wished. Colby telegraphed Wilson on Friday night that he was going to ask that the rules be suspended, then he would nominate the President. On Saturday morning Glass, Cummings, Burleson, Robinson, and Daniels met with Colby to express their opposition to his plan. The men convinced Colby to forget his scheme. Early that same morning the campaign managers for Palmer and Cox had met to stop McAdoo. By the sixth ballot McAdoo had 368½ votes and Palmer 251½, while Cox had gained 195 votes. Finally, on the twelfth ballot, Cox took the lead and continued to be the front runner, but he still had too few votes to win.

On Sunday July 4, all the campaign managers counted votes, traded support, and otherwise sought any advantage they could for their candidates. McAdoo's supporters almost all agreed on Cox as a second choice should their man prove unable to obtain the necessary votes to win. Yet no agreements on a ticket were reached during the weekend. On Monday the first ballot indicated there was very little change in voting. By the thirty-fifth ballot McAdoo and Cox clearly were the frontrunners, with the latter having the best opportunities to win. McAdoo forces soon sensed that they could not win and thus jumped on the Cox bandwagon. The Democrats in the final analysis had nominated a safe candidate. And, after considerable discussion and several nominating speeches, Franklin D. Roosevelt was nominated as Cox's vice-presidential candidate.

φ φ φ φ

Because the Democratic convention of 1920 met in San Francisco, and it was near there that Will Rogers then was on location filming a movie, he no doubt had hoped to attend some of the sessions in person. But when the phone call reached him about the serious illness of his children, he left San Francisco immediately, driving all night to reach home. It was too late. His son Fred had died June 17; the humorist remained at home for several days.

How Rogers managed to write his humorous columns during this sad period is difficult to imagine. Fred died at 4 a.m., and Rogers' first article about the Democratic convention was dated that same day. From the original articles it was obvious that Will typed them himself, but the typing, spelling and punctuation were even worse than his usual careless style. Some of the pages were typed on both sides; on some he started at one end of the paper and covered one-half page; then he put the same page in the machine again, this time upside down, and continued to type. The writings may have been taken by someone else and put on the wire for NEA—one of the rare times he may have allowed someone else to help edit his material. Possibly they were phoned in or there could have been an editor on the Los Angeles *Record* who assisted during this critical period. The *Record* carried the articles and in one issue of the paper indicated that Rogers was doing them for the *Record* exclusively.

Rogers did not compare the Democratic convention to a chautauqua. He used another current "fad"—a Ouija board seance which he spelled phonetically. Although he probably devised the analogy on the spur of the moment, there was a deeper implication in his "gags".

Again, as he had with the earlier convention, he pretended to be at the source of that power—with President Wilson in Washington, rather than in San Francisco. Wilson, like Penrose, was actually ill and also had telephone communications with the convention. This gave Rogers a convenient device to report current happenings as he learned about them from the daily papers, making them seem current, even though he was not there.

Many of his printed observations were keen as he sliced through the political speeches and platform promises, but a close examination of the articles covering the Democratic convention reveal that he was possibly using the same comments, or simply revising the comments, that he had used earlier. He made a noble effort under the circumstances, but it is in the later convention articles that he can be seen at his best.

(Texts for the following articles are from the News Enterprise Association "tear sheets." Variations are from the *Oklahoma News OKN*. — The Editors)

NEA, June, 1920

Article #1 Democratic Convention

WILL ROGERS SAYS

By Will Rogers (Famous Oklahoma Cowboy Wit and Goldwyn Motion Picture Star.) [1]

SOMEWHERE IN THE WHITE HOUSE, June 00.—After thanking Penrose for all his favors to me and complimenting him on sneaking Harding[2] over, I asked him, how can I get the real advance information on this Democratic weegee seance?

Pen said: "Well, they are doing a lot of knocking and asking questions out in 'Frisco, but if you want to go where the answers to the knocking are coming from, why go to the White House."

I said: "But President Wilson[3] is sick. He can't be their control during this seance."

"Say, I was supposed to be sick, too," said Pen, "but I put it over, didn't I? He has just as good a telephone as I had."

I said: "I have a letter here from Colonel House[4] that might help me seeing him."

Pen said: "I wouldn't mention it, if I were you."

I said: "I believe he will see me. He used always to come to hear my jokes when I was with the Follies and laughed at them, too—especially the ones on Republicans."[5]

Pen said: "Why shouldn't he see you? You are not a Republican senator."

So, when I arrived at the White House, all I could see was some men putting in telephone wires. There wasn't an officeseeker in sight.

I met Admiral Doctor Grayson[6] coming out. I asked him, "How is the president?" Admiral said: "I don't know, as the doctor has not come this morning."

Then I met Tumulty, our president during most of this administration. I said to Tumulty: "I want to see Mr. Wilson and I don't want a single office or a favor."[7]

Tumulty grabbed me and rushed me right in and said, "You are the only person who ever called here that didn't want something."

The president seemed glad to see me when he found I was not looking for an appropriation and said, "Well, will you tell me the latest Republican joke?"

I said: "I know a good one. Nine-tenths of the Republicans never even heard it until Chicago—Harding."

I asked Mr. Wilson: "What do you think of Bryan's chances this seance?

Mr. Wilson said: "I think they are just as good as they ever were."

I asked him: "Mr. Wilson, they say you caused Senator Delegate Jim Reed[8] to be unseated, is that so?"

The president said: "I didn't unseat him; I simply phoned the ushers not to let him in."

I said to him: "Do you think you will run?" He said, "Well, if I don't I will put the boy in."

I said: "What do you mean, 'the boy'?" He said: "Why, my boy—McAdoo."[9]

I said: "But the boy said he wasn't running."

Mr. Wilson said: "Of course not. At the start let Palmer and Cox[10] get deadlocked like Wood and Lowden. Then I will phone them to stick the boy in."

I said: "Ah, you mean to put him over a la Harding."

The president said: "Well, you stick with me during this weegee convention and you will be on the right end of the 'phone."

NEA, June, 1920

Article #2 Democratic Convention

WILL ROGERS SAYS By Will Rogers (Famous Oklahoma Cowboy Wit and Goldwyn Motion Picture Star.) [11]

SOMEWHERE IN THE WHITE HOUSE, June 00.—Well, President Wilson and I sat at the old 'phones in the White House today and listened to the opening of the Democratic weegee convention.

After Cummings[12] had finally given out and had to stop, I turned to the president and he said: "It's all right, but he left out part of it."

I said: "If you write anything and then rehearse a man for days how to say it, you are pretty apt to know if he leaves anything out."

He said:[13] "Well, what he left out was certainly not about the Republicans. He had that part in there."

* * *

I said: " But, Mr. President, there were fewer high-toned phrases and big words in there than in most of your speeches."

He said: "Yes, I had to make it very plain. Did you ever have a good look at a delegate? Why, Tammany Hall[14] delegation has to take an English interperter along."

* * *

He said: "Was that speech as long as Bryan's are?"

I said: "Yes, for you know Bryan's speeches are interrupted every four years by elections and then he goes on again."

* * *

I didn't tell him, but the way Cummings' speech sounded every time the Americans had to retreat in the war, it was the Republicans that did it, and every time they advanced, it was the Democrats.

I Said: "But what about a platform?"

He said: "Oh, we don't need much of a one. All we do is point with pride and let the Republicans view with alarm."

* * *

I Said: "How do you stand on the liquor question?"

He said: Just like the Republicans do on all questions—straddle."

* * *

I said: "But who will be nominated?"

He said: "Don't make me laugh. The boy will walk in."

NEA, July, 1920

Article #3 Democratic Convention

WILL ROGERS SAYS By Will Rogers (Famous Oklahoma Cowboy Humorist and Goldwyn Motion Picture Star.)[15]

SOMEWHERE IN THE WHITE HOUSE, Washington, July 00.—When I arrived at the White House today Wilson was feeling a bit blue.

I asked: "What's the matter?"

He said: "Oh, it's the old Democratic complaint threatening me again."

"What old complaint?" I asked.

He said: "Why, Bryan."

"Why, you don't dread HIM do you?"

The president said: "No! It is that he's so quiet, like a mother with a child. If it's talking there is no danger; it's during these long quiet spells that she knows something is the matter."

* * *

I said: "Well, I got a grouch on, too, Mr. President. I am a Cherokee and it's the proudest little possession I ever hope to have, but yesterday they nominated another of our tribe, R. L. Owen,[16] and credited him with everything from striking oil in Oklahoma to driving the sharks off the eastern coast but never a mention of the Cherokee."

* * *

"So when Irv Cobb[17] stated that Owen's sole support would be the entire Cherokee tribe, I want to tell my old friend Irv that he lost one of them yesterday."

* * *

"My-Four-Years-in-Germany" Gerard,[18] was the next name offered up for advertising. If that's all it takes to get nominated, I claim a place, as I am writing a book called "My Four Years With the Ziegfeld Follies,[19] or Famous Men I Have Met at the Stage Door."

* * *

I said: "President Wilson, why didn't you go out yourself?"

He said: "After one has visited the conventions of the old world, these here seem like slumming."

I said: "Mr. Wilson, if you want to get rid of 'half of one per cent' Bryan,[20] why don't you have the boys promise him a seat in his next cabinet?"

President said: "I would, but Will, he won't do.[21] I tried him once."

* * *

I said: Well, everything is all O. K. out at the weegee-seance islands."[22]

He said: "But I am afraid when they get to voting that some of the candidates, with a couple of quarts of Old Crow, will stampede the convention."[23]

* * *

"I said: "But, President, the boy says he's not a candidate."

Mr. Wilson said: "Well of course, if he don't feel like taking it, I suppose I will have to be inspired for another four years."

NEA, 1920

Article #4 Democratic Convention

WILL ROGERS SAYS By Will Rogers (Famous Oklahoma Cowboy Humorist and Goldwyn Motion Picture Star.) [24]

SOMEWHERE IN THE WHITE HOUSE, Washington, July 00.—I dropped in on President Wilson today just as he was saying over the phone to Frisco to keep Senator Reed in Oakland.

* * *

I said "Why do you want him unseated?"

President Wilson said: "Hasn't he been, for over a year, trying to unseat me?"

* * *

I said: "By the way, Mr. Wilson, where are all your hired help, such as cabinet officers and all the crew?"

He said: "Oh, they are out in Frisco doing what they can for the boy."

* * *

I said: "You are not looking for a third term?"

He said: "No, but all my cabinet are."

Then I said: "This weegee seance out there is not so much a case of political principle as it is a case of hold your job."

* * *

I said: "If the boy is elected, are you going to have him keep these same hired hands?"

The president said: "If Colby[25] can swing the Progressive vote, we will keep him. But if he don't, why I will have the boy let him go."

* * *

I asked him about this lilliputian, Carter Glass.[26]

Mr. Wilson said: "On account of his size I sent him out there. I knew he could get a lot of news for me where a bigger man couldn't get in."[27]

* * *

I said: "Is Secretary Daniels[28] out there, too?"

The president said: "Yes, he is out there, getting on and off boats. If it wasn't for him the weekly moving picture reviews would have nobody to show."

* * *

I said: "What do you think of the chances of this fellow Marshall?[29] He is vice something or other."

The president said: "I have heard he's a good man but I have never met him personally."

* * *

I said: "They say there is a lot more enthusiasm around this weegee board than at the Chicago Chautauqua."

The president said: "Yes, but that don't mean anything. A noisy vote don't do any more than quiet one does."

* * *

I said: "But aside from all this, Mr. Woodrow, who will be nominated?"

He smiled and said: "May I not mention to you casually that the boy will crawl in?"

(The next two articles were not in NEA collections. However, the *Cleveland Press* and OKN carried both articles verbatim.—The Editors)

Cleveland Press, July, 1920

Article #5 Democratic Convention

WOODROW TOLD ME AND I TOLD HIM—

By Will Rogers

Cowboy Humorist and Movie Star

SOMEWHERE IN THE WHITE HOUSE, July 2— Yesterday I asked President Wilson if he was going to listen to the rest of the nominating speeches over the phone.

He said, "Will, do you want me to be sick again?"

* * *

"How is the weegee seance out in Frisco going, anyway, Mr. Wilson?" I asked.

He said, "It was going all right and was knocking and getting the answers from me here till they found Bryan moving his hands around in the dark trying to find where the wires were located."

"Mr. President," said I, "in all these years of worry about what to do to get rid of Bryan, how is it that none of you thought of making him vice president?"

* * *

I said, "Why don't you all declare yourself one way or the other on the liquor question?"

He said, "Well, we can't. If we declare wet we lose the bootlegger vote."

I said, "Prohibition has certainly drove the price of votes up. Votes that used to be bought for a half dozen 5-cent beers now cost a $4 bottle of hair tonic.

* * *

I said, "Mr. President, I read your platform and it says we advocate generosity to soldiers, but don't want to tax the people more. How are you going to do that? Let the soldiers float a loan among themselves? Do you realize that we were last in war, last in peace and last to do anything for our returned soldiers?"

* * *

I said, "What about Ireland?"

He said, "Well, the trouble with Ireland is the English landlords own all the land."

"Well," said I, "the best way to settle that is to make every English landlord go to Ireland and collect the rent personally. That would not only solve the problem but eliminate the landlords."[30]

* * *

I went on: "I see the platform says you advocate free speech. I don't see what good that would do. Your parties have called each other everything I ever Heard."

* * *

"How about Mexico?" I asked.

"Well, we could intervene," he said, "but if the U. S. took it over most of the Americans down there would have to hunt another country."

I said, "Instead of going to war, wouldn't it be cheaper just to outlaw these American cases and let them come home?"[31]

* * *

I said, "President, some of the candidates are running out of money out in Frisco and are paying the delegates off with I.O.U.'s. Why do the Democrats nominate so long before they ballot?"

He said, "I don't know, Will, unless it is so the delegates can get a chance to look around a bit before they sell."

* * *

I said, "I see the boy says he don't want it. You say you don't want it. The Republicans this year considered it an honor to be nominated, but the Democrats seem to consider it a duty."

Cleveland Press, July, 1920

Article #6 Democratic Convention

WILL ROGERS SAYS

By Will Rogers

Cowboy Humorist and Movie Star

SOMEWHERE IN THE WHITE HOUSE, Washington, July 3—President Wilson doesn't hear so well over the phone, so I'm telling him just what is happening at the weegee seance in Frisco.

* * *

I said, "There is somebody praying."

He said, "Yes, even a Democrat needs a little religion every four years."

* * *

I says, "Midget Friday Glass is reading the platform. He says the Democrats are for your League of Nations, but if they see they can't win with your league, they will reservate enough so they can win with prohibition.

"I think they condemned the Republicans in there somewhere, but I won't be sure.

"They praise the war. They said it was one of the best wars the Democrats ever fought.

"SOLDIERS' COMPENSATION: They are going to give the boys farms, but by the time they got them they will be too old to tend them.

"MEXICO: They said there were fewer Americans being killed there than ever. Sure, they will keep on being killed till they get the last one.

"LABOR AND CAPITAL. They say labor should be paid well, but capital should not be charged too much.

"IRELAND: They expressed sympathy for Ireland, but from the looks of its casualty lists lately, England needs it more.

ARMENIA: The delegates showed they didn't know where it was, but it must have sympathy. Tammany Hall needs sympathy more than Armenia.

"RURAL CREDIT: They showed the Federal Farm Loan Bank had made it easier for farmers to borrow and harder to pay back.

"MERCHANT MARINE: They advocated a merchant marine, even if we have to sell boats to get it .

"HIGH COST OF LIVING: The Republicans eat too much."

* * *

I said, "Well, Mr. President, I have good news for you; they adopted the platform just as she is.

He said, "Sure! I could have told you that when I wrote it and sent it out there."

* * *

I said, "Bryan just took the floor. He was cheered for 15 minutes and then voted against 6 to 1. Do you think Bryan is disappointed that the prohibition plank was left out?"

Mr. Wilson said, "No. That would have left him nothing to talk about."

* * *

The president said, "Who led on the first ballots?"

I said, "Don't make me laugh. You laugh. You know who did—the boy."

* * *

The president said, "Well, I guess I am a kind-a bad fixer, eh! The platform and the candidates!"

"Well, Penrose's judgment has been vindicated again," I told him. "He said you would put it over. Give me a little credit, too. When all the writers picked Chicago and Frisco, I picked you and Penrose and you have both come thru nobly. But who will it be?"

He said, "May I not tell you again, Will, as I have told you from the start, that unless someone cuts my telephone wire, the boy will creep in?"

REPUBLICAN CONVENTION OF 1924

On June 10, 1924, the Republican Party held its national convention in Cleveland, Ohio. With Harding gone, the convention opened with the slogan "Keep cool with Coolidge," and the conventioneers did just that. To the chagrin of local night club owners and others expecting to profit from the arrival of noisy delegates, the quiet and orderly convention was a definite disappointment. Coolidge had insisted that the convention be "dry"; therefore little opportunity for noisy fun existed. Coolidge clearly was in control of the party and the convention.

Coolidge was the only candidate nominated. The delegates rather perfunctorily gave him a four-minute ovation, and on the only ballot taken, he received 1065 votes. The only business left for the convention was to select a vice-presidential candidate. Coolidge let it be known that he wanted Senator Borah, but the latter adamantly refused the offer. When balloting began for vice president, sixteen men received votes. Governor Frank Lowden received 222 votes, Senator William S. Kenyon of Iowa got 172, and Charles Dawes 111. By the second ballot Lowden began to gain votes and immediately thereafter his total reached 766, enough to win the nomination. Then the convention chairman, Representative Frank W. Mondell of Wyoming, read a letter to the delegates in which Lowden absolutely declined the offer. The convention was so confused that a recess was called to decide what the next move should be.

Disagreement existed during the recess because the congressional leaders wanted to nominate Senator Charles Curtis of Kansas; administration supporters and representatives supported Herbert Hoover. The delegates, who were tired and bored with the parliamentary railroad, had different opinions also. They seemed to think that Charles G. Dawes would be a more exciting candidate. On the third ballot with preliminary sparring completed Dawes received the nomination with 682½ votes.

The short Republican convention had been lackluster and pro forma. While the two major parties seemed capable of encompassing all prevalent political views, this was untrue. There apparently was no place in the country for a certain faction of liberals. Hence, with dissatisfaction rife within both parties, liberals met in Cleveland on July 4 and launched a type of farm-labor movement called the Progressive Party. Their candidate was as expected, Senator Robert LaFollette, progressivism's best known leader. The group chose Senator Burton K. Wheeler of Montana as his running mate. The new party afforded opportunity to bring a truly different and reform type of party platform, and that is exactly what was drawn and adopted. Fighting monopolistic domination of public and private life, the party called for public ownership of railroads, natural resources, and water power, and popular referendum on such things as war, arms reduction, direct nomination of presidential candidates and popular election of federal judges. Significantly, this was a broad and far reaching program that many people were unready to accept. Party leaders knew they could not hope to win the election, but they hoped to cause the election to be thrown into the house of representatives where they might obtain a part of their platform for supporting a candidate.

φ φ φ φ

Will Rogers often said that because he was born on election day—November 4, 1879—he had a "natural right" to comment on politicians or politics. As long as he could remember, politics of one kind or another had been important at the Rogers ranch near Oologah, Oklahoma. His father, Clement Vann Rogers, was active in tribal affairs of the Cherokee Nation long before Will was born, and the elder Rogers continued until the time of his death in 1911, serving on various commissions and boards, as judge and senator of the Cherokee Nation and as a delegate in 1906-07 to the constitutional convention for the new state of Oklahoma. Rogers County, Oklahoma was named in honor of Clem Rogers—not his more famous son.

With so much concern and political awareness in the Rogers home, it was no wonder that Will Rogers was interested in such affairs; and his interest grew as he took his rope and gum to the stage in New York where he met many of the big names in the news. Taking notes for his "gags" from the daily newspapers, he found politicians were his best targets and soon it became a mark of distinction to be panned by the cowboy-philosopher in his act with the Follies. As politicians all knew, Rogers never sought to hurt anyone, never ridiculed any person; he only kidded about the "fool things" they did. And his humor was based on truth.

In 1924 Will Rogers first attended a presidential nominating convention in person. By then he was probably better known than most of those about whom he wrote. He had established himself as a writer through his weekly syndicated columns; his movies were being shown across the country; and he was a star in the Ziegfeld Follies. His income was more than $150,000 for the year of 1924; yet he still wore his battered hat and his one wrinkled suit, and remained "just an old country boy, trying to get along."

In 1923, a newspaper in Toledo, Ohio, had called him the most popular speaker in the country and claimed he had "the most forceful mind in America today" (21 January, 1923, *Toledo Times*). "It is claimed his satirical shafts could accomplish any object aimed at," the story continued. "It is even reported the Republicans and the Democrats have each caught the idea of securing Rogers as a spellbinder for the next presidential campaign. It is believed he would be the greatest drawing card a campaign ever had."

When the Republican convention opened in Cleveland, Ohio, Rogers had been in New York, preparing to open with the *Follies*. When he wrote his first convention article on June 8, 1924, it was natural for him to call it "Coolidge's Follies." With him in the press stands were William Jennings Bryan and others about whom he wrote. He authored five articles and remained until the convention closed before he returned to Atlantic City for the Follies opening on June 18.

(Texts for this convention are based on the *New York Times* unless otherwise noted. Variations are from the *Tulsa Daily World TDW*.—The Editors)

New York Times, June 9, 1924

Article #1 Republican Convention

COULD HAVE NOMINATED COOLIDGE BY POSTCARD SAYS WILL ROGERS, STARTING FOR CLEVELAND

by Will Rogers[1]

As I pen these lines I am waiting for my train to carry me to Coolidge's Follies in Cleveland. At first I was going to say the Republican Follies, but it's not. They have nothing to do with it. The whole thing is under the personal supervision of Mr. Coolidge.[2]

It's a one-star show. Now can you imagine Yaps like us going to Cleveland from all over the country when Mr. Coolidge is not going to be there himself? It's like going to see Sir Harry Lauder's show without Sir Harry.[3]

I am leaving tonight with New York's delegation of Unnecessary Delegates. They preach economy, and here are hundreds of thousands of dollars being wasted to ship all these Destructive Delegates to a place to announce something that everybody in the United States knew six months ago. He could have been nominated by post card. Why didn't he suggest taking this money they are spending to tell him he is nominated and give it to the poor in each State? Don't say there is no poor. There must be some Democrats in every State.

As for drafting a platform, that's just a lot of Apple Sauce. Why, I bet you there is not a Republican or Democrat office-holder today that can tell you one Plank in the last Election Platform without looking over the minutes. These Misled Delegates that journey to Cleveland will have just as much chance of helping to frame that platform as a Bow Legged girl would have at our Stage Door. Mr. Coolidge framed that Platform. I doubt if Lodge even has been allowed to see it.[4]

Now there is another thing. There is nothing certain in politics except Salary and rake-off. Of course, these hundreds of delegates were instructed for Coolidge. But every Delegate is, after all, scarcely human—he is just a Politician. So wouldn't the promise of jobs under Hiram Johnson beat merely belonging to the Party under Coolidge?

Or suppose this Dakota Bunch start a Filibuster and tie up the Convention and neither Coolidge nor Johnson can win. That would mean a Dark Horse Candidate. So I am taking Will Hays and Valentino along with me.[5] Both will be made-up ready to go on in case of Deadlock.

If these Delegates vote the way they were instructed to vote Back Home they will be the first politicians that ever did what the people told them to do. And if they do, this will be the first convention in the History of the World where the Man won who had the most votes to start in with. Things must be in a pretty bad way in the Republican Party when they have only Two Men who think they are good enough to run. Why, in the Democratic Party they have a Thousand who think they are good enough. According to that, the Democrats must have the most Able Party.

Of course, lots of people are banking on the excitement coming from the nomination of the Vice President. Why, Mr. Coolidge has had him picked out months ago, ever since Congress overrode his first Veto. Some say it is Lowden.[6] But I don't think they can ever persuade him that he can never do any better.

Imagine the Republicans worrying over who they will pick for a Vice President. Just think of the Poor Democrats. They are worrying who to pick for a President. If they can get a good man for President they would be willing to let the Vice Presidency go.

Lots of people can't understand the popularity that Mr. Coolidge is deservedly enjoying all over the country at the present time. I can tell you. It started the minute he opposed Congress and the Senate. The People said: "If he is against Congress he must be right." It was the surest fire political move anyone ever had a chance to make. If he agreed with Congress he would have been as dead as they are today.

But tomorrow I will see their Show. They say they are Good. I WILL SEE.

New York Times, June 10, 1924

Article #2 Republican Convention

WILL ROGERS SAYS CLEVELAND OPENS CHURCHES TO GIVE THE DELEGATES SOME EXCITEMENT

by Will Rogers[7]

CLEVELAND, June 9.—This is the first Vice Presidential convention ever held in the history of politics.

I suppose four years from now they will hold a National Convention to nominate the Assistant Sergeant-at-Arms of the House of Representatives.

All my life I have been longing to attend a convention and see the excitement and hear the shouts. Now, when I do get a chance I draw this one.

The city is opening up the churches now and having services so the delegates and visitors can go and hear some singing or excitement of some kind.

There is not a band in town. The Oklahoma delegation brought a fiddler, but when he heard all the silence he started crying and broke his fiddle.

They have a few flags out, but even they are all wet. A bell boy was pinched for paging a guest too loud.

My disappointment would be just like a sick man who had been promised a trip to a circus for forty years. Then when he is able to go out they take him to Grant's Tomb.

But if you think my case is bad look at the city of Cleveland. They have waited hundreds of years for one of these. Now they draw this Chautauqua.

I have been coming to Cleveland for years playing, but I never saw it so quiet and sad.

You would think somebody was going to steal their depot, which they have loved and cherished for hundreds of years.

Billy Sunday Needed.[8]

Cleveland is negotiating now with Billy Sunday to come here and hold a revival so the town can get back some of its old excitement, and the money that they lose on this.

But we are all just victims of circumstances. Who would have ever thought that the day would come when people would be going to a convention just to nominate a Vice President.

Why at the last Republican Convention they were days nominating Mr. Harding and just as they were putting on their hats to leave, some one happened to think, "Why, we haven't nominated a Vice President. That's customary is it not?" So some one who happened to have read of the Boston police strike suggested Mr. Coolidge, so they nominated him that minute, and the others went home to read the next day who he was.

In the old days it was not, "Who will we nominate for Vice President?" It was "Who can we get to take the thing?"[9]

I searched all morning trying to find the Democratic headquarters.

I walked up to a big fat colored delegate from below the line, who was plastered with badges, and asked him, "can you tell me where the Ku Klux Klan headquarters are?" He said, "My Lord, are they got up here, too?" he just quickly walked out from under about eight badges, some of them reaching back as far as McKinley.[10]

You can tell a New England delegate, he will be eating a box lunch in the lobby, which he brought from home.

Nine hundred delegates have rooms in town and 900 alternates live in the lobbies of the Hollenden and Cleveland Hotels.

There would be room for twice as many people if the ones who are in there would take off all their badges.

Coolidge Vetoes Lodge.

Senator Lodge, who has staged every show up to this, is made Vice Chairman of the Ushers Committee.

They say they won't nominate one of the Old Guard for Vice President, they want new faces. Tomorrow at the convention, I am going to put into nomination Fanny Brice.[11] Fanny has the newest face I know of; she just had it overhauled this year.

They want a man they say for Vice President, who will get the farmer vote. If the farmers don't make any more between now and November, than they have the last three years, they won't be able to come to town to vote.

They wanted Lowden on account of him owning a farm. He makes enough out of his Pullman Car stock to keep the farm going.

But the trouble is there is such a small majority of farmers in this country that own any great amount of Pullman Car stock.

Mr. Stearns, late of Boston, Mass., is a caller in our midst.[12]

New York Times, June 11, 1924

Article #3 Republican Convention

WILL ROGERS ENTERS CONVENTION TO LEARN, / BUT SAYS HE'S AS IGNORANT AS BEFORE

By WILL ROGERS.[13]

CLEVELAND, June 10.—The Republican Vice Presidential conscription convention opened at 11 o'clock *this* morning with an array of badges that was deafening. I had the thrill of my entire life. I entered the convention press stand with William Jennings Bryan. We were the only two aliens in the entire hall—he the solitary Democrat and I the sole remaining Progressive Bull Moose. Both of us entered, not to jeer, but to be instructed.[14] We came out three hours later more ignorant than when we went in.

As we walked over from the Hollenden Hotel everybody recognized Bryan and spoke. Finally a traffic policeman recognized me, and shook hands and said, "I saw one of your movies last night; they flatter you."

Well, I never in my life felt so grateful for having some one recognize me, and to make it doubly gratifying, he didn't know Bryan. [15]

We sat together in the press stand. Everybody thought I was a plain-clothes man sent along to protect Bryan from the Republicans. I can't blame them, for Lord knows my clothes were plain enough.

As we entered the hall everybody stood up. Both of us looked at each other rather embarrassed, as we didn't know which one the demonstration was meant for. But we were soon set at ease on the subject, when we found that they were rising to sing one of our national anthems, which, by the way, the Republicans don't know any better than the plain people.

It will take America two more wars to learn the words of our national hymn. Sam Blythe[16] was on the other side of me, and when some didn't stand up for the anthem he remarked to me that they were the New Thought.

Bryan and I had no sooner got in the hall than they commenced to pray. The preacher started reading his prayer, which was new to me. Where I come from if a man can't think of anything to pray about offhand, why, there is no need of him praying. If they couldn't find a Republican that knew how to pray they should have called in a Democrat. They are all praying this year.

The prayer was very long, but, of course the parson may have known his audience and their needs better than me.

Then Mr. Bryan turned to me and said: "You write a humorous column, don't you!"

I looked around to see if anybody was listening and then I said: "Yes, sir."

He said: "Well I write a serious article, and if I think of anything of a comical or funny nature, I will give it to you."

I thanked him and told him: "If I happen to think of anything of a serious nature, I will give it to you."

When he said he wrote seriously, and I said I wrote humorously, I thought afterward we both may be wrong.

I want a whole article to touch on Mr. Burton's keyring speech (a keyring speech is one where the speaker encircles everything good his party has done and leaves outside the ring everything bad).[17]

I listened to it, and it sounded to me like the minutes of the last Congress. Once Mr. Burton referred to the free silver campaign of ninety-some-odd. Mr. Bryan turned to me and said:

"I had forgotten that campaign myself. How did he ever remember it?"

So you see Mr. Bryan was handing me a lot of funny ones, and if you will read his article and there happens to be anything of a serious nature in it that is worth while, you will know that I did my part even if he don't give me screen credit.

I came back to the hotel with him and we had lunch together, and

I learned a great many things about politics from a man who has survived longer than any other big leader, and who is still going strong.

In my weekly article I want to tell you some more about our visit.

The biggest applause Mr. Burton got was when he said the Republican Party should remain intact, including La Follette.[18]

From the monologue standpoint the speech was bad. His finishing gag was in the middle. Bryan said "The speaker suffered from a premature climax." I will have to give him a couple of good serious ones to make up for that one.

New York Times, June 12, 1924

Article #4 Republican Convention

WILL ROGERS BOOMS HAYS FOR VICE PRESIDENT; WOULD SUBSTITUTE HOLLYWOOD FOR CONGRESS

by Will Rogers[19]

CONVENTION HALL, CLEVELAND, June 11.—The second riotous day of the Vice Presidential Convention opened amid wild excitement. As the Secretary read the number of delegates present the house went wild.

Yesterday they prayed for "blessings which are at Thy command," and today their prayers were answered, with rain, for the thirty-fourth straight day in this city.

The convention was billed to start at 10:30 this morning, but it didn't start until 11:15. No one had the nerve to start it.

William Jennings Bryan and myself again accompanied each other to the wake. I started him an hour earlier today than yesterday, so he would have time to shake hands with everybody who knew him on the way. I tried to find that policeman who knew me yesterday, I guess they had discharged him.

The festivities opened with 8,000 badges in the hall.

If all the money spent on political badges and political literature was spent on farm relief, we would have the most prosperous country east of the Alleghenies.

I don't want to appear disrespectful or lacking in devotion to prayer, but when prayer has been the outstanding feature of both days I can't help but record the facts. They are getting longer each day. I don't know if that is through necessity or not.

This one today was a keynote prayer.

Today's was by a different parson. It was the only strictly political oration I ever heard delivered in the guise of prayer. I had never heard prayer have a text like sermons. His was "Republican Party

Unity". The only reference to anything pertaining to the Bible was the word "Amen" at the finish.

He was by far the best orator that has appeared.

Mr. Bryan and I are the Weber and Fields of the convention. You remember one of them used to get just as many laughs as the other.[20]

So today in this article I am taking the serious side of the convention and he is taking the comedy.[21] Of course he assists me with serious suggestions, for instance, here is one he told me today:

"Senator Lodge passed by a little girl and her mother up in Massachusetts, and the little girl said, 'Oh, mamma, ain't Mr. Lodge the meanest man in the world?" and the mother scolded the child very sharply and said, 'How often have I told you not to use the word ain't!' "

A lady was the best thing on the program today. She was to introduce Mr. Mondell of Wyoming as the Chairman of the convention. She simply walked down front and said, "Convention, I submit to you Mr. Mondell."[22]

If that had been some politician introducing him, they would have had to drag in the glory of every last Republican President as far back as Lincoln, and it would have taken an hour for him to have thought of them all.

Now the lady in being so brief and concise—it was either she was smart or else she couldn't think of anything good to say about him.

What she left out he immediately said. He said, "This Chairmanship is the greatest honor that can come to any man." Now he knows that is a lot of applesauce, for a Chairman at one of those conventions is nothing more than an auctioneer with a hammer, receiving and taking the delegates' yes's and noes.[23]

When the lady got up Mr. Bryan applauded all over the place. He said to me "Why don't you applaud the lady?" So I gave him this funny one to use in his humorous article today:

"Why should I applaud her? I never saw her before."

Then he gave me this serious one for my serious article today:

"The compliments to the ladies are the only thing we Democrats can applaud at a Republican convention without sacrifice of our republican principles."

Mr. Mondell in his Chairmanship keynote speech pulled the same gag that Mr. Burton finished his with in the middle yesterday:

"We want Republicans that will stick together, not Republicans in name only."

Well, I give Mr. Mondell credit. He copped the best gag Mr. Burton had yesterday, and it went almost as big as it did yesterday.[24]

I want to leave before they wear it out entirely. This Professor Burton will get the use of it tomorrow, when he fools everybody by nominating Coolidge.

They are holding that big surprise back for the finish.

My candidate has come.[25] He just got in this morning and phoned me. I told you I would deliver him. It's Will Hays. I started him Monday for President, but he has degenerated down now till Vice President is about all I have for him. He can hold both jobs, preside over the Senate and Hollywood both. In fact, I think we should move the studios from Hollywood to Washington in exchange for the Senate and Congress. I bet you the City of Washington would trade in a minute. But I would hate to be the one to suggest it to Hollywood.

Tomorrow I am going to desert Bryan and let him find his own serious idea and go with Will Hays. I won't have to stop so much on the street on account of some one recognizing my companion.

New York Times, June 13, 1924

Article #5 Republican Convention

WILL ROGERS BREAKS AWAY FROM CLEVELAND; LIKENS HIS MOVE TO OTHER FAMOUS EVENTS

By Will Rogers.[26]

I have just done something that,[27] when the facts are known, will make me one of the Immortals and when I die my headpiece will read, "Here lies the Body of the First Man that left the Cleveland Convention."

In every gathering, be it War or Peace, there must be one outstanding feature. No I don't say that I was the only one that knew enough to leave. Neither can Sergeant York[28] explain to you what made him do what he did in France. It's just an intuition that comes to every man to do something now that every other man wants to do but he just can't rake up the courage. That's why some of us will go down as Heroes, while the others will always be with the mob.

Pershing's[29] fame will live throughout the ages not as being the man most responsible for winning the war for us but by announcing his arrival personally to Lafayette. Not through a butler or courier, mind you, but personally.

Take Abraham Lincoln. A new angle on the reason that his memory is honored through eternity is (according to every speaker that was allowed to open his mouth at this convention) that "Lincoln was a member of the Republican Party." Had Lincoln been unfortunate enough to have been a member of the Progressives and done the same thing he did, why, a Republican convention would never have heard of him.

Of course to most of you who never attended a Republican convention, why, Lincoln's fame was based on a remark (while a member of the Republican Party), consisting of eleven words. That's all. Some historians have since added two other linnes, but in the original Lincoln saying there were only these eleven words. Both political parties are based on it: "You can fool most of the delegates all of the time."

That's enough: you don't need to fool only a comfortable majority.

McAdoo will always remain in the public's mind not because he held more jobs creditably during the war than the Kaiser thought he held but by his now historic paragraph:

"Young man, go West."[30]

Grant has a Tomb for Tourists erected in New York for a witty remark he once made more than for his war record. It's as follows: "Politics is hell."[31]

Washington gained fame not through being the stepfather of his country but through a picture of him crossing the Delaware before we manufactured our own ice. But the fame of that is rather clouded by Eliza and Little Eva doing the same thing. So his glory is only 50 per cent, as great as it would have been if he had done it first and alone.

Mr. Coolidge has gained well deserved fame by being our first public official to know when not to say anything.

I quote all these various cases of fame to illustrate how my case has a combination of them all. Pershing said:

"Lafayette, I am here."

I said:

"Cleveland, I am gone."

These others stand on something they said. I rest my case on what I did. I claim a man should be known by his deeds and not by mere words. I didn't stay and talk. I acted. I saw my duty and I done it.

Now I want this distinctly understood, that I have nothing against Cleveland. I love Cleveland because I knew them before this catastrophe struck them. She will arise from her badges and some day be greater than ever. But I simply couldn't stand the incessant sweeping by of bands, the din, the roar, the popping of corks, and the newness and brightness of the speeches, and the "fairness to other political parties" uttered from the platform. I just had to have a rest and return to the solitude and quiet of a Ziegfeld rehearsal, where everything is still and orderly as a prayer meeting.

P. S. Since I arrived in New York they read a platform.

P. S. It is now six hours later and everybody has forgotten what the platform was.

P. S. (third time). Before they forgot it, why, they nominated Coolidge. I'm telling you this as a scoop on the other papers.

They held off choosing a Vice President until the finish of the show. This is the first time a Vice Presidential nomination has been strong enough to hold an audience till the finish.

It has been rumored around town today that I left to prevent my being nominated as Vice President. I wish to state that that was exactly the case.

Well, so long, readers—both of you. Will meet you at the Democratic convention again. What it lacks in class, in comparison to the Republican one, why, they will make up in noise.

Tip to prospective delegates who are coming:

Leave your watches and jewelry at home. Bring nothing but your alternates. It's a cinch you can't lose them.

DEMOCRATIC CONVENTION OF 1924

The Democratic National Convention of 1924, which began in Madison Square Garden on June 24, was so destructive that it might truthfully be said to have destroyed the party of Bryan, Wilson, and Cleveland. No new party structure would arise out of the ruins until the election of Franklin D. Roosevelt in 1932.

Early in 1924, with stories of Republican corruption on the front pages of every newspaper in the country, the Democrats were jubilant. They believed that a Democratic return to the White House was in the offing. But there were more than a few problems; just as in 1920, the party was without a leader. Cox had been beaten so badly in 1920 that he was no longer a viable power in the party organization. There were only two obvious front runners, and both men—William G. McAdoo of California, and Alfred E. Smith, governor of New York—represented the divisions within the party that would bring its destruction.

McAdoo was a rural Georgian who exemplified all the virtues of small-town Protestant America. As an heir of the W. J. Bryan tradition, he was a "dry" native American Anglo-Saxon who appealed to Southern and Western Democrats. Alfred Smith was the antithesis of McAdoo. He was the product of Tammany Hall, the New York political machine; he was a wet, and in an era of rampant nativism his Irish-Catholic background was a severe political handicap. McAdoo and Smith reflected a polarity in the minds of many Americans; as the country grew increasingly urban and industrialized, native Americans began to resent the tensions which were a part of change. Many saw in Al Smith all of the worst aspects of the new America—urban, wet, immigrant, Catholic. The Democratic party was to be torn apart by this tension and fear.

The Ku Klux Klan, filled with racial bigots and religious cranks, powerfully influenced opinions in many sections of the South and West. To the Klan, Al Smith personified all the things "good people" should oppose; and, the organization decided, the New York Catholic must be defeated at all costs. The Klan had no candidate it really could trust, for McAdoo had not agreed to the Klan's program. But, he was a prohibitionist and a Protestant. That McAdoo never spoke for or against the Klan was to his advantage.

A surprising development changed the political scene. Early in the campaign McAdoo was the apparent candidate for the Democratic party; however Senator Walsh's committee investigating the Teapot Dome oil scandals involved the presidential hopeful in the proceedings. This was the first indication that any Democrats were involved.

Edward L. Doheny, one of those implicated in the Teapot Dome affair, testified before Walsh's committee that he had hired McAdoo to represent him as legal counsel. Although this occurred after McAdoo left government service, he had received $25,000 a year for five years. But the oil scandals eventually involved members of both major political groups. Despite McAdoo's innocence, the Smith forces employed a guilt-by-association campaign to destroy McAdoo's chances for the nomination, even though he did well in the primaries, capturing North Dakota and defeating local candidates in Georgia and Florida. By convention time it appeared that McAdoo might have as many as 500 first ballot votes, far short of the 751 required to win.

As expected Smith had the support of the big city bosses—a mixed blessing during an anti-urban era. Smith did what he could to avoid the close association with Tammany. He appointed as his campaign manager, Franklin D. Roosevelt, a known anti-Tammany foe who was also protestant and dry. Recovering from his bout with polio he had contracted in 1921, Roosevelt's task was to reconcile the anti-Smith forces of the party in the South and West. Before the delegates officially gathered for the convention, it was obvious that both Smith and McAdoo controlled enough votes to veto the other's nomination. As they both represented such opposite views on practically every issue in the country, a deadlock also was certain.

Complicating matters more was the plethora of favorite son candidates. Almost every registered Democratic leader in the party seemed at one time or another to be a candidate. John W. Davis of West Virginia and New York was an important dark-horse candidate. With a long record of yeoman service to the party, he had been Ambassador to London and enjoyed a reputation as one of the foremost constitutional lawyers in the country. He had money, was pro-League of Nations, and appealed to conservatives in both parties. And Davis appealed to the labor voters in the country because of his excellent record on their behalf. William J. Bryan denounced him vehemently, but Davis still was a viable compromise candidate.

McAdoo and his forces faced a set back, however, on the first day of the convention when the Iowa delegation which had supported him offered former Secretary of Agriculture E. T. Meredith as their favorite son. Complicating the bad news was the announcement by the North Dakota delegation that they were switching to Smith because of McAdoo's refusal to state his position on the Klan. On the second day of the convention Senator Walsh of Montana was elected permanent convention chairman and the roll was called for the nominating speeches. For two and one-half days, 43 speeches were made on behalf of sixteen candidates.

Franklin Roosevelt nominated Al Smith and thereby created one of the most dramatic moments of the convention. From crutches, Roosevelt moved the entire auditorium to applause—even the anti-Smith forces. In the last few sentences of his nominating speech Roosevelt gave Smith the name of "the Happy Warrior," a sobriquet that would follow him for the rest of his life. Will Rogers described the convention as a wild scene where delegations marched and yelled for an hour. Much of the demonstration was for Roosevelt and not Smith.

The Klan issue surfaced during the fifth day of the convention. Homer Cummings read a proposed majority platform; then a minority plank concerning the Klan was added. The platform Cummings read called for religious toleration and asked for racial harmony; the minority plank openly condemned the Klan and its activities. For several hours delegates and spectators roared as speakers tried to talk for or against the platform. William J. Bryan's speech showed he was old, tired, and out of step with the world, when he spoke in favor of the Klan. His comments enraged many delegates and people in the galleries; he was loudly booed. When an Underwood supporter from the state of Georgia spoke in favor of the minority plank, the band played "Marching Through Georgia" and outraged Southerners. When the vote on the anti-Klan plank was taken, supporters of Bryan, the Klan, and others won by less than one full vote. They had won a bitter victory, but one that spelled disaster for the party.

The deadlock between McAdoo and Smith caused so much contention and confusion that, after the sixty-sixth ballot, a delegate moved the rules be suspended and an evening session without spectators be held. His motion was quickly defeated. Two ballots later an Arizona delegate with a sense of humor suggested casting a vote for Will Rogers—he got little support for this idea. On the next ballot McAdoo reached his peak with 530 votes, twenty short of the simple majority. On Saturday the convention adjourned for the weekend.

During the balloting on Monday McAdoo's strength declined appreciably, and Smith finally received a plurality of votes on the eighty-sixth ballot. This was a trend that continued, for on the eighty-eighth ballot on July 8, it was evident that McAdoo definitely was finished. Interestingly, Senator Samuel Ralston's name reappeared on the seventy-fourth ballot, and by the ninety-third ballot he appeared to be enjoying a stampede, for he had 196½ votes, Smith 355½, and McAdoo 314. News of the death of Calvin Coolidge, Jr., the President's son, had prompted adjournment on Monday night. A second recess also was called for Tuesday evening.

During Tuesday night more political maneuvering occurred during which both Smith and McAdoo considered withdrawing their names, but neither proved willing to put party or country above personal ambitions. When the convention reassembled, delegates learned that sixty-six-year-old Senator Ralston had the good sense to withdraw his name again. As a result of Ralston's withdrawal eighty-one votes returned to McAdoo, and John W. Davis moved into third place. Davis supporters had waited for this moment, hoping that they could present their candidate as a compromise nominee. Thereafter Davis gained votes. On the ninety-sixth ballot McAdoo realized he could never win. In response to pleas by party regulars, he agreed to remove his name from the list of nominees. It was 3:00 a.m. after the ninety-ninth ballot that the convention learned of McAdoo's actions. The convention adjourned until the next day, hopefully to choose a candidate.

During the night Smith thought of his position and the future of the party, and, like McAdoo, realized he could not win. To continue the fight would only further splinter the party. He decided to throw his support to Senator O. W. Underwood, a move that caused the dry McAdoo votes to switch to Davis for the nomination. On ballot 103 Davis stampeded the convention finishing with 844 ballots to Underwood's 102½. The hotly contested Democratic convention was over.

The delegates adjourned after Thomas Walsh quickly rejected offers to become the vice-presidential candidate. A conference of party leaders met later to nominate a vice president. Actually, that evening twelve nominations were made—Walsh being absent and sending a letter requesting he not be considered—but in the final analysis Davis wanted Charles Bryan, W. J. Bryan's brother, and the convention gave him what he wanted. The die was cast, the party was terribly torn by factions, and the election of another Republican president would clearly show that fact.

φ φ φ φ

Fortunately for Will Rogers and his fans, the Democratic convention opened in Madison Square Garden the same day the *Follies* opened at the New Amsterdam Theatre in New York, and he was able to appear on stage and still cover the political "show" for the newspapers. And his scribbled notes show that he was able to use some of the same "gags" for both purposes.

Crowding the theatre were many conventioneers who came to hear Will Rogers' comments as well as to enjoy the color and pageantry of the performance and the beauty of the Follies girls. There were other shows in town, but only one Will Rogers. With the convention in full swing it was natural for him to talk about politics on stage and write about the convention as though it were just as big a production as Ziegfeld ever designed.

Rogers stayed at the Astor Hotel in New York, spending as much time as possible at the convention, fussing about the long dry speeches, the noisy demonstrations, and keeping the press stand in stitches with his humorous asides. When the time came, he would rush to the theatre, stroll out on stage, and entertain the audience with the version of what he had seen during the day. Many of the "gags" he typed on scraps of paper—sometimes comments or just key words or names—then he would mark an X beside the ones he had used in his articles so he would not repeat himself. No doubt the same ones were incorporated into his act on stage, but with many spontaneous modifications as he "worked" with his audience, improvising as the audience reacted. Then he would rush back to the convention, visit with friends, and gather material for his column the next day. If he grew weary and sometimes nodded or dozed a little during the proceedings, it is not surprising.

It must have been difficult for him to find time to interview candidates when he constantly had to avoid being interviewed himself. Whatever he said or did was news. This was especially true after the Arizona delegation gave him one vote—actually, two half votes—for the presidential nomination on July fourth.

He was interviewed in his dressing room at the theatre that night. A story in the *New York Times* July 5 reported the interview:

> What do you think of being nominated for the nomination, Mr. Rogers was asked.
>
> Wait a moment, he replied, I cannot talk statesmanship clothed in the habiliments of the art of Thespis. I must change from my stage costume.

So he put his necktie on and then began:

> This is a very serious moment in the destinies of the nation. The Democratic Party is locked in a strangle hold and can make no progress. My candidacy represents nothing more than the effort of the plain people—of which I am one, very plain, that's why I'm in the Follies—to remedy this disastrous condition of affairs.
>
> It is my duty to go directly to the scene of the conflict and marshall the forces of right and justice. I do not seek this office, but respond to public demand in the spirit in which Spartacus left his plow in the furrow. I leave my Ford in the ditch and go to lead the movement to which the unanimous vote of that one Arizona delegate—who deserves a high place in the country's roll of patriots—calls . . . .

The story continued for several paragraphs, and the reporter and editors of the *New York Times* knew there was no need to explain that Will Rogers was "spoofing" the readers with the same sort of political "hot air" he had been hearing for more than a week at the Democratic convention. The readers in 1924 knew this already.

As the convention struggled through the nomination of some 60 candidates, including Rogers, plus the unending seconding speeches by those who hoped to draw attention to themselves or their state via radio, the Oklahoma humorist's comments on the dullness and repetition became more obvious. He remarked that no theatre audience would ever sit through such a "show." Yet he actually did write a running report of the conventions of 1924. No longer was he simply writing gags or jokes as he had for the conventions of 1920. This time he was on the scene, watching with shrewd eyes, hearing with well-trained political ears, and writing about events as they happened.

Playing the role of the naive observer or the bewildered innocent, he was able to expose the dysfunctional nature of many convention practices by "poking fun" at events of the day. Rogers' readers were able to sift through the deluge of information poured forth from the newspapers and spot the comic and ridiculous antics present in the well planned pageantry. From time to time, his real exasperation at poor leadership shows in his articles. To a man like Rogers, whose mind cut through all the rhetoric and bombast, quickly sifting the truth from the pretense, it must have been difficult to sit through so much confusion. He managed to keep his columns humorous, but they came very close to having a cutting edge as the days dragged by. In his article written July 9, he emphasized the length of the convention by pretending the item was written by Will Rogers, Jr., who was carrying on the life's work of his father, covering the Democratic convention. When the convention finally ended, Rogers said he had not been forced to make a single joke—he just reported what happened.

Rogers evidently contracted with McNaught Syndicate to cover both conventions for a set fee, but he had not counted on having to do so many articles. He published five on the Republican convention, but he wrote eighteen on the Democratic "Follies." Even though he was noted for his boundless energy, Rogers must have been physically and mentally exhausted from doing the shows and covering the conventions. The heat was intense, the necessity to travel from one place to another, and the additional appearances he made in between, must have sapped his strength. His writing seemed as effortless as did his personal comments on stage, but the notes that exist are proof that he had to put forth considerable effort to find humor at the conventions. Most of these notes he worked into the articles in one form or another; others he probably used on stage.

As a follow up to the Democratic nominations, he typed rough notes for telegrams to major figures, complete with imaginary replies. To John W. Davis, whose running mate was Charles W. Bryan, he offered congratulations, adding: "I hear you are to be associated indirectly with one of the Bryan Boys. For God sake pick the right one. If I had to be beat by some man I would rather it was you than anybody." In the pretended reply from Davis, he wrote: "Thanks Will for your kind suggestion, I will pick the right Bryan and watch the other one. Will if you want to be my Ambassador to England you can have the Job and my knee Pants."

To Al Smith, he wrote: "I told you Al you would be the Lucky one that they would nominate Davis . . . Well Al . . . we will go back to our Respective Follies, Me to the Amsterdam and You to Albany . . . We will make a joint Campaign in 28 Al and I will take you away out west as far as Pittsburg." Typing Smith's reply, Rogers said: "Thanks for the Message Will, Honest counting is all that beat me, If we had had Tammany Counters up there it would have been over in one day. Thanks for your 10 Gallon donation to the entertainment Committee." To McAdoo, he pretended to wire, "Its tough Mac but you wouldent have liked Washington any way . . . . . "

Also in his typed notes, he made several "resolutions" that he would have liked to introduce. In one he praised the New York taxi drivers for not running over any more of the delegates and newsmen than they could help; in another he expressed appreciation for the grade of beer served to the press. On behalf of "his paper," the *New York Times,* he wanted it understood that they had nothing to do with bringing such a convention to the city; and finally, he thanked the bootleggers of New York for their "hearty cooperation in keeping the price within the reach of all. They made up in Bulk what they liked in price," he added.

As if in mock apology for his humorous comments, Rogers finished his notes with: "No one could possibly do anything to mar the dignity of the Convention. When the whole thing was applesauce."

(Texts for the following articles are based on the *New York Times* unless otherwise noted. Variations are from the *Tulsa Daily World* TDW. — The Editors)

New York Times, June 23, 1924

Article #1 Democratic Convention

WILL ROGERS FEARS THE MADISON SQUARE SHOW MAY

RIVAL HIS IN MAGNITUDE OF ITS APPEAL[1]

by Will Rogers

Sunday morning, at the depot at Atlantic City, two special trains were standing side by side. One was our train carrying the Ziegfeld Follies Company back to New York after a week's tryout of the new show. The other was for a bunch of Delegates going to the Democratic Convention in New York. Nobody seemed to know which to take, so, being an accommodating kind of a person, I called out:

"On your left for the Ziegfeld Follies show and on your right for the Democratic Consolation Show."

Now both shows open Tuesday. The Democrats go to Madison Square Garden, where Ringling Brothers' Circus always plays, and we go to the Amsterdam Theatre, a beautiful theatre consecrated solely to Art.[2]

We think we have the best show we have ever had. They think they have the best show they ever had.

It's the first time in the theatrical history of New York City where two shows of equal magnitude both opened on the same night.

It means "Men versus Women." They are featuring Men, and we are featuring Women.

I don't mean to appear partisan, just because I am with the Woman Show, but I think Women will outdraw Men as an attraction every time.

Can you imagine any one going into a big barn of a place to see Al Smith, Oscar Underwood, or that old Gentleman Ralston, when they can go into a comfortable theatre and see 100 of the most beautiful Creatures on earth? I tell you it's not in the cards.[3]

Now, take Bill McAdoo; he is a dandy, nice fellow, and I like him personally, but do you think I would go into a place to look at him when I could see Ann Pennington's knees?[4]

Of course, they may get a few of the riff raff, because some people will go to see anything. There are some people so old-fashioned that they still listen to a radio.[5]

But the class won't be there. They have got to get the class in their show to draw them in. Why, we have Imogene Wilson in our show, and she is better known than all their candidates put together.[6]

And the constuming: to compare that is a joke! Can you imagine my old friend William J. Bryan's old alpaca coat stacked up against the creations Evelyn Law and Martha Lauber will have on?[7]

Mind you, I am not criticizing any man's grooming (in fact, I couldn't). But when you come into New York to open, you naturally have to compete with what New York rival attractions have to offer.

Now, these politicians' suits are all right in the Chautauquas[8] (they know they are, for they have tried them for years), but not for New York.

The only thing they have on us is the badges. We are simply outbadged. Now, if you just want to look at badges and no beauty, why there is where you want to go, for as a badge display it is a total success.

Of course, we could put badges on our girls, but who wants to see a Follies' girl overdressed.

By an odd coincidence, both shows carry monologists. I have my little monologue in the Follies, and they are featuring in their consolation show another friend of mine, Pat Harrison of Mississippi.[9]

Now I can modestly and truthfully say that in comparing us two-why they have the advantage, for Pat will not only beat me for humor, but he will lay it all over me for distance.

There is only one point where I will beat him, and that is on account of his being a politician. I don't think he has had a chance to learn anything about it, and that is sound logic.

Then another overwhelming advantage he has over me is, I only had one week in Atlantic City to break in my monologue and he has had years doing this same one in the Senate.

There is no race of people in the world that can compete with a Senator for talking. Why, if I went to the Senate, I bet I couldn't talk fast enough to answer roll call.

Both shows are holding dress rehearsals Monday night. They are trying out their platform, the one they are to speak from, not the one they are supposed to stand on after nomination, as of course that one won't be strong enough to hold up Carter Glass.

The city is doing all it can to make their stay here remembered. The Mayor issued orders that no delegate was to be robbed until after the convention was called to order.

It was a beautiful Sunday here. The New York churches were crowded with New Yorkers. Coney Island was crowded with delegates.

It may have been a coincidence, but every preacher in town preached on "Honesty in Government."

My side kick, Mr. Bryan, arrived and sent his three trunks full of resolutions direct to the stage door. One trunk was leaking.

New York Times, June 24, 1924

Article #2 Democratic Convention

CONVENTION A SUCCESS SO FAR, SAYS ROGERS; WOULD ADJOURN BEFORE NOMINATION SPOILS IT.[10]

By Will Rogers

Democrats win first big victory![11]

Republicans run a bad last!

New York City scores big victory!

Cleveland, Ohio, runs second!

New York and the Democrats swamp Cleveland and the Republicans without ever having to start their convention. New York has had more convention in one day than Cleveland and the Republicans had in a week.

It can adjourn right now (which is 6 o'clock on the evening before it's billed to start) and it will have been a better convention than the Republicans had.

In fact, I suggested to them that if I was them I would adjourn before they nominated somebody and spoiled it all.

Excitement? Why, there are more bands playing in this town than there were delegates at Cleveland.

A State that didn't send at least two bands had their badges taken away from them.

If they had had that many bands and delegations parading all in different directions out in Cleveland, why, they would have had to borrow some streets from Toledo or Youngstown.

Al Smith copped off Fifth Avenue for his parade, and it took five hours for his followers to stagger by a given point.

Mr. McAdoo phoned me to come over to the Vanderbilt Hotel at 9:30 to meet the California delegation. Their train came in at 9. I got there, chatted with him, then had a very pleasant visit with Mrs. McAdoo, and I was tickled to death when she didn't ask me anything about politics.[12] We discussed the best way to bring up babies and raise them so they will never know that their parents had anything to do with politics.

About noon the Californians arrived. We found out the Los Angeles delegation had been selling lots to customers all along the line of march. That is what kept them so late.

Mr. McAdoo came out on the balcony of the hotel and made a very good speech, while the delegates went through the crowd and took first payments for choice corner lots in Hollywood.

Why, even Arizona, with the smallest representation (they are allowed one delegate, one-half a delegate-at-large and one alternate not to weigh over ninety-five pounds, stripped), why, when they arrived behind their band they created more excitement than Mr. Coolidge's home State of Massachusetts delegation did at Cleveland.

My home state of Oklahoma got here and wanted to parade the whole town on their way to the hotel and they haven't found them yet. They will be so worn out they will be no good for voting purposes.

Hawaiian Islands arrived with a vote and three-quarters and eighteen ukeleles.

They search every grip coming in here at the depot. That of course is done to protect the local dealers here. The town is closed up tight as a drum for everybody that don't control a vote. More badges have had drinks wasted on them today than in the entire three previous years of Republican rule. Theatre managers, hotel proprietors and boot leggers all agreed on a minimum price during the convention. They figure the bulk of business done will make up for the lower prices.

Tomorrow is what they call Credential Day.[13] Every delegate has to show he is a bona fide delegate with a vote before a Tammany man is allowed to start saying, "Well, here's how we get you."

What a wonderful convention this would be in history if they just wouldn't start the balloting at all.

The only thing that can spoil this convention is for them to nominate someone.

New York Times, June 25, 1924

Article #3 Democratic Convention

ROGERS SEES HARRISON AS RIVAL MONOLOGIST; LEARNS FROM HULL WHAT THE CONVENTION IS FOR[14]

By Will Rogers

Well, the Democratic scandals got started yesterday.[15]

Cordell Hull, the Chairman, announced that Cardinal Gibbons would offer the opening prayer. He was informed by some Republican that Cardinal Gibbons had been dead for three years, but that he might prevail on Cardinal Hayes to act instead.[16]

Hull evidently knows more about politics than the ministry.

The thing was almost an hour late starting. You could tell the delegates who had been entertained by Tammany men the night before. They looked awful, and must have felt terrible.

The building is literally lined with flags. I could never understand the exact connection between the flag and a bunch of politicans.

Why a political speaker's platform should be draped in flags, any more than a factory where men work, or an office building, is beyond me.

A man handed around in the press stands some thick paper-back books. I asked, "Is this the life of Old Hickory?" He said, "No, that is Pat Harrison's keynote speech."

Jealousy is a hard thing to overcome, but I must admit my rival monologist of the United States Senate, Pat Harrison, told things on the Republicans that would have made anybody but Republicans ashamed of themselves.

When he mentioned old Andy Jackson he just knocked those Democrats off their seats. Then, as he saw they were recovering, he hit 'em with the name of Thomas Jefferson, and that rocked them back. Then he mentioned Woodrow Wilson, and that sent them daffy.

I am not up on political etiquette, but it struck me as rather strange, after paying a tribute to a wonderful man, that the delegates should raise up and start shouting and singing "Hail, Hail, the Gang's All Here, What the H____ Do We Care." They hollered and shouted and sang "John Brown's Body" and "Tipperary." Even my old Side-Kick Bryan, was prancing around the hall shouting. Now, he has been brought up different. He has read the Bible, even if it was just to get quotations from, but he knows, even if those other delegates didn't, that that was no way to pay tribute to a martyred President.

As poor as the Republican Convention was I will give them credit, they didn't sing "Hail, Hail, the Gang's All Here" when the speaker mentioned Lincoln.

The whole thing looked like a sure stampede for Wilson. So there will be a terrible disappointment when the delegates find that he, like Cardinal Gibbons, has passed beyond and won't be able to accept.

As usual, they opened by singing our anthem. After they had all finished Chairman Hull announced that Miss Anna Case[17] would sing it.[18] I suppose he did that just to show what a sucker she could make out of the 12,000 who had just sung it. It made me feel terribly embarrased, for I thought I had done a pretty good job of it at first.

Chairman Hull pulled another beaut. He read what the convention was gathered here for: "That it was to nominate a man to run for President, and take any other drastic means necessary."[19]

Just to give you an idea of what a big thing this convention is, Mayor Hylan came all the way from Palm Beach to be here.[20]

Mayor Hylan then made a welcoming speech to the convention. It was "Honesty in Private and Government Affairs." I don't see why he should lecture the delegates; they are not going to get away with anything out of this town.

But he did have a sure fire finish to his act. He said, "I have told them to issue you little cards that will be good for every so-called private place in New York."[21]

Thursday they start balloting and as fast as a Presidential candidate is eliminated he has to leave the hall. I look for the building to be empty by Thursday night.

If they look for a compromise candidate I want ex-Vice President Tom Marshall. There is a smart man and he has a sense of humor.

I will have a big inside story for you tomorrow that just broke this minute, and I will have the whole angle of it in tomorrow's article.

I suppose they will have Ben Franklin lead us in prayer tomorow.[22]

New York Times, June 26, 1924.

Article #4 Democratic Convention

WILL ROGERS COMES OUT FOR VICE PRESIDENT; CLAIMS ALL QUALIFICATIONS EXCEPT DRESS SUIT[23]

by Will Rogers.

The following is one of the bravest statements made in a political decade:

In the entire three years of preparation by the Democratic Party to groom some man for this present crisis there has never been a mention of a man to run for Vice President.

You see, every man that wants to run at all wants to be President, and a man would take his life in his hands to go and ask one of those fellows if he was willing to run for the second place.

It's bad enough to be nominated on that ticket for President, much less Vice President.

So I just got off and held a caucus with myself and said somebody has got to be sacrificed for the sake of party harmony. I hereby and hereon put myself in nomination, and to save some other man being humiliated by having to put me in nomination, why, I will just nominate myself.

Here is an enclosed certificate to show that this is bona-fide:

I, Dr. Isador Moskowitz[24] of 234 East Mott Street, have examined the enclosed patient, Mr. Will Rogers, and find him to be of sound mind and body (in fact, sounder in body than mind). This certifies that if he wants to run for Vice President I see no way of preventing it.

Signed, Isador Moskowitz, whose doctor's commission expires June 1, 1925.

So I, Will Rogers, of Claremore, Oklahoma; Hollywood, California, and 42nd St. and Broadway, New York, do hereby step right out and declare myself, not only as a receptive but an anxious candidate for the husband's position (meaning second) on the forthcoming Democratic ticket.

On first hearing this it may sound like a joke, but when I relate to you some of the qualifications which I possess, why, I think any fair-minded man will give me serious consideration.

But the trouble is there are not any fair-minded men in politics.

In the first place, they have got to nominate a farmer who understands the farmers' condition. Well, I got two farms in Oklahoma, both mortgaged, so no man knows their condition better than I do.

He has also to be a man from the West, Well, if a man came from 25 feet further West than I lived last year, he would have to be a fish in the Pacific Ocean.

Dawes was nominated on the Republican ticket on account of his profanity. Now I have never tried cussin' in public, but I guess I could learn to get used to it before a crowd.[25]

Another big reason why I should be nominated is I am not a Democrat.

Another still bigger reason why I should be nominated is I am not a Republican.

I am just progressive enough to suit the dissatisfied.

And lazy enough to be a Stand Patter.

Oil has never touched me. The reason I know it never has is, I drilled a well on my farm in Oklahoma, and I never even touched it, much less oil touching me.

I never worked for a big corporation.

When the President can't go anywhere, why, the Vice President has to go and speak or eat for him.

Now, I could take in all the dinners, for I am a fair eater.

I could say, "I am sorry the President can't come, but he had pressing business." Of course, I wouldn't tell the reason why he didn't come, so I am just good enough a liar to be a good Vice President.

I am not much of an after-dinner speaker, but I could learn two stories, one for dinners where ladies were present, and one for where they were not.

Of course I have no dress suit. The Government would have to furnish me a dress suit. If I went to a dinner in a rented one, they would mistake me for a Congressman.

I have the endorsement of my friends William J. Bryan, Pat Harrison, Al Smith, McAdoo, Ben Turpin, Bull Montana, Izzy and Moe, Senator Walton, Ring Lardner, Bugs Baer, Irvin Cobb, Rube Goldberg and Kin Hubbard.[26] I know I can hear a lot of you all say, "Yes, Will, you would make a good Vice President, but suppose something happened to the President?"

Well, I would do just like Mr. Coolidge—I would go in there and keep still and say nothing. He is the first President to discover that what the American people want is to be let alone.

It won't take much to launch the boom. We will wait till about tomorrow, and when some dark or even light horse is eliminated, we can take their headquarters, and buy their buttons and badges cheap.

P. S. I was born in a Log Cabin.

New York Times, June 27, 1924

Article #5 Democratic Convention

WILL ROGERS DOUBTS SANITY OF DELEGATES; THE MAN I'M ABOUT TO NAME' AGONIZES HIM[27]

By Will Rogers

Well, of all bunk I ever saw collected in one building, it was in there yesterday.[28] It was like a menagerie at feeding time.

We heard nothing from 10 o'clock in the morning until 6 at night but "The man I am going to name." Then they talk for another thirty minutes and then, "The man I am going to name." There have been guys going to name men all day, and all we ever got named were about six out of a possible 200.

Franklin Roosevelt started in early in the morning with the "Man I am about to name." He had the opportunity of a lifetime to make a name for himself comparable with the Republican end of the Roosevelt family. But no, he must say, "Man I am about to name" for ten pages.

If he had just said, "Delegates, I put in nomination Alfred Smith; try and find out something against him," why, the people would have classed it as a nominating speech that would have lived through the ages. But he must talk what we have heard for four days—"Corruption, honesty in government and the man I am about to name."

But when he did get to the end and named Al you would have thought somebody had thrown a wildcat in your face. The galleries went wild and about ten State delegations marched and hollered for an hour.[29] Talk about our civilization! Why, if they ever took a sanity test at a political convention 98 per cent would be removed to an asylum.[30]

By an odd coincidence Mrs. McAdoo and Mrs. Al Smith[31] were in almost adjoining boxes. I worked my way over there during the demonstration and talked with Mrs. McAdoo about when she was going to bring the boss to our show. I love to talk with her, we never have to talk politics. It's either children or shows. She seemed to be enjoying the Smith demonstration, knowing of course that most of the hollering and marching was not done by delegates with a vote.

Then I went over to Mrs. Smith's box and talked with Mrs. Smith and their two boys, two regular kids. I just wanted to see how they took this. Well, they thought it was great, but wanted to know if I would give them a rope and show them how to catch some of their pets when they got out.

Mrs. Smith is a charming, plain, every-day woman, and I watched and studied these two, one of which will probably be next First Lady of the Land.[32] They are similar in a way. Both are plain, home-loving mothers and the greatest thing that I can say for them is, I'll bet you if either or both of their husbands are defeated at this nomination, that outside of the disappointment that they will feel for their husband's sake, neither one of them will have any great personal regret, for they strike me as being ladies that would rather rule around a nursery than around a White House reception.

While on this "human interest" tour the next box I stopped at was Barney Baruch's. I guess he is about the only scandalously rich man that is not a Republican. He is one of the few dollar a year men during the war that earned it. He had his wife and two lovely daughters with him and they were pulling for McAdoo.[33]

My next stop was at Mayor Hylan's box. He asked me to come in and chat a while. Father Duffy, the "Fighting Chaplain" of the New York Division during the war, a man whom I love and admire as any man I ever knew, was also with the Mayor.[34] The Mayor endorsed my Vice Presidential boom.

Some one after saying fourteen of these, "The man I am about to name" finally decided to name Governor Ritchie of Maryland as a possible President. Well, Maryland broke out and next to Smith or McAdoo it was by far the next most foolish.[35]

Only Maryland and Delaware were in on this demonstration but if they had as many votes as they have noise he would be our next vetoer.[36]

Maryland has a flag that looks as if they were advertising a Turkish cigarette.

They kept marching by, trying to get the District of Columbia to join them, not knowing, of course, that the District has no votes. But one more emblem would have broken up their Turkish flag color scheme.

Kansas had a man who is a Governor that they were "about to name" for about forty minutes before even the speaker who was nominating him could think of his name. It was Davis. This race will be clogged up with Davises before the end of the week.[37]

Some bird from Michigan made such a flowery and glowing tribute to one of his fellow-statesmen that it did not look to me as if a soul in Michigan could fill the bill but Henry Ford, but he fooled us by naming their Governor.[38]

You could never tell by a man's talk who he was going to nominate. They all kept the names until the last word. It was safer.

A fellow named Igoe from Illinois told us seventeen times that he was from Illinois and was raised on a farm. Now, he didn't no more have to tell us he was raised on a farm than I would have to tell my audience I was raised on a farm. After it was all over, we found out, much to our astonishment that he was one of the twenty-one that were only seconding the nomination of Al Smith. I thought he was at least going to nominate ex-Mayor Bill Thompson of Chicago for President.[39]

I guess the two or three States that did not nominate the Governor for President must have done away with the Governor system and put in the commission form of government.

It got so bad there for awhile I signaled the Oklahoma delegation to nominate Jack Walton, our ex-Governor.

That seems to be the penalty of a man being Governor during a Presidential year. Some Yap will humiliate him by naming him as their favorite son for President.

One nominator talked so long I knew it couldn't be Mr. Ralston he was going to nominate, for he would have died of old age before he was named.[40]

One man from Iowa spoke for eighty minutes on the forty years' war. Nobody knew what in the world he was talking about. Then he finally said, "I second the nomination of Al Smith." It was the only surprise of the day, because everybody figured he was trying to borrow something from the convention.[41]

Illinois has forty delegates and they are all for different candidates and all have to make either nomination speeches or seconding speeches. According to the speeches, a candidate is harder to second than he is to nominate.[42]

Oh yes, a woman from Oregon seconded McAdoo for the ninth time.[43] She didn't have to come.[44] She could have stood on the banks of the Columbia River in Oregon and we could have heard her perfectly. I bet she busted every radio east of the Mississippi. She made a sucker out of the loud speaker they had for the building.[45]

New York Times, June 28, 1924

Article #6 Democratic Convention

WILL ROGERS DROPS VICE PRESIDENTIAL HOPES, WEARIED BY WINDY SPEECHES IN THE CONVENTION[46]

By Will Rogers

Every year in New York they hold in Madison Square Garden a six-day bicycle race. There are two men to a team and one of them is on the track all the time, night and day, for six days and nights. These men do this for fabulous prices.[47] They are experts in this particular line. They train for it, as it requires stamina, skill and strategy to last during the entire week. Now, off-hand, you would consider that the silliest thing that a human being could do was to ride a bicycle six days and nights.[48]

Well, I saw something yesterday that for stupidity, lack of judgment, nonsensicality, unexcitement, uselessness and childishness has anything I've ever seen beaten. It was the Democratic National Convention.

Comparing it to the six-day bicycle race would be like comparing Mutt and Jeff to a Rembrandt.[49]

Imagine, if you can, thousands of people gathered in a hall at 10:30 in the morning from all over our Union, the representative people being forced to sit there from then to 6 in the evening and listen to the very same identical speech made over and over again by fifty different people. Now that would be all right for one day, but you must remember that this has been going on for four days. Just think of taking up the valuable time of twelve thousand people, day after day, with:

"The man I am about to name to you, that matchless leader; the man who can carry us to victory in November, that son of Democracy, not only loved by his own State but respected and admired by all, that only true successor to that great man Woodrow Wilson."[50]

Now, that was wonderful, to pay a fine tribute to the memory of such a man as Wilson, and it was done beautifully by Pat Harrison the first day and who caused a real outburst of enthusiasm. But when you hear it dragged in for five straight days, every one in the same way, just to receive applause, it's bad.

"Never an Original Remark."

To show you that I must not be alone in my judgement, yesterday there were several speakers who were never allowed to finish.[51] They were interrupted all the way through. Where these delegations get these speakers from Heaven only knows. They tried a lot of women, and outside of one from Pennsylvania, the first one that spoke, why, they were just as bad as the men.[52] It does seem that out of all this barrage of everlasting talk, that maybe just accidentally some one would have made an original remark, or perhaps coined some epigram that could be remembered. But no, not even by accident has a sage remark been dropped.

You can't do it when you all are doing the same speech. Here are delegates brought here on a very serious business, to nominate a man for the highest office is the gift of this nation. They pay their own expenses here and are paying high hotel rates, and lots are from a part of the country where every dollar has to be made last as long as it can.

And I want to tell you that it is a shame that men are allowed to get up there on that platform and take up the time of eleven hundred honest, patriotic men and women who have come here for a purpose, and want to get it over and get back home. I say it is a downright imposition for speakers to get up there when they have no more to say than has been said by 90 per cent of them during this convention.

You must remember that these delegates are like prisoners in a way. They have got to listen to you, so every one of you who get up there and take up their time are simply hitting a man when he is down. Not only doing that, but you are robbing him. Can you imagine a theatre audience sitting there listening to the same old hokum over and over again? Why, they would get the hook on you so fast these delegates would be back home in three days.

Wouldn't Go on the Family

The stuff that they pull there is an insult to the intelligence of their audience. The American people must be the most tolerant people in the world. But even they will turn, and they are commencing to turn in this audience.

Why, will you tell me, should a man be seconded by some one from almost every State? I will tell you why: Just to gratify the ambition of some local man or woman who want it said they got up before the convention and seconded for the forty-second time Mr. So-and-So.

Practice some of your oratory on your own family at home and see how quick they will walk out on you. Don't pick on an audience that through courtesy and patriotism has to stick to hear how little you have to say.

And even in nominating your man, why should it be necessary to tell for two hours what he has done? If he has not done anything that the people already know about, he has no business being a candidate; and if he has, they already know it. You are insulting them by telling them something they already know.

If a man had had sense enough to have gotten upon the platform and said: "Delegates, I present to you for President Mr. John Smith" (or whoever he might be presenting), and then sit down, there would have been the wildest excitement in that hall you ever saw and his candidate would have probably been elected on the spot, just as a relief and a rebuke to those terrible orators.

I covered the Cleveland convention and said it was terrible, but I want to tell you this is worse, for theirs didn't last as long, and they did not allow every voter to second the nominations.

One guy from Montana, Maloney, forgot his speech and didn't say anything. He was the hit of the day. They applauded for five minutes. That should have been a tip to the other speakers. But no, if he has learned something at home he can't change it. Maloney can remain proud of himself for the rest of his life, for he had by far the best speech at the New York convention.[53]

Sees Deaf and Dumb Vote Won

Another speaker, through the crowd interrupting him, never got to name the man he was talking about. The candidate gained hundreds of votes right there by this man never mentioning him. If some of these candidates can be elected after these speeches then they have got to find voters who are deaf and dumb.

There is a society in this town that stops us when we abuse or unnecessarily annoy a bucking horse or wild steer right in this same Madison Square Garden. Now, why in the world don't they get busy and protect a delegate? No trained animal was ever tortured like these delegates have been for four days. They are visitors here and it's not fair to them. New York can certainly do as much for a delegate as they can for bucking bronchos.

The six-day bicycle race goes six days and never gets anywhere. But then, they didn't start anywhere. This thing talks six days and never says anything.

The only purpose I can see that the whole thing has answered is that it has educated the convention up on who the Governors of the Democratic States are. If I was a Governor I would have it in my contract that I was not to be nominated at a Presidential convention.

I thought yesterday, when you had to hear all this unnecessary spouting[54] about each man, what their wives must have thought of all these new wonderful men that they had been married to all these years and were just finding out.

Now, I never propose a thing unless I have a solution to it. Make every speaker, as soon as he tells all he knows, sit down. That will shorten your speeches so much you will be out by lunch time every day.

Or make them be censored and not allow one man to repeat what some other man had already said. That would cut it down to just one speech at each convention.

I did want to run for Vice President, but I have changed since yesterday;[55] I want to go down and take my rope, and when the speaker has said enough, rope him and drag him back to his delegation. I will be a bigger help to my country in that way than any way I can think of.

Now, my readers, I hope you will pardon me for not being funny in this article. But I like these delegates, and I want to try and do them a service that they will thank me for as long as they live.

New York Times, June 29, 1924

Article #7 Democratic Convention

PLATFORM MAKERS' PRAYER IMPRESSES / WILL ROGERS, WHO SAYS IT'S A BIT LATE[56]

By Will Rogers.

Well, it was 6:30, and they had just read the platform. I had it before me, forty-five pages. If it came out in the open on every question and told just where they stood, they could have saved themselves, not only forty-two pages of paper, but perhaps their election in November.

When you straddle a thing it takes a long time to explain it.[57]

It favors fixing everything the Republicans have ruined, keeping everything that they haven't, right up to its present standard.

In the Republican platform at Cleveland they promised to do better. I don't think they have done so bad this time. Everybody is broke but them.

They have been five days working on a plank on the Ku Klux and finally brought in the same one the Republicans used.

Some guy from Maine offered an amendment naming the Klan by name and they debated it for two hours. There were 12,000 civilians and at least a hundred thousand cops in and around the building. There were ten policemen standing in the aisle by the side of each Texas delegate.

I tell you it don't take much strategy for a man to keep his mouth shut around this hall now.

At the morning session Homer Cummings told what a hard time the committee had had getting the platform ready. He kept on telling the audience that he had not been to bed until 3 o'clock any morning and that yesterday morning[58] he went to bed at 6 A. M., and kept on talking about bed. I was sitting on the speakers' platform with Joe Tumulty, President Wilson's Secretary, and Pat Harrison.

Joe said, "Cummings is telling us a bedtime story."

He told how they had fought over the Ku Klux plank, and at 6 o'clock yesterday morning some one happened to think of the Democratic Party.[59] Well, it was such a frank statement that it made a hit, because most of the audience were interested in the party kinder indirectly, and they were glad to know that their Resolutions Committee had given the party a thought even if it was at such a late hour that the thought would perhaps do them no good.

He said there were fifty-four men on this committee and that they thought of prayer, and that they all recited the Lord's Prayer. (Can you imagine fifty-four typical political bosses reciting the Lord's Prayer at 6 o'clock in the morning?)

Then he explained to the convention that after they had finished that, William J. Bryan lifted up his voice in an invocation for guidance and help in this hour of stress.

Evidently Mr. Bryan was not satisfied with just the Lord's Prayer so he improvised one that he thought might be an improvement over the original, especially for this occasion.[60]

So you can see at a glance what drastic means this convention is forced to resort to.

The thing that struck the whole crowd so forcibly was (and Congressman Upshaw of Georgia remarked it to me):[61] Why did they wait till this late in the convention to pray?

I told my good friend, Mr. Bryan, when we were in Cleveland together and listened to their opening invocation, I said to him: "You better listen to that, for you fellows will have to do some praying in New York." So he can't say I didn't warn him.

And this is only a sample of what they will have to do in November.

I have always said that W. J. Bryan is the most valuable man the Democratic Party has got. Where would they have been on this prayer proposition if it had not been for him? Because Tom Taggart, George Brennan and Norman Mack would be absolutely useless in an emergency of that kind.[62]

New York Times, June 30, 1924

Article #8 Democratic Convention

WILL ROGERS RUNS INTO ONE DELEGATION THAT HE ADMITS HE IS UNABLE TO ROPE[63]

By Will Rogers

June 29, what a day to conjure with. It will go down in Democratic political history as one of the memorial days of their party.[64] It is Sunday, and they have adjourned and can't do anything. If you can keep a Democrat from doing anything, you can save him from making a mistake. That is why this will always be a remembered day.

Saturday they fought, balloted and orated all day, and perhaps it will go down in voting history as being the nearest to a dead heat that was ever run. Only for the fact that the State of North Carolina is the only State in the world that was ever mathematically able to divide a delegate into fractions, was one side able to defeat the other.

When North Carolina announced to the Chairman that three and eighty-five one-hundredths of a delegate were in favor of the Klan amendment, and that twenty and fifteen one-hundredths of a delegate were against it, why, there was a round of laughter that broke up what was the most tense moment ever witnessed in a convention hall.[65]

I left the press stand on a run. I wanted to see what manner of architectural anatomy a man or woman must have to be only fifteen one-hundredths per cent of a delegate, and how many men and women it took to constitute eighty-five one hundredths per cent of a delegate.

Well, that stopped the show. They had to wait until they got the professor of mathematics from Columbia University (they had to wake him up, as it was 2 o'clock in the morning), and he came in to see what process of arithmetic they had used to arrive at this odd subdivision of a human being.

Well, this professor and the Chairman could not do anything until they had called in some surgeons from Bellevue, because this was evidently a case of compound fractions, assisted by assorted sizes of operations in surgery.

Fourteen thousand people in the hall and 14,000,000 radios had to stand at attention while the doctors held a clinic over the North Carolina delegation.

And the funny thing about it was that it was only North Carolina apportioning out her delegates so that every voter could come and see New York that the noes were able to defeat the yeses.

And I don't know yet how they got at eighty-five and fifteen. I can understand ninety and ten, or sixty-six and two-thirds or one-third, but eighty-five-fifteen-can you savvy it? They must use some other total than a hundred.[66]

If a delegate is three-seventeenths of one vote, what would that make an alternate?

Singer's Midgets are the smallest number of people to one body I ever saw, and you can't even divide them up to go down as far as twentieths.[67]

Can you imagine a New York hotel preparing twenty-four rooms to receive North Carolina's twenty-four delegates and along come 480 to sleep in them, chaperoned by 480 alternates?[68]

How would you like to ask the North Carolina delegation out to dinner with you?

So, up to now, the two high spots in the entire convention are Maloney of Montana, who forgot his speech and hence was the best thing, here,[69] and the display of higher mathematics by that grand old Commonwealth of North Carolina.

I met and had a very pleasant chat earlier in the day with the Governor of North Carolina.[70] He invited me to come down some time. Now I don't know, if I went, whether I would meet him or twenty Governors. I am not going anywhere on a five-one hundredths per cent invitation.

Ex-Secretary of War Baker made a very impassioned emotional speech on the League of Nations. If he had been successful in his amendment he would have had credit for demoting his party out of about four million votes next November.[71]

They have conscripted sixteen men for President. They always do that, as you can't tell how many may back out on you.

The delegates are already getting color blind. They can't tell a dark horse from a light one.

I am still in for the Vice Presidency, but I don't think they will ever get down as far as the R's.

If they elect McAdoo they won't have to have a Vice President. He is so used to holding so many jobs in Washington that when he calls a Cabinet meeting all he will have to do is to talk to himself.[72]

Bryan made a great speech Saturday night,[73] but he didn't sway any of New York's vote. They are used to getting something for their votes besides oratory.

I can walk into that convention with one lone case of gin[74] and sway more votes than all the weeping of Baker, the elocution of Bryan, the epigrams of Pat Harrison, the briefness of Maloney, or the mother love of Mrs. Pennsylvania Brown.[75]

For it's just as Senator Pittman told Secretary Baker, politics is a business.[76]

Today they start balloting,[77] and I suppose some man will win the nomination by the narrow margin of a left forearm of a North Carolinian.

Saturday will always remain burned in my memory as long as I live, as being the day when I heard the most religion preached, and the least practiced, of any day in the world's history.

New York Times, July 1, 1924

Article #9 Democratic Convention

CONVENTION'S LONG STAY LOOKS LIKE SCHEME TO BOOST CITY'S CENSUS, SAYS WILL ROGERS[78]

By Will Rogers

Well, they have been balloting all day at the Democratic side show at the Garden, for that is what some misguided people think is the nominating place.

The real nomination is taking place in a room at some hotel with less than six men present.

And when it is known it will be as big a surprise to those delegates as it will be to you out in Arizona, and you will have just as much to do with it as they will have had.

They have been here so long it looks like a scheme on New York's part to hold these people here until after the next census is taken.

Every day somebody prays. Yesterday it was the audience.[79]

I sat up on the speaker's stand and I found a book of rules on one of those things.

An uninstructed delegate is one whom his district sent here with a free rein to use his own judgment, but when he comes back he is supposed to give up 50 per cent of whatever his vote brought.

An alternate is a man sent along to watch the delegate and see that he turns in the right amount, and it is also his duty to get out and drum up trade and keep track of prices and see what they are bringing other places. He, according to the rules, is to receive 10 per cent of the gross.

A delegate at large is one who gets a room and bath at the hotel.

The Chairman of a State delegation is a man that announces how many votes his State cast. The qualification for this job seems to be for a man that can't count. After he has announced the votes, they poll the delegates and he sees for himself just how near he guessed.

Another rule reads, no money shall change hands among buyers or sellers while on the floor of the convention.

This is purely a Democratic rule; the Republicans have no such restrictions. That is why they are the most prosperous party.

On account of this rule they had to adjourn this afternoon;[80] they had gone as far as they could; nobody would change his vote for nothing.

The rule is similar to one I wanted to introduce in Washington, that no Senator be allowed to buy liquor from another while on Government property.

Last night delegates were invited to dinners at the Ritz who up to then had watched their hats in Childs.[81]

Favorite son Governors who have been holding their States to the last finally told them:[82] "Boys, leave me and get out and do the best you can, but remember one thing: don't ever let it be said that our glorious State is cheap."

Personally if I was a Governor I would hold my delegation until at least today. Why, they will get twice as much for them as they did last night.[83]

The Government has an income tax man watching all transactions. In selling you have got to figure on a tax.[84]

One of my friends from Oklahoma won't even sell, he is just giving options.

Tammany is getting desperate. They say they will carry this convention if it takes every quart of liquor on Manhattan Island.

Politicians that buy[85] votes with wood alcohol should be careful and not deliver the drink until after the delegate has voted.

Prohibition has certainly raised the price of democracy. Votes that you used to be able to buy at conventions with a half dozen nickel beers are now thinking nothing of asking a case of Scotch.

An the tough part about it is that they are no better votes.

Some man ought to be running here on an out and out "wet" ticket and be carrying some of his samples. He would walk in.

I guess there are some men here who don't spend anything for delegates and it is easy to see who they are. They are the ones with no delegates.

The only mistake I can see is some of them have not bought enough.

I hope they don't go just too far and get them so they won't be able to vote tomorrow,[86] as I want to see this thing over and get back to the serious business of trying to entertain people.

If they are smart they will nominate some man we don't know.

I didn't think at first that the Democrats were serious about really nominating some one this year, but they tell me they have to put up somebody or they will lose their franchise.

New York Times, July 2, 1924

Article #10 Democratic Convention

WILL ROGERS SEES DARK HORSE TURN WHITE AND DESCRIBES THE 'SCIENTIFIC PHENOMENON' [87]

By Will Rogers

Well, folks, I have just come from a private visit with the Presidential nominee of this convention.

I didn't go there as a newspaper man to interview him; I was invited there by he himself.

I had never met the man before, but there he was, all alone in the private home of a friend, listening to the radio news of the convention.

He was one of the dark horses. I was there for perhaps thirty minutes or more. Now, they say a leopard never changes its spots. But I want to testify that just in thirty minutes I witnessed a human being (who may be our next President) change his color from a dark to a very flesh-colored light.

When I walked into a big private living room to meet him in there alone this fellow looked so black I thought they had made a mistake and I was, perhaps, meeting a Republican delegate from Georgia to one of their conventions.

But he was so pleasant, and seemed so glad to see me, and

repeated a few of my convention jokes, that I kinder overlooked his terrible darkness.

The radio was started going. They reached the M's, and Mississippi voted for John W. Davis.[88] Well, Sir, the figure opposite me commenced suddenly to grow lighter. He almost began to look like a white man. He kept on talking, asking questions about the convention, and offered me a cigar. That is the only political thing I noticed about him during the entire visit. Not smoking myself, I refused, but even if I was a smoker I have seen so many casualties from campaign cigars that I would have refused anyway.

I can truthfully say to you Drys that he is a Dry. That is, he was while I was there.

The radio started on another ballot, and it reached the M's again, and Missouri went from McAdoo to Davis. Well, there, right before my eyes, was transpiring a scientific phenomenon (I guess that is what those Birds would call it). Here was a political dark horse turning white, and I am the only human being that was there to witness it. I want to tell you that outside of the time Bryan asked me to have luncheon with him it was the biggest thrill I ever got.

A big political leader dashed into the house and remarked: "John, it's going just like we figured." I offered to withdraw, as I knew they had important business, but "No," he said. "You stay right here." And I sat there and heard the inner workings of a national convention.

Some day, with both men's permission, I might tell you what was said. I will start my little newspaper career by taking a tip from our President, Mr. Coolidge, by keeping my mouth shut. I feel mighty proud that these men trusted me enough to discuss things before me without even pledging me to secrecy. So I just listened, but I have plum forgot what they said.

You won't be disappointed in him. He is a real congenial, smiling he man.

I was awfully glad to meet him, as I already knew the other two leading candidates, Mr. McAdoo and Al Smith. They are all great fellows. I hate to see one win because I will hate to see the other two lose.

How would this do? Put in all three and put on three eight-hour shifts. My good old friend Gompers will support me in that plan.[89]

Divide the work. Let Mr. Davis, on account of his European experience, attend to all foreign affairs, also social ones. Let McAdoo handle the money, the labor questions and the railroads, and let our Al take a big stick and club those politicians into line and make them do something. A combination like that would be unbeatable. Elect them for life; then they wouldn't have to worry about where they were going from there. They could give all their time to their work.

I haven't room for it here, but I want to tell you I have spent the day talking to all the prominent ladies, exchanging a few old jokes for some real inside political information. The queen of all of them is here and will be at our show tonight—Mrs. Alice Longworth.[90] I got a lot of impressions from her. I also sat in Mrs. McAdoo's box and discussed California, and a little weeny bit of politics with Princess Bibesco, daughter of Mrs. Asquith.[91] She told me jokes faster than I could reach up and get them. So some Sunday I want to give you the ladies' angle on this thing. All of them.

The big break of this voting will come when Senator Saulsbury's[92] votes are released.[93]

Fashion will get you sooner or later. I noticed today[94] that the Arkansas men delegates have had their hair bobbed.

There are only two things that will get applause here now. One is a change in a whole State's vote and the other is an announcement that "some prominent Republicans have been indicted in the oil scandal." If they can just get enough of these Republicans in jail that they have indicted, why, the Democrats can win this election, just on account of there being none left out to vote.

I wanted the announcer to do like they do at the six-day bicycle race, offer $100 for a two-vote sprint.

Smith is going out to try and pick up a lap on the field.[95]

Mississippi changes her vote so often, they must be voting from the names in the telephone book. If the convention lasts long enough Ziegfeld will get it.

Ohio is still displaying a wonderful memory. They are with Jimmy Cox.[96]

Sallie Turner is still having Missouri polled.[97] Their names are better known to the convention than the candidates'.

This whole thing is just being dragged along to educate the Northerners[98] and the Southerners up to eat hot dogs. It will go down in history as the hot dog convention. By the end of the week these delegates will start barking, for the right candidate. I would rather have the dog privileges here than the nomination.

New York Times, July 3, 1924

Article #11 Democratic Convention

WILL ROGERS NAMES THE ONLY MAN, HE SAYS, WITH WHOM THE DEMOCRATS CAN SURELY WIN[99]

By Will Rogers.

(Nominating speech to be made by Will Rogers and to be

released to the press as soon as they get it. Don't wait for speech to be made.)

Old men and women of this assembled convention (for you are old if you were here when it started), Mr. Toastmaster, welcome guests and Republicans:

I have been sitting here day after day, and week after week, and listening to your fighting and wrangling; I have seen the smartest of your leaders and the shrewdest of your politicians trying to unfathom this disreputable mess in which you have entangled yourselves and the grand and glorious name of the old Democratic Party, a party which enrolls upon its books that grand nom de plume of Thomas Jefferson, that sturdy old oak, Hickory Jackson, and, in occasional cases, Bob La Follette.[100]

Oh, my friends, I am too good a Democrat not to be appreciative of what the party has done for me, not to try and warn you while there is yet time.

We are not gathered here just to name a nominee of the next election, but we are here to name the next President of the grand and glorious United States, of which this party today is the sole refuge for the true patriot.

In naming a man for this high and lofty office there are certain traditions and specifications which we must always hold in mind, if we want to reach a successful victory in November.

The man we name must be a man of unquestioned integrity. The man I am about to name has that very essential quality.

The man we name must be a man who is not now connected with these intersectional fights and feuds here on the floor. The man I am about to name is absolutely aloof from them.

The man we name to carry us to victory must be geographically strong enough to carry a majority of New England. The man I am about to name knows these mysterious canny people.

The man we name must be able to go into the far Westland and reap a majority. The man I am about to name possesses the attributes to do that very deed.

The man we name must be able to remove any doubtful States into the realm of certainty. The man I am about to name can give you a majority that will look like a census report.

The man we name here must be a man who never earned, outside of public life, a fee of over $10. The man I am about to name has that honorable reputation.

The man we name here must have no taint of Morgan or Wall Street. The man I am about to name never saw Wall Street.

The man we name here must have absolutely no affiliation with the Klan. The man I am about to name is not a member of the Klan.

The man we name must be of no minority religious creed. The man I am about to name belongs to the creed whose voters are in the majority.

On account of the present length of the convention, the man we name must not be of too many score of age. The man I am about to name has many useful and unworried years of public service ahead of him.

The man we name must have had no connection with oil. The man I am about to name never used oil, except at Government or State expense.

Oh, gentlemen of the grand and glorious Democratic Party, let us not make a mistake. We have our greatest chance this year to bring home victory. That great scandal in our opponents' party and their close affiliation with predatory wealth has given us an unbounded opportunity.

Don't let us disrupt the party when we can win. We will go to a sure Democratic defeat if we name the wrong man. Oh, my friends, let us be connected with a victory in this glorious year of 1924. Why court defeat?

The man I am about to name is the only man in these grand and glorious United States who, if we nominate, we can go home and have no worry as to the outcome. Don't, oh, my Democratic Colleagues, listen to my friend Bryan. He named ten candidates: ten men can't win! Only one man can win. Oh, my newly made friends, have confidence in me. Trust me just this once and I will lead you out of this darkened wilderness into the gates of the White House. Oh, my tired and worn friends, there is only one man. That man I am about to name to you is Calvin Coolidge.

New York Times, July 4, 1924

Article #12 Democratic Convention

SURVIVORS OF CONVENTION WILL GET BONUS AFTER SIX YEARS, SAYS WILL ROGERS[101]

By Will Rogers

I am in favor of taking the platform and making a motion that the convention adjourn and let the election go by default.

This thing has got to come to an end. These delegates and visitors may not know it, but right where they are sitting and sleeping every day is New York's municipal swimming hole.[102]

Summer is on us here and you visitors are depriving New York of their annual bath.

I suggested to Tex Rickard, who runs the Garden (when Taggart, Mack and Brennan are not here), that he turn the water on during the balloting.[103] I think the delegates would welcome a bath while here.

I met an old man on the street yesterday with a long beard. He could remember when this thing started.

New York invited you people here as guests, not to live.

One delegation told me yesterday that they either had to move to more modest quarters or to a more liberal candidate.

These halves, and quarters and eighths and sixteenths of delegates make it awful hard for a buyer to get to all of them. You may buy off fifteen and the fellow who controls the sixteenth will try and hold you up and you are stuck.

In years to come children will say, "Father, were you in the big war?" and father will say,[104] "No, son, but I went through the New York convention."

In six years the people of the United States will be paying a bonus to the delegates who survive this convention.

And the tough part of it is that it is not like the convention that you read about in the papers sixty-four years ago that had to move from Charleston to Baltimore. They can't move this one. They have tried it and no other town will take it. A second-hand convention is one of the hardest things to get rid of in the world.

For instance, why should Claremore, Okla. (the best town on Dog Creek), bind themselves to sit day after day and listen to: "Alabama, twenty-four votes. Alabama, twenty-four votes for Oscar W. Underwood. Total votes cast, 1,098. Necessary to elect, 732. No one having received the required two-thirds, the secretary will call the roll again."[105]

If any of you feel badly at not having been able to attend, why there is your convention right in those last few lines above.

If Alabama changes her vote we will never find it out, for just through force of habit they will say "Underwood" for days to come.

But she will run at least another week, for Bryan is going to make another speech.[106]

Today is the Fourth of July,[107] I suppose somebody will read the Declaration of Independence, and then Alabama will vote twenty-four for Underwood instead of Thomas Jefferson.

After it is read, somebody will bring in a minority report on it.

Some one prayed again today at the opening.[108] But they are beginning to lose interest even in prayer, as none of their prayers up to now have been answered.

Oh, what a bone-headed move I made by signing up with the

papers to write this convention for so much for the whole thing. I have spent more in taxi fares and lead pencils than I have been paid. The next one I will be smart enough to get paid by the month.

I have a nominating speech that I want to take the platform and make, but Bryan has blocked my every move. He is jealous of two monologuists going on the same bill. You have to have unanimous consent to be allowed to speak and I have all the thousand and ninety-seven votes—all but Bryan's. The Democratic Party has got to start breaking in some younger man to take Bryan's place in a few years. So why don't they take me.

But I guarantee you one thing, my friends. While I may never be able to put my man before the convention personally, I am going to do exactly like Bryan and devote the rest of my time to keeping the other fellow down if he shows his head and also to keep W. J. Bryan off that platform. Because in naming two dozen candidates yesterday, he failed to mention my name. You may have noticed me with a bundle under my arm. Well, that was my rope, and if he rises to speak on a point of order he exits via the rope.

The thing has just got to break pretty soon, as the women delegates' badges are wearing holes through their shirt waists and the convention may turn into an exposure in two more days.

Another reason I know it can't last much longer is that the women who sit in front, on the speakers' platform, are about to run out of different hats to wear.

They would rather lose the election than wear the same hat twice.

Princess Bibesco, with a bright new one on yesterday,[109] was all that kept the Oklahoma men delegates from bolting the convention.

I am sitting at my typewriter sound asleep, but I can still write "Alabama twenty-four for Oscar W. Underwood." That is better known right now in the building than the Lord's Prayer.

The Secretary will call the roll again.

New York Times, July 5, 1924

Article #13 Democratic Convention

CONVENTION MET TO CELEBRATE BIRTHDAY OF PRESIDENT COOLIDGE, WILL ROGERS THINKS[110]

By Will Rogers

The biggest celebration ever held in honor of a President's birthday was held in Madison Square Garden yesterday [111] in honor of the fifty-second birthday of Calvin Coolidge.

A man must be a pretty good President when the opposite party holds a demonstration all day and night in his honor.

They wanted to make him a present of an opponent, but it takes two-thirds to agree. Why, two-thirds of the Democrats never agreed on anything. There are not two delegates from any one State speaking to each other. How on earth are they ever going to get 732 to agree?

Met at 1 o'clock and my friend, Mr. Augustus Thomas, the orator and playwright, read what was called the Declaration of Independence.[112] Nobody knows how they ever found a copy of it. The J. P. Morgan private library has most all those old things, so I guess he loaned it to them.[113]

The delegates seemed mildly amused as he read this strange old legend.

On its completion, a delegate at large from Georgia offered an amendment to the Declaration of Independence which Mr. Walsh read.[114]

Ohio called for a poll of their delegation in case the Declaration came to a vote.

Mr. Thomas explained before starting to read it that it was written by Thomas Jefferson, a Democrat.

Had its author happened to have been a Republican it would have been denounced as a Senatorial Oligarchy.[115]

In this Declaration one paragraph said the Fourth of July was a national holiday and by this declaration was to be always considered such.

So the Democrats moved to amend the rules of the Declaration of Independence so they could work on July Fourth.

A candidate nominated on this day would not only be considered null and void by the voters in November, but it would be illegal for him to even run second.

Two days ago I came out for the nomination of Calvin Coolidge. Well, that was just like Mississippi or Louisiana. I wanted to give everybody a complimentary vote for a ballot or two. Cal hadn't got anything up to then, so I thought I might start a little jam his way. But on the next vote when I saw nobody was going with me, why I immediately switched, for I am like all of them. I want to be on the band wagon with the winner. Ohio will quit Baker[116] quicker than I quit Coolidge as soon as they see who will hand out the next Post Offices.[117]

Being with a loser may get you credit for being a game guy but it don't bring you in any Federal pork chops. You are a Favorite Son just as long as the winner is uncertain.

Mr. Walsh then told the Secretary to read the roll of States and see if there had been any new sales during the night. Every delegation had remained either honest or unfortunate during the night until he commenced to get down into the M's. Missouri voted no progress. Michigan reported no luck. But Minnesota had disposed of two votes, Smith being the lucky purchaser. All other delegates and alternates rushed over to get the quotations on what they had been able to get for them. Order was finally restored.

They then read a telegram from Mr. Ralston of Indiana saying he wanted to withdraw. This telegram had been here all week, as I know and everybody knows that he never did want to run. Never intended to.[118] But, anyway, Taggart did not read it until today.[119] Everybody was anxious to see who Taggart had sold to. But he is a pretty good business man. Prices were not quoted but McAdoo had been able to get 20 and Smith had got the other 10, showing you that they must have come pretty high or one candidate could have handled the whole lot.

This was the biggest individual deal recorded during the entire week and all the other delegates' mouths watered at Indiana's good fortune. Then they read another telegram, supposedly from Jimmie Cox. A Mr. Moore had been carrying it around all week and it was so torn that he could hardly make it out. It sounded just like Ralston's. But why shouldn't it? One man sent them both.

Well, everybody was all hopped up as to who would get these. But he fooled everybody by giving them to Newton Baker for Secretary of War, not for President. Mr. Baker will have the pleasure of hearing his name called for a few ballots while Mr. Moore is arranging the most advantageous terms possible for their ultimate disposal.

Jimmie Cox[120] is a very capable, smart man politically. He never intended to run and I think he did great by letting the boys use his name until they got a chance to clean up a little something. You should have heard the applause these resignations got. It should be a lesson for some of these other candidates who are still sticking in, most of whom are Senators.

A Governor will resign but you give a Senator a vote and you can't blast it from him.

I'm sending a telegram tonight to be read at the convention and signing Saulsbury's name, releasing his six votes, as they told me today they had come to New York to be in a crowd.[121]

I doubt very much if I can shame these Senators into it.

Bryan didn't speak today.[122] I'll bet you that this is the first Fourth of July in fifty years he did not lecture to the fortunate dead at Arlington or somewhere else.

If this deadlock keeps up I want to take the floor and nominate a candidate. I am not kidding. I want to nominate Tom Marshall of Indiana. I can nominate that man and break this tie. Think it over.

His is the best compromise you have. Do not know him personally and never saw him but I am for him. Now let us get busy. If you listen to me I will get you delegates out of debt by Christmas.

Pardon me, the Secretary has just started in on what will become America's national yell: "Alabama—24 votes for Oscar Underwood."

New York Times, July 6, 1924

Article #14 Democratic Convention

HE'S THE DARKEST OF THE DARK HORSES NOW, SAYS WILL ROGERS, CONTROLLING TWO HALF VOTES[123]

By Will Rogers

Arizona, voting under the unit rule, voted one vote for me.

The Secretary then read the finals: 1,098 votes cast, 732 necessary to nominate. Mr. Rogers having not quite received a majority, we will proceed with the roll-call. ALABAMA—Alabama votes 24 votes for Underwood.

On the following ballot I failed to pick up any additional strength. In fact, if I remember right, my lines began to weaken. I think I lost strength. Yes, come to think of it, I did show weakness; I lost my entire delegation.[124]

I was at the Follies (the uptown ones) working at the time but heard the news over the radio. Before I could get there after our show, why, the moneyed interest had gotten busy. You see, I had no floor leader to keep them whipped into line. So my strength dropped back right to where it was when the convention started.[125] So while it may look like I have lost. I have really held my own. This spurt that I took was not normal, and was wholly beyond my strength. It was all done to test out the other fellow.

I went down today[126] to round up my lost forces, and found it was not only one but it was two with a half vote each. I was tickled to death it was not from the North Carolina decimal fraction delegation, because it would have broken me to have bought hot dogs for all of a total vote of one.

Well, sir, I will say that these two half portion delegates from Arizona were by far the most intelligent men I have met during the entire convention, and had we more of their farseeing statesmanship this deadlock would be wisely and promptly broken.

I had never met or heard of the men before. I had, by the way, heard of Arizona, and I want to here compliment the State on the men they produce.

They both told me that I could get them back any time I would buy them a hot dog sandwich. So I told them I hoped I would never need them that bad, but to stand by in case of a deadlock.

It's not only my own vote that I control, but it's the strength that I can swing. I can pull that one Doheny vote too. He wired me to put it with mine so that we maybe could raise some more.

So I am the dark horse. I am so dark that a black cat looks illuminated to me.

I am so dark that a Georgia negro would look like a snow man beside me.

Still, Chairman Walsh (who acted as house detective for the Democrats during the late Republican burglary) only has two, so he is only one vote lighter than I am.[127]

My campaign contributions would do credit to Calvin Coolidge—I haven't spent a cent.

I am such a dark candidate that they can't vote for me in the daytime.

Cox of Ohio wants me to take over the rent of his headquarters.

Ralston wants to sell me the remains of his campaign buttons. He said he knew that I didn't look that old now, but that I would before this convention was over.

They voted today to take the convention to Kansas City, and Kansas City[128] rejected its coming there by 1,010.[129]

My friend the Governor of Alabama's term as Governor has expired while here. He goes back home a substitute to an alternate.

In next Sunday's article I want to discuss my platform and policies, in comparison to the ones adopted by the other party. The Republicans have a springboard for a platform.

I am up with Bryan's one vote now, and if they vote to let the candidates take the stand I will beat him in a debate, because he has given out, and I am fresh.

I have had three offers today[130] to bolt this convention and go to La Follette's out in Cleveland, but nobody else is gentlemanly enough to withdraw here, so why should I?

Oh, glory be to goodness the thing has stopped. Taggart of Indiana made a motion that they adjourn until Monday and decide what to do. Can you imagine being here two weeks tied up and nobody thinking of that before? I bet you it was those two smart men from Arizona that thought of it.

If it hadn't been for those two men thinking of the right thing to do, both times, why, this convention would have been a failure.

Pardon me, I can't go any further. I just got my whiskers caught in my typewriter.

Alabama, 24 for Underwood.

New York Times, July 7, 1924

Article #15 Democratic Convention

WILL ROGERS SEES M'ADOO AND WON'T QUIT; TRUSTS CAUSE TO BRYAN, WHO SLEEPS ON JOB[131]

The Democratic Convention was apparently beginning to get humorous even to its leaders, so the only way they could stop it being funny was to adjourn it.

So they adjourned and held another miniature one[132] with only the managers of the candidates there, which meant, perhaps some seventy or eighty men.

Taggart of Indiana figured that it wouldn't be as funny as the big one, as there would be one-tenth as many in it.

But I heard all about it and it was, because sometimes a little man is just as comical as a big one.

Here is an illustration: It was suggested that the head of the ticket, which is Mr. McAdoo, drop out, then on the next ballot Smith drop out, then so on, all the way down the line. The proposer suggested they go on down as far as Saulsbury, who has only 6 votes, and stop there. [133]

Somebody said: "Why stop there, go on down to Arizona's candidate, Rogers. If you are going go all the way through with it."

Now, this is none of my made up jokes.[134] It actually happened in conference, so you see the smaller gatherings have not been able to remove any of the unconscious humor from them.

Who in the history of any gathering ever heard of eliminating from the top down to pick out a man? Imagine going to horse races to bet on the horse that would run last.

You who are not here will say, "But this is absurd, it can't be so." I tell you it is so. Just because it is so silly is why it is liable to receive consideration.

Nothing that has had any sense to it has ever passed here yet. If a man could just think up something crazy enough, you can get it by here.

For instance, one man from Texas proposed that all the low candidates drop out of the race for one day only, and then come back the next day, then the high ones do the same on some other day.

In other words, certain candidates were to run on certain days. For instance, McAdoo on Mondays, Smith Tuesdays, Wednesdays they would vote on Underwood, and so on down the line. He didn't say so in his resolution, but I suppose that they were to ballot on me on April Fool's Day.

Now that is crazy enough, ain't it? Well, I want to tell you that it came very near passing. The two-thirds rule is all that saved it.

Mr. Bryan and I write for the same syndicate, and we meet every evening around 6 in their office writing and filing our stories. We always have a friendly chat (as I don't think he reads my articles; he only reads his own).

He said that he was going to this conference of candidates' managers. I said, "How is that?" He said, "Why, I am my brother's manager." I said, "Why, your brother only has two votes; so that you won't feel lonesome up there with those two, why, you can also represent me with my one."

I got afraid after that he would sell me out. But no, what do you think he did? He goes up there in this important conference and goes sound asleep.

Can you beat my luck picking out a campaign manager to represent me like that? I felt terrible about it at first, but when I got to thinking of what the other members of the conference gained by his going to sleep, I figured that I could sacrifice my interests just to have them enjoy a few minutes peace.

With Bryan asleep at a conference, I bet you it was the most successful one he ever attended.

I should have let Taggart handle my votes for me. He is far and away the best man. Why, if I do decide to sell he can get me twice as much as any other man.

I have been asked repeatedly if I was going to withdraw. No, sir, I am not. Why should I show myself as being the only gentleman in the race by withdrawing?

The press of this town is slowly coming back to normalcy, and beginning to see clear. Mr. Heywood Broun, by long odds the most able writer, and far-seeing citizen of this country, today came out for me unquifocily (I can't spell that darn word, but it means without reservations, besides you don't want a President for his spelling. Some of the worst President we ever had were the best spellers).[135]

I have only one regret in regard to Mr. Broun selecting me for his praise. That is, he is on a New York paper. And New York City's leading papers have been so universally wrong in all that they have predicted, that it is almost fatal to have them support you.

New York papers have killed off more deserving candidates by supporting them than W. J. Bryan has by opposing them.

I have just come from the McAdoo headquarters and had a chat with my old California neighbor. He didn't seem too busy to run Barney Baruch out of there while he talked with an ordinary cow-puncher.

He said: "Bill, are you going to withdraw?" (I guess it was the only time one candidate has met another during the week). I said:

"Are you?" He said: "No, sir-ee. I am going to stick."

I said: "Well, I am, too. If the top man won't withdraw I don't see why the bottom man should."

Here is how I feel. They are going to drop the men at the top first, one on each succeeding ballot, clear on down till they reach the end. I guess I am now sitting mighty pretty if that goes through.

I will give Smith the Post Office in New York and McAdoo the one in Hollywood.

I will move the Capitol to Arizona, give them the Boulder Dam on the Colorado, and won't even allow California to get the waste water (unless they come through with some support here).

Oklahoma, my native State, has voted for everybody on the last census report but me. So from now on in all my writings I will tell the truth about them instead of lying as I have been doing.

I am in the race to stay. Tomorrow I will announce my platform, and it won't be the top of a picket fence, either, that no one can stand on.

Yesterday was Sunday.[136] Candidates went to church for political purposes that next Sunday can get back to normal again.

Just think, we have to get up in the morning and start again: Alabama, 24 for Underwood.

New York Times, July 8, 1924

Article #16 Democratic Convention

WILL ROGERS PICTURES CONVENTION IN ACTION; LOATHES ITS FUTILITY, HOLDS LEADERS TO BLAME[137]

By Will Rogers

Madison Square Garden, New York City, July 7.

Chairman Walsh (raps twice with the gavel without head coming off gavel)—The National Democratic Convention is now called to order.[138] Brother Isaiah of the Thirty-sixth Presbyterian Church of Patterson will ask the blessing. (Brother Isaiah prays for the same thing that they all have been praying for for twelve days. He closes with no apparent success.)

Chairman Walsh—The clerk will proceed with the roll-call of the States.

Delegate on the Floor—Mr. Chairman!

Mr. Walsh—For what purpose does the gentleman from Missouri arise?

Delegate (or, rather, three-fifths of a delegate)—Mr. Chairman, I want to present the following resolution: "Resolved, That we suspend the rules and vote on the abolition of the unit system."

Another delegate from Missouri arises—Mr. Chairman!

Mr. Walsh—For what purpose does another delegate from Missouri arise?

Delegate—Mr. Chairman, our delegation was instructed by our primary to come here and vote for our candidate as long as he had a possible chance to live through the convention.

Mr. Walsh—We will vote on the suspension of rules. All those in favor say Aye; those opposed, No. The noes have it. Mr. Secretary, read the roll of States.

Secretary—Alabama, 24 votes.

Governor and Chairman of Alabama—Alabama votes 24 votes for Oscar Underwood.

Secretary—Arizona, 6 votes.

Chairman of Arizona—Arizona votes 3½ for McAdoo, 1½ for Underwood and ⅛ for John W. Davis (And so on all through the various States and Territories.)

Mr. Walsh—The clerk will read the finals of the 498th ballot.

Secretary—McAdoo, 413½; Smith 362⅛; J. W. Davis 71.9; Underwood, 49 1-7; Glass 78.5. Total number of votes cast, 1,098; necessary to nominate, 732.

Mr. Walsh—No candidate having received the necessary number of votes to nominate, the clerk will proceed with the roll-call.

Delegate on Floor—Mr. Chairman![139]

Mr. Walsh—For what purpose does the gentleman from Oklahoma arise?

Delegate—Mr. Chairman, I want to present the following resolution for the consideration of this convention: "Resolved, That we suspend the rules and vote on the abolishing of the unit system."

Another delegate from Oklahoma arises—Mr. Chairman!

Mr. Walsh—For what purpose does the gentleman from Oklahoma arise?

Second Delegate—Mr. Chairman, our delegation was specifically instructed by our State primary to vote for our candidate as long as there is a possible chance of getting any post offices.[140]

Mr. Walsh—We will vote on the suspension of the rules. All those in favor of the resolution signify by saying Aye; opposed, No. The noes have it. Mr. Secretary proceed with the roll-call.

Secretary—Alabama, 24 votes.

Chairman and Governor of Alabama—Alabama votes 24 votes for Underwood.

Secretary—Arizona, 6 votes.

Chairman of Arizona Delegation—Arizona votes 3½ votes for McAdoo, 1½ for Underwood, 1 for John W. Davis.

Secretary—Arkansas, 18 votes.

Chairman of Arkansas Delegation—Arkansas votes 18 votes for Robinson.

(And so on through fifty-two of them).

Mr. Walsh—The clerk will read the finals of the 499th ballot.

Clerk—McAdoo, 412⅜[141] Smith, 362 9/16 (a clear gain of 4½ sixteenths); J. W. Davis, 70 4-30; Underwood, 49 12-24; Glass, 77 98-12. Total vote cast, 1,098; necessary to nominate, 732.

Mr. Walsh—No candidate having received the necessary number of votes to nominate, the clerk will proceed with the roll-call.

Delegate on Floor—Mr. Chairman!

Mr. Walsh—For what purpose does the gentleman from North Carolina arise?

Delegate—Mr. Chairman, I want to present the following resolution: "Resolved, That we suspend the rules and vote on the abolition of the unit system."

Another Delegate from North Carolina—Mr. Chairman!

Mr. Walsh—For what purpose does the other gentleman from North Carolina arise?

Second Delegate—Mr. Chairman, Our delegation was specifically instructed before we left our home to stay with our candidate as long as Madison Square Garden remained an insane asylum, and I see no reason so far why our instructions should not hold good.

Mr. Walsh—We will vote on the suspension of the rules. All those---

Now, readers, I will take a dying oath that is precisely and to the very letter what has been going on in a so-called civilized nation foı six days and six nights. Underwood alone has received more votes during the week than Mr. Harding did during the great landslide. The resolution to suspend the rules has been voted on more times than Bryan has made the same speech at Chautauquas.

One entire day of twenty-four solid hours has been consumed in "For what purpose does the gentleman arise?"

Mind you, this is witnessed by ten thousand supposedly normal people every day. They have worn out nine gavels and one hundred and ten million people's patience.

And not a bit of blame is due to the delegates. They are here trying to do the best they possibly can. They are conscientious, good American citizens. It's the so-called leaders. If a man in the Democratic party is ever referred to again as "leader," he will at least have the good sense to know that whoever calls him that is kidding him.

Can't you just imagine Charley Murphy[142] turning over in his grave?

Bill Stone or Roger Sullivan would have had these people back home so fast they wouldn't have had time for their badges to tarnish.[143]

The candidates are hiding; they don't come to the Garden. It should be the leaders that should hide.

Oh, Goodness, maybe after everybody gets out of there tonight, some good humanitarian will burn the building! He will come clear, whoever does it, and perhaps be nominated.

New York Times, July 9, 1924

Article #17 Democratic Convention

WILL ROGERS JR.' REPORTS THE CONVENTION FOR HIS FATHER, WORN OUT BY LONG SERVICE[144]

By Will Rogers.

Will Rogers Jr. attends the convention to take up the duties of reporter to replace his venerable old father.

By Will Rogers Jr.

Papa called us all in last night and made his last will and testament, he called it. He said he had carried his work on just as long as he could and he realized that he was unable, on account of his old age, to go further with it. He put in the will that I being the oldest was to take up his life's work, that of reporting the Democratic National Convention.

He herded us all and told us of how he had given all the best years of his life to this and out of respect to his name and memory that we children should carry on. And that our children were to do likewise and that we should raise them to always know that their mission through life would be to keep reporting the progress of the Democratic National Convention at New York. And it was in the will that if we didn't we would forfeit any claim to any royalties that might still be coming due from books that he had written on the early life of the convention.

Mama wants to send him to the Old Men and Old Women's Home for Survivors of this Convention, but he won't go. Poor Mama is worried about him. He won't talk rational. He just keeps saying, "Alabama" and "for what purpose does the gentleman arise," and "if we can't elect our candidate we will see that you don't get yours" and "unfit"[145] and release." We don't know what it all means.

Now, Mr. Editor,[146] I am only a little boy and I am not much of a reporter but Papa told us we didn't have to be very good; that all we must practice was endurance. But you will, Mr. Editor, please take my story, won't you, for Mama's sake, for she knew how poor Papa hated to give up and how proud he will be if I can only keep his life's work going?

Mama got our Dad's old press badge and patched it up so it would stick together and I went down today.[147] The hall was full of all those feeble people and it looked kinder like a church; everybody was sleeping. All but one man, who was standing and reading aloud out of a geography the names of States that are situated in the Western Hemisphere and that don't belong to Canada.

Papa had given me an old worn and torn paper with a list on it that he had used to mark off the numbers on when this convention started. He told me to always keep it for comparisons. Also that a museum had tried to buy it from him. I go to school and our teacher had told us what a wonderful country this is we live in, and how it had stuck so well together and, sure enough, when this man kept reading these names and figures, why, on Dad's old paper were a lot of the same ones.

I kept waiting for him to call out the name "Wisconsin" that Dad had, but this fellow didn't have it on his, and according to Dad's old paper we at that time had California and anybody knows that Japan has owned California for years. On Dad's old paper they still had the Philippine Islands, which is now Japan's Naval Base. But as for the candidates, the names were just the same. None of them had dropped out. Their sons were carrying on their father's work too, trying to hold what votes they had. Saulsbury Jr. had six. Underwood Jr. had a few more than what was on Dad's paper, as the State of Alabama had more population and had naturally increased its number of delegation.

An old man sat by me and I got to talking to him and he seemed to want to be friendly and talk of his early life. He said his name was Coogan, "Jackie Coogan," I think he said, and that he used to be in some old fashioned thing called moving pictures, and that he could remember as a child when this started that men used to be wakened up and have to call out the numbers when their States were called.[148] But now they have little phonographs and every time a State is called, why the phonograph says "Two and nine-eights for Smith Jr. and one and sixty-five fifths[149] for McAdoo Jr." and so on.

A man has a hammer and he couldn't keep them awake with it any longer so they adjourned, and the attendants wheeled them all out. It was only about three o'clock in the afternoon and they were to be back again at nine. I went home to tell Pop what had happened and to write my story. He said, "It's looking better, son; they are adjourning earlier and starting later. Maybe the miracle will happen" and his old eyes began to gleam as he seemed to vision the end of his glorious dream.

Then I told him very enthusiastically "Oh yes, Pop, it looks great because a man with a family name of Brennan got up, and one named Cramer, and said they would adjourn and hold a conference of leaders and would have something to report by tonight."

Well, I wish you could have seen my poor old Dad. He went into spasms. He pulled his hair. He raved. None of us could do anything with him. He had been all right before I had mentioned this leader and conference business. He then said:

"Son, those same men's fathers started holding those conferences forty years ago. Going to report something to the convention tonight? That is exactly what is the matter with this convention now, it's those conferences. If they had let the delegates confer instead of the leaders, why, your poor old father could have spent a life of usefulness instead of one listening to a man read off numbers, which we all knew better than he did.

"Son, if it's the Taggarts and Rockwells and the Macks and Cramers and[150] all of them that are conferring you will die like your poor old father, right at your post, listening for something to happen.

So please, Mr. Editor, take this story and tomorrow,[151] when I come home to dear old Dad, I will make him feel good.[152] I won't tell him they are going to hold another conference.

New York Times, June 10, 1924

Article #18 Democratic Convention

WILL ROGERS HAILS DAVIS, AS 'CLASS OF RACE'; THANKS BRYAN FOR EFFECTING NOMINATION[153]

By Will Rogers

Who said miracles don't happen? Didn't the Democratic National Convention nominate a man at last?

This should bring more people back to religion than any other one thing. It has been a demonstration of faith, because, after all, God is good.

It is generally conceded and understood that a comedian has no sense, and that we are only to make people laugh and not to think.

About six days ago (seems like six years) I devoted a whole article to my prediction of John W. Davis's nomination. I told you of being invited to his home and chatting with him for half an hour or so during the balloting. I told you what a fine, upstanding, pleasant man he was, and that I had learned something there that I would some day divulge to you (and some day I will).

Well, a lot of things have happened since then. But nothing has happened any different from what I heard at that time. But there I go trying to make a comedian sensible again.

There is one expression that fits Davis better than any. It applied during this convention. It applies during the coming election, and I hereby offer it as a campaign slogan: John W. Davis is the CLASS OF THE RACE.

Race horse men who bet continually pick horses more for their class than they do for their past performances.

This convention wound up in a personal triumph for William Jennings Bryan. My old friend W. J. is the greatest character we have in this country today. He is a very unique man. Most of us only attract attention twice on earth. One is when we are born and the other is when we die.

But Mr. Bryan even improves on a bear: a bear hibernates all Winter, but Bryan hibernates for four years, and then emerges, and has a celebration every four years at every Democratic Convention.

In the meantime, he lectures in tents, shooting galleries, grain elevators, snow sheds or any place that he can find a bunch of people that haven't got a radio.

No one has ever been able to understand the unique and uncanny power that he seems to hold over the Democratic Party, especially near nominating time. Since 1896 he has either run himself or named the man that would run.

And then all during the convention here you would hear the expression, "Well, poor old man Bryan! He has lost his grasp on the delegates. Here is one where he won't be able to name the man." But not me: I never wavered; I was as sure of his success ultimately as I was as sure of Davis's.

He got the floor and he made a speech, in which he told of seven men who might possibly be good men for the job. But he hinted at the man who would be nominated. Then he wrote articles for the papers, and in them he told what John W. Davis had done.

Well sir, my readers, right there is where Bryan named and nominated the next Democratic nominee. As I said before, it is canny the confidence those delegates have in Bryan. When he came out against Davis, Davis was a nominated man. Those eleven hundred delegates said, "If Bryan is so set against him he must be the right man."

Had W. J. Bryan never taken that platform and in a veiled way denounced Davis, and had Bryan never written a line in the papers against Davis, Davis would never been nominated.

So you see, Bryan leaves with an unbroken record since 1896. He has never failed to be the man responsible for the man the Democrats would name.

Personally I know Mr. Bryan to be a very shy man and I think he framed it just this way. I think he has been for Davis all the time, and he knew how he could do him the most good.

In closing my little article after a seige of all these weeks, I want to say that this will perhaps be the last Democratic convention I will ever cover. For I doubt if they ever have another one. Physically, and financially, and artistically, it has been a total loss to me.

I will cover the next war for a given sum but I won't cover the next convention on a straight yearly basis.

And artistically it was a failure for me, as I was not able to write something funny every day, for three weeks, just about a man reading off numbers. So I want to apologize to you. I couldn't make the grade.

Physically, I haven't had any sleep[154] since Walsh wore out his first gavel.

And, by the way, there is a man that emerged a hero. Before he quit, he was the biggest favorite in that Garden, and they pulled a bonehead by not nominating him for 1924 race.

I want to tell you in my weekly letter about having him in the Theatre one night, and all the other notables we have had all these weeks.

Now, as to what the convention has done for me politically. I think that I can well report progress. Having no one to nominate me, and not being a member in good standing of theirs (or either party, in fact),[155] I think one vote was not so bad. I feel, and so do my two Arizona constituents (who voted a half vote each), that with proper campaigning we can at least double my strength by the next convention.

And I want to take this means of thanking those two men for their unwavering support during the entire fifteen minutes which they stuck so staunchly by me.

In closing, I want to be like Mr. Bryan's speech here one night. Everything he ever has or ever got, he said, he owed it to the Democratic Party. Well, I also want to say that every vote I ever got for President in my life I, too, owe to the Democratic Party, and that they were not far-sighted enough to have gone through with it is, of course none of my business.

If I could have only gotten Bryan[156] to have just made one speech against me I would be having my picture taken for the campaign buttons.

Oh, yes, they met again last night, but I wouldn't go down. There was some loose talk about naming a Vice President. I doubt if they do it at all. But I couldn't afford to do down there and take a chance to be named for a job like that.[157] Thank goodness there is some dignity left in me.[158]

Well, by-by, folks. I am going to get my whiskers bobbed, and then go to sleep and stay there for four years.

REPUBLICAN CONVENTION OF 1928

"Cool" Calvin Coolidge had brought political stability to the Republican party and the nation when he had assumed the nation's highest office after Warren Harding's death, and had been elected in his own right during the elections of 1924. It seemed only natural that he could win again if he desired to run. However, while on vacation in the Black Hills of South Dakota on August 3, 1927, the President delivered a bombshell to Republicans—he would not again run for office. Actually Coolidge had used the word "choose" to run for office and this left some doubt about a possible draft for the nomination. From this date Republican campaigning began in earnest. Herbert Hoover took Coolidge at his word and began at once to campaign for his party's nomination. Many Republicans in the senate believed Coolidge was sincere in refusing the nomination, and they also began to make plans for a new candidate.

Hoover made several attempts to ascertain Coolidge's attitude about accepting a draft for the nomination, but Coolidge was noncommital. Hoover then tried to get Coolidge's support for the nomination by visiting the White House and offering to discuss the nomination. The President remained taciturn and evasive.

There was considerable opposition in the senate and house to Hoover's nomination. Vice-President Dawes, Senators Charles Curtis of Kansas, James Watson of Indiana, Guy Goff of West Virginia, Frederick Steiwer of Oregon, and Frank Willis of Ohio wanted to block Hoover's nomination at any cost. Curtis, part Osage Indian, was the leading senatorial candidate. He hoped for a deadlocked convention in which he would win the nomination in a scene reminiscent of Harding's last minute triumph. Other men such as Andrew W. Mellon and national committeeman Charles D. Hilles wanted a deadlock so they could then draft Coolidge.

When nominations began on July 14, John L. McNab led off the nominations with Hoover's name. A twenty-four minute demonstration followed. James E. Watson was nominated, followed by a surprise nomination of Coolidge by an Ohio delegate. But Hoover's preliminary work had been so effective that on the first ballot the delegates nominated him with 837 votes. Only the business of selecting a vice-presidential candidate remained, and the omnipresent Senator Borah solved that problem when he insisted that Curtis be selected. Curtis was awarded the nomination with a vote of 1052 out of 1089. Thus the Republican convention ended on a note of harmony.

φ φ φ φ

Knowing fully what he faced at the conventions of 1928—the heat, the crowds, the long hours and dull speeches—it would have taken an unforseen tragedy to keep Will Rogers away. Politics was the mainstay of his humor, just as his rope and gum had been in his early years on stage. And even the two plane crashes he survived on the way east to the convention in Kansas City failed to stop him.

In the four years between conventions, Rogers' star had risen. With his wife, Betty, and their three children settled in California, Rogers enjoyed stronger ties to a real home than he had known since his mother died. He delighted in entertaining the stream of visitors—ranging from the "big" names in politics and business to the entertainment world to his cronies from cowboy days to "kinfolks" from Oklahoma. The three Rogers children were teenagers, with activities and friends coming and going from their beautiful home in Beverly Hills. Sometimes Rogers stayed home for two or three weeks at a time—writing his columns, making movies, playing polo, riding with his children and friends. But never for long. His own restless nature, his need to seek new horizons, as well as the demands of his public kept him active.

In 1926 Rogers and his wife had made an extended trip through Europe. It was on that tour that he began his daily "piece for the papers" titled "Will Rogers Says." This column brought his humor to breakfast tables throughout America each day and greatly increased his need for fresh materials for his writing. It was then he wrote the series of five articles for *Saturday Evening Post* which later were compiled into a book, *Letters of a Self-Made Diplomat to His President;* from his experiences on a side trip to Russia he wrote the book, *There's Not a Bathing Suit in Russia & Other Bare Facts,* published in 1927. When Rogers returned home, President Coolidge invited him to dinner, and he spent the night in the White House. Rogers served a real diplomatic service in 1927 when he went to Mexico to join his good friends, Ambassador Dwight Morrow and flyer-hero Charles Lindbergh.

What passed for homespun humor or crackerbarrel philosophy came from his vast knowledge of the world, his acquaintance with leading figures around the globe, and his unceasing curiosity about things great and small. In January, 1928, he and Mrs. Rogers attended the Pan-American Conference in Havana and in February he began a lecture tour that took him to more than 60 towns and cities from New York to Florida and throughout the southern and midwestern states. Whenever he came close to Claremore, Oklahoma, he stopped to visit with old friends and relatives. From the White House on the Potomac to the white house on the Verdigris where he was born, Rogers found fans, spread good cheer, and mined nuggets for his humor.

He wrote and spoke without discrimination about people and places and things from everywhere. But being mentioned in his columns was more effective than any advertising money could buy, and many public figures sought him out. When he said the worst thing Henry Ford did was make cars and panned the "tin lizzies," more Fords were sold. When he revealed that he had been served "fish hash" at the White House and compared the stoic President to the Sphinx of Egypt, it made Coolidge more human, and brought protests from Rogers' Democratic friends that he was turning Republican. He quickly pointed out, however, that he belonged to neither political party. He had friends—and found humor in people—from all walks of life. In 1926 and 1927 he wrote two articles for the *Saturday Evening Post* concerning the Democratic party. In the first article he pretended to be searching for an issue to hold the party together and in the second he advised his good friend Al Smith of New York to stay out of the presidential race to avoid splitting the party.

As the convention drew nearer, editorial writers and others urged Rogers to get involved seriously in politics—to run for office. The editor of *Life*—the popular humor magazine of the 1920's—persuaded him to let the magazine run a series of articles promoting Will Rogers for President. And, although there is some evidence that he regretted the deal, it caused considerable excitement, sold magazines and made him $500 per article.

In the issue of May 17, 1928, an editorial in *Life* proclaimed: "What this Country needs is a Bunkless Party." Without it, *Life* foresaw a political campaign which would be "a colossal waste of time, for those actively engaged in it and for those of us who have to read about it in the newspapers and listen to it over the radio." Major candidates would have to straddle fences, especially on the issues of prohibition and farm relief, and be forced to "take refuge in the same bunk," the editorial said. The search was on for "a bunkless candidate who will run for President on an honest, courageous and reasonably intelligent platform." In the following issue, Will Rogers was endorsed by such prestigious Americans as Henry Ford, Harold Lloyd, Glenn H. Curtiss, Ben Lindsey, Babe Ruth, General William Mitchell, Ring Lardner, and Charles Dana Gibson.

Even though the campaign was in fun, it spoke of a certain sense of alienation between average Americans and their national parties, injecting directness and honesty into an atmosphere of compromise. The issue of "Americanism" had been used in 1924, and was still important in 1928. *Life* lauded Rogers as pure American: "Equipped as he is with a generous supply of genuine Indian blood, he's a lot closer to 100% American than are most of the people who brag of it." *Life* also pointed to Rogers' extensive travels as a basis for support: "Will Rogers has seen something of the world. He knows more about our foreign relations than do all the eighteen august members of the Senatorial Foreign Relations Committee. He was famous as an Ambassador of Good Will when Lindbergh was still toting mail between St. Louis and Chicago."

The cover of *Life* May 31, 1928, carried a full page portrait of Will Rogers, the proud nominee of the Bunkless party. Playing on the famous Coolidge statement as well as Will's ever-present gum chewing, *Life* announced that their candidate "Chews" to run. In the 27 articles which followed— some of which Rogers wrote himself and others which were compiled from his notes by editors when deadlines proved impossible for the entertainer-journalist to meet—the candid debunker held to his promise of "sincerity." Instead of suggesting that someone better might have been selected, Rogers congratulated *Life:* "You boys was inspired." For his platform Rogers had a handy slogan: "Whatever the other fellow don't do, we will . . . . No one man would want a broader, or more numerous planked platform than that . . . . William Howard Taft could stroll with Marie Dressler and Sophie Tucker on either Judicial Wing and not take undue precaution of stepping off."

For those in search of rewards of a tangible nature, Rogers had a disappointing prospect: "Our support will have to come from those who want NOTHING and have the assurance of getting it." And, finally Rogers promised to resign if elected. All of these promises were in point-for-point contrast with the serious pronouncements of the official candidates.

In his pretended keynote address, Judge Ben Lindsey summarized the appeal of Rogers to voters of the twenties: "genuine honesty; freedom from cant, hypocrisy, and shame; the courage of independence. And above all . . . that God-given quality of unashamed simplicity that enables a man to be the friend of cowboys and kings—to earn the trust and confidence of all the people."

The June 7 issue satirized the ambiguous positions both parties had assumed on the prohibition issue. Rogers proposed his own fence-straddling position: "WINE FOR THE RICH, BEER FOR THE POOR, AND MOONSHINE LIQUOR FOR THE PROHIBITIONIST." The issue for June 21 carried a similar anti-bunk expose of farm relief, a topic of real concern to Rogers.

As his campaign gathered momentum, the editors quoted from the daily press on the serious ramification of his candidacy. A Denver paper claimed, "Rogers is bigger than the presidency. He can make and unmake presidents and lesser public officers and he adds daily to the gaiety of nations!" A Bridgeport, Connecticut, newspaper saw him as uniquely capable of dealing with an adversary which recently had destroyed a president's peace plans: "Nobody can see through politicians at Washington more clearly than Rogers. Nobody holds them in less awe. As president, he certainly would not be afraid of the senate. Much more likely, the senate would be afraid of him. Every time one of the senate windbags began to gas, Rogers would utter a piercing remark of perhaps ten words, and deflate him. . . ."

Life's August 9, 1928, issue had Rogers challenging Hoover—"To Joint Debate—in Any Joint You Name." Emphasizing his own persistant critique of the unstable prosperity of the twenties, Rogers described the topic for debate: "You may say the Issue is 'Prosperity' You will try and show that we are prosperous, because we HAVE MORE. I will show where we are NOT prosperous because we haven't PAID for it YET." Preserving his neutrality, Rogers extended the same invitation to Al Smith in the next issue of *Life,* suggesting Madison Square Garden at midnight as the proper place and time for the confrontation.

In the August 23 issue of *Life,* Rogers' irritation with the farm programs of both candidates surfaced. In Smith's case, the attempt was obviously futile: "How is Smith going to get the farmer's vote all over the country when he never received a single vote of a farmer in his own state in all the years he has been running?" The efficient Hoover was equally out of place on the agrarian circuit: "Hoover will put efficiency charts in the hen-houses so each hen can read her Egg Quota for the day. He'll set up time clocks for the cows to punch. But will the cows and chickens co-operate?" In contrast, the Bunkless candidate declared himself to be "the only candidate that is running on either side that has ever looked a mule in the face or (otherwise) down a corn row." With devastating directness, Rogers said: "I can tell you in a few words what the Farmer needs, HE NEEDS A PUNCH IN THE JAW IF HE BELIEVES THAT EITHER OF THE PARTIES CARES A DAMN ABOUT HIM AFTER ELECTION." The October 19, 1928, issue of *Life* contained a serious statement by Rogers concerning the anti-Catholic propaganda being produced to slander Al Smith, which showed Will's persistent stand against bigotry and "monkeying" with someone else's religion.

Throughout the campaign, Will Rogers had shown that the American public's spirit was superior to such a dispiriting performance as they faced every four years. The institutions of power were less than perfect, but the ability of Americans to laugh at themselves through the journalism of their self-appointed representative reassured them that they could gain a perspective of their own foibles.

On Wednesday, June 6, 1928, Will Rogers left California, flying east for the Republican convention in Kansas City by way of Chicago and to Jackson, Michigan, where he had a speaking engagement. The first leg of his journey was in a new monoplane air mail carrier of the Western Air Express piloted by Fred Kelly. Dr. L. D. Cheney was the only other passenger. As the plane attempted to land at Las Vegas, Nevada, the right wheel broke and the plane went over, nose first, and landed on its back. Newspapers reported that the men "narrowly escaped death," but Will reportedly was only "dazed" while Dr. Cheney was cut near his eye by flying glass. Making light of the incident after he landed in Salt Lake City at 5 p.m. Wednesday, Rogers assured reporters that he was not hurt and that Kelly was in no way responsible for the crash. Just a few hours later, Will survived another crash when the Boeing air transport "smashed its undercarriage" in a landing at an emergency field in Cherokee, Wyoming.

Will said they were both "incidents, not accidents," and "as harmless as the conventions will be." Humorously he related that he was saving the blood on his shirt as a souvenir. His only complaint was that somewhere along the way he had lost his overcoat. After filling his pre-convention commitments, he finally landed on the soggy field at Kansas City airport June 9. With mud spraying up past the cabin windows, he remarked it would be a good place to train trans-Atlantic flyers. A welcoming committee was ten minutes late in arriving at the airport. Rogers left ahead of them, and they departed in pursuit of "the only cowboy in the world whose conversation is worth $7.50 a ticket," the papers reported.

According to the St. Louis *Post-Dispatch* (June 11), William Allen White called the convention the "dreariest public occasion since the burial of William McKinley." Meanwhile, the report continued, things were livelier "in an improvised canteen" on an upper floor where "a dozen men listened to the foremost wits in the country."

Henry L. Mencken, his ruddy face glowing, was denouncing Will Rogers to his face as "the most influential editorial writer in America:"

> "Look at the man," he shouted. "He alters foreign policies. He makes and unmakes candidates. He destroys public figures. By deriding Congress and undermining its prestige he has

virtually reduced us to a monarchy. Millions of American free men read his words daily, and those who are unable to read listen to him over the radio . . . . I consider him the most dangerous writer alive today."

"Come on, now, Henry, you know that nobody with any sense ever took any of my gags seriously," remonstrated Rogers.

"Certainly not," was the retort. "They are taken seriously by nobody except half-wits, in other words by approximately 85 per cent of the voting population."

While Mencken may have been "shouting" as reported, his outburst must have been "for show." He and Rogers remained friends and continued the give-and-take of men who understand each other.

That night (June 11), Rogers gave a benefit performance at Shubert Theater in Kansas City to raise funds for the children's department of the Salvation Army. According to the *Kansas City Times* the next day, Rogers said: "Our old forefathers some 150 years ago, when they laid out the Constitution of this country, made it almost foolproof! I really don't want to take anything away from any of our politicians or any candidate who might be nominated here . . . but I really do, honestly and truly, believe that it doesn't make much difference who is president." Noting that "'some nut in a spirit of seriousness" suggested him for the presidency, Rogers said the only thing to recommend him was, "I would be the only President this country ever had that was funny purposely!" Adding to his experience during his stay in Kansas City, Rogers went to see a marathon dance that had been going for six days and nights, led the "Rogers Cowboys" polo players in a match with Fred Harvey's team, winning 12-4 on the Country Club field, and bought a new brown suit. Known for traveling with only one suit, the fact that he purchased a new one earned him space in O. O. McIntyre's column: "'I went out with Will Rogers this morning while he purchased a suit of clothes. Will refuses to pay more than $50 for a suit, and when he puts it on he wears it until Mrs. Rogers makes him buy a new one."

During the convention, a Kansas City policeman, "Happy" Smith, was killed in an attempt to stop a daylight robbery not far from convention headquarters. Rogers volunteered to do a benefit performance to raise funds for the widow and five children of officer Smith, performing on stage for an hour and a half before about 1800 people in Ivanhoe Auditorium on June 17.

Whenever Rogers was spotted on his way to the press stands or in the crowd, the delegates yelled for him to speak, and he "entertained" his fellow journalists continuously. A reporter for the *Topeka* (Kansas) *Journal,* (June 13), said, "'Will Rogers sat about two rows in front of me, and I could tell by the laughter that he was throwing away priceless quips and jokes, scattering what brings him in so much per joke with reckless disregard for expense." The *Kansas City Star* commented on Will's transformation from a humorist to a social and political philosopher, adding, "He catches the salient points of current trend, the newest thing, and he rarely misses fire . . . All is game to him, but he knows how to be startlingly personal without being offensive."

A writer for the Arkansas (Little Rock) *Democrat* (27 June) summed it up by saying: "As was expected, the best 'stuff' about the convention at Kansas City came from Will Rogers . . . But for the delegate at large of all the American people, the news issuing out of the gathering would have been dead as the proverbial door nail. Will saved the day for all of us with his humor."

(Texts for the following articles are based on the *New York Times* unless otherwise noted. Variations are from the *Tulsa Daily World TDW*.—The Editors)

New York Times, June 11, 1928

Article #1 Republican Convention

WILL ROGERS' VIEWS OF THIS CONVENTION

He Finds a Dog-in-the-Manger Party Forming, Ready to Thwart the Majority. Has Slogan and Yell Ready. Also Reveals a Great Secret—He Personally is for Mrs. Coolidge on a Vindication Platform.[1]

By Will Rogers

Special to the New York Times

KANSAS CITY, June 10.—Flew in here yesterday from Chicago and made a forced landing on the backs of twenty-one candidates, who were laying out in the grass on their stomachs trying to figure out some way to stop Hoover.[2] The propeller struck one in the head and that gave him an original idea.

He says: "Boys, let's be honest with ourselves." Well, that was a laugh right there. "Let's don't kid ourselves. There just don't seem to be any prominent demand for any of us to be President, so what can we do?"

Well, just then the iron tailpiece on the plane skidded off another so-called favorite son's head and set him thinking seriously. "Well, if nobody wants us what do you say we all get together and stop the fellow that the majority want?"

"That's a great idea," says all the rest, in what sounded like unison.

Formation of a New Party.

"What will we call our party?"

"Let's call it the Dog-in-the-Manger Party."

"That's great. Now, members, can we trust each other?"

"We can till this candidate is stopped, and then it's every fellow for himself."

"Now, that's understood. We all sign an agreement that we won't start killing each other off till after we have all killed the first fellow off. Is that understood? We are gentlemen till our main mission is performed, and then we revert back to type. Is that plain to all of you?"

"It is."

"All right, members, let's get to the manger and guard it with your lives!"

"What's our slogan?"

"Keep the party in the hands of politicians."

"What's our yell?"

"Three long groans."

So that is the party that was formed by my pilot foolishly landing on them.

Suppose Mellon Didn't Arrive.

I only claim one distinction in arriving at this convention. I am the only one that has arrived that wasn't bringing a letter from Coolidge.

Mellon[3] is on a special train with the Pennsylvania delegation. I am just thinking what would be the consequences if something happened to Mellon himself on the way out. They wouldn't know any more who they were to vote for. I doubt if he has ever told them where the convention was being held and he may not get here.

Three hundred thousand farmers were supposed to come to the convention to show that they needed relief, but the roads are so bad out here that they couldn't make it.

If the farmers got here they wouldn't know how to ask for relief. Everybody here is looking for personal relief. They haven't got any time to monkey with somebody's troubles.

Absentees Missing Nothing.

Don't any of you feel down-hearted because you are not here. You are not missing a thing. I have been here before and heard Jim Reed make one speech and cause more excitement in the town than all these Republicans combined.

The convention opens Tuesday and closes when Coolidge makes up his mind.

Of all the tips you get around here, everybody gets a different one. The bell-boys where the delegates are staying are the only ones that haven't got a tip since the thing started.

General Pershing is the latest tip that's going the rounds. Well, we had one elected on "He kept us out of war." Why not elect one on "He got us out of war"?

A Great Secret Revealed.

Now, here is something that I have tipped you all off to before, and that is who I am for, myself. Well, here it is, out for the first time; I am for Mrs. Coolidge. I want her to run on a Vindication platform. And if the Republican Party paid its just debts she would be nominated.[4]

New York Times, June 12, 1928

Article #2 Republican Convention

WILL ROGERS PUTS IT UP TO MR. MELLON[5]

And Gives the Times Results He Got From Interviewing the Convention Enigma. Who's Vare?[8] Mellon Asks. Admits Also It Doesn't Pay to Save Country's Money—Can Smith Beat Hoover?—He Won't Get Chance.

By Will Rogers

Special to the New York Times

KANSAS CITY, Mo., June 11.—"Well, I just got tired milling around the hotel lobbies all this time, and I just made up my mind to go right where the Convention was being held. So, when Mr. Mellon come, I just headed for his quarters. He had always been mighty nice to me and laughed at my little jokes at all the dinners. So he had a Senator who was acting as a doorman and let me right in.

To make sure that I would get in I took my tax receipt with me to show him that I did all I could to make his department make a good showing. For I know how hard he is trying to make us forget Alexander Hamilton.

"How are you, Mr. Mellon? The whole town has been waiting for you," I says.[6]

"Hello, Will, I am glad to see you. How is your personal campaign getting on?"

"I am doing about as well as all the other candidates here with the exception of the one that will be nominated."

No Word of Coolidge Moving.

"Did you bring the letter from Coolidge?"

"Yes, I have it right here."

"Well, let's open it and see what it says."

"No. I can't let you see it, Will. It's confidential, and it's not to be shown till the proper time on the convention floor."

"Can you give me any kind of hint that Coolidge will or will not run?"

"No; only I never heard him say anything about moving."[7]

"Well, who are your Pennsylvania delegation for ?"

"Well, I haven't told them yet."

"If Hoover will keep you in your present job, will you be for him?"

"Certainly, but he hasn't said that he would."

"Would you like to be President yourself?"

"No, I care not who is a country's President, just so I can handle its money."

"Who is Vare for?"

"Who's Vare?"

"Why, ain't he from Pennsylvania?"

"Not that I ever heard of. He might be from Philadelphia, but not from Pennsylvania."

"How much money did you save for the country during your term?"

"All that Congress appropriated."

"Do you think it did any good to save it?"

"Not a bit. We would have been better off if I hadn't saved it."

Can Smith Beat Hoover?

"How long will the convention last?"

"Till I show them this letter."

"Can Smith beat Hoover?"

"He can, but he won't."

"Why?"

"Because he won't get a chance."

New York Times, June 13, 1928

Article #3 Republican Convention

AS WILL ROGERS SAW CONVENTION OPENING[9]

Well, Hoover's Stopped—From Being Secretary of Commerce, He Says; Note on Keynote Prayer; Note on Fess's Speech (Which Almost Got to Paying a Dividend)—All Over but the Finish[10]

By Will Rogers

Special to the New York Times

KANSAS CITY, Mo., June 12.—If you are interested in Vice Presidents and such things you will perhaps be interested in this convention. Nobody in the history of conventions ever saw a convention start out and end so quick.

A man that couldn't even get into the United States Senate arrived here the evening before the convention opened and announced who he was for and they started paying off.

Mellon came here with the Pennsylvania delegation and there his authority ended. Mellon had the money, but Vare had the votes.

The allies "stopped Hoover." They stopped him from being Secretary of Commerce.

If you haven't had a room to stay in while here, you can get one now. There is six candidate headquarters that are to be sublet.

Keynote Prayer and Keynote Speech

The convention opened with a prayer, a very fervent prayer that Al Smith be not nominated.

It was a keynote prayer, if the Lord can see his way clear to bless the Republican Party the way it's been carrying on, then the rest of us ought to even get it without asking for it.

Then they brought on Simeon D. Fess (be careful how you spell that or you will confuse the name with evolution). He delivered what is called the keynote speech.

A keynote speech is press notices for the Republican Party, written by its own members. Here are just a few things that I bet you didn't know the Republicans were responsible for—radio, telephones, baths, automobiles, savings accounts, enforcement, workmen living in houses and a living wage for Senators.

The Democrats had brought on war, pestilence, debts, disease, boll weevil, gold teeth, need of farm relief, suspenders, floods, famines and Tom Heflin.[11]

He told of so much money that we had saved, that I think if he had talked another hour he would have paid us a dividend.

When he got to Coolidge, I thought sure he was referring to "Our Saviour" till they told me, "no it was Coolidge." The way he rated 'em was Coolidge, the Lord, and then Lincoln.

Could Finish in Ten Minutes

It was an impromptu address that he had been working on for only six months. He made no attempt at oratory. He just shouted. He dramatized figures. When he told how many million we had saved, his voice raised, but when our savings had reached the billions, why his voice reached a crescendo. All expenditure was spoken in an undertone.

They adjourned till tomorrow for the sake of the hotels. They could have finished this convention in ten minutes today.

Men who yesterday wouldn't allow their names to be associated with the Vice Presidency are today announcing they would consider being drafted.

Jim Watson is even wondering if he can get his Senate seat back again.[12] Goff is gone back to the nineteenth hole.[13] Lowden has left for his Pullman. Hoover is drawing plans for one of the biggest engineering feats he ever embarked on. So it's all over but Hoover and Curtis.[14]

New York Times, June 14, 1928.

Article #4 Republican Convention

DOWN TO A DOG FIGHT SAYS WILL ROGERS[15]

Men Who Wouldn't Even Speak to a Vice President Now Trying to Be One. No More Heard of Mellon; He's Just the Treasurer Again—Suppose Hoover Demanded Vare as a Running Mate!

By Will Rogers

Special to the New York Times

KANSAS CITY, Mo., June 13.—The whole show has degenerated into nothing but a dog fight for Vice President.

All we have done today is listen to Senator Fess explain what he forgot to say yesterday. It seems he left out Roosevelt's name yesterday, and it took him all day to alibi for it. I don't know who he forgot today that he will have to bring up tomorrow.

They had a time seating the Texas delegation, as there was no law in Texas to apply to a Republican primary. Texas never thought they would come to a point where there would ever be any Republicans there. They also have no laws against the shooting out of season of reindeer or musk ox.

The Indiana delegation took a day off and went to visit the most prominent Republican Indianans at Leavenworth.

They just played the National Anthem, and when they finished Fess asked the band leader to play something else "while the Chairman was trying to think of something to say." They are still playing.

Men who two days ago wouldn't even speak to a Vice President, are now trying to get to be one.

They have weeded the Vice Presidential candidates down now to just the following: ninety-six Senators, 435 Congressmen and forty-seven Governors. (Forty-eight Governors, I should have said; Oklahoma has been admitted.)

They took a vote on the floor of the convention of the Georgia delegation and fifteen voted black and three white. They stopped everybody in the house from smoking. The Republicans are coming out against cigarettes and tobacco.

We don't hear any more of Mellon. He is just the Treasurer since Vare delivered the Pennsylvania delegation to Hoover. Be a good joke to Senate[16] if Hoover demands Vare run with him as Vice President. That will get him in the Senate.

They say Dawes is flying here to keep them from sentencing him to another four years listening to the Senate without ear-muffs. The only man laughing at the whole convention is Jim Reed, a Democrat.

New York Times, June 15, 1928

Article #5 Republican Convention

MR. ROGERS REVIEWS DAY'S PROCEEDINGS[17]

Regrets Absence of 'Hot Dogs' in Convention Building, but Hopes for Houston. He Suggests a Ticket; Looks Like Hoover and Heflin to Him, He Says—Not Enthusiastic About Smoot's Speech.[21]

By Will Rogers

Special to the New York Times

KANSAS CITY, Mo., June 14.—Let's get out of here and go to Houston. They haven't got hot dogs to sell in the convention building. Now, Jesse Jones, don't you get high hat down at Houston and not serve any there.[18]

There is nothing to do here when a speaker comes on. You have to listen to him.

The convention met last night and then adjourned in five minutes. That was the most successful convention the people of the country have ever enjoyed. They met again at 10 this morning, but unfortunately didn't adjourn. It looked like they had, but they hadn't.

Yesterday a Catholic priest offered the prayer. Today it was offered by a Jewish rabbi. Both are for Smith. They both prayed for guidance for the Republican Party, but not guidance to be elected.[19]

It's going to take more than prayers to get those farmers back in good humor.[20]

Reed Smoot from Salk Lake read what sounded like a cross between a financial report and a World Almanac. He spoke heartily of prosperity. But our national deficit was still thirty billions when he finished.

The crowd couldn't hear him and shouted for him to speak louder. Then when he did speak louder and they did hear him, why they got sorer than a boil and wanted him to speak low again.

He brought up Nicaragua, but he left the marines down there. He said that he would protect American lives down there, even if we had to send some there to protect.[22]

He was two hours reading Republican press notices, the favorable ones. The farmers that spoke received much applause but no material relief.

On to Houston for hot dogs and excitement with every speech.

If they had taken these words from the dictionary this convention would have been over a week ago: "The great Republican Party."

It looks like Hoover and Heflin to me.

New York Times, June 16, 1928

Article #6 Republican Convention

KNEW 'TWAS A CINCH, WILL ROGERS SAYS[23]

But Does Think It Low Down for Republicans to Pay Curtis That

Way. McNab Who Said Too Much; And the Women Orators, Terrible—Where Curtis Got the Votes That Named Him.

By Will Rogers

Special to the New York Times

KANSAS CITY, Mo., June 15.—Wow! She is all over. Hoover and Curtis. What have I been telling you for days about Curtis? I knew he was a cinch for that.

The Republican Party owed him something, but I didn't think they would be so low down as to pay him that way. He used to be floor-walker of the Republican Party on the Senate floor. Now he will be time-keeper.

Everybody at the convention who wanted the job themselves voted for Curtis. So that means he got eleven hundred votes.

He and Hoover were both nominated last night. Hoover, early in the evening in the convention, and Curtis later at the hotel.

Borah[24] nominated him with the shortest, best and most sensible speech of the entire convention.[25] Most of these men don't nominate candidates; they just handicap 'em.

Whoever nominated Jim Watson should be made to learn it; then repeat it to himself before each meal so long as he lives. And then we wouldn't be even with him. Even Jim didn't deserve such a speech.

Another preacher prayed this morning and had to read his prayer. There hasn't been a one that could make an impromptu prayer.

This one was a Methodist, and he wanted us "to look to the hills for wisdom," and here we went and nominated Charley Curtis from the plains of Kansas, where a five-foot ash heap would constitute a precipice.

This preacher prayed for Plymouth Rock. Lord, it's Boulder Dam we are after, now! There is no appropriation goes with Plymouth Rock.

This guy McNab nominated Hoover in two minutes last night with a splendid speech.[26] Then come an ovation of twenty minutes. To show you how good this first little speech was, it took him almost an hour to spoil it. He was afflicted from what William Jennings Bryan once told me about a speaker at the last Republican convention. "He is suffering from a premature climax."

If McNab had quit it would have been the greatest speech any Californian ever uttered.

I hate to say it, but the women that spoke were all terrible. Well, they were pretty near as bad as the men, and that will give you an idea how bad they were. Charley Curtis's daughter was modest and beautiful.

The prominent Republicans of the great State of Georgia certainly did themselves proud at this convention. They couldn't answer a roll-call without taking a census of the delegation.

Well, we are on to Houston. Kansas City did a mighty fine job of entertaining and caring for everybody but so will Houston.

DEMOCRATIC CONVENTION OF 1928

The Democrats who assembled in Houston, Texas, on June 26 were unanimous in their desire to avoid the factionalism and divisiveness which had characterized the convention of 1924.

Even rural Americans conceded that Alfred Smith was obviously the strongest candidate the party could nominate. Reelected as Governor of New York in 1926 by a vast margin, Smith had the support of every northern state east of the Mississippi and most western states. He virtually had no opposition for the nomination. McAdoo had had enough of campaigning during the 1924 convention at Madison Square Garden, and he wanted no part of the nomination. The location of the convention was a compromise to the southern, "dry" Democrats who had not been able to attend a national convention of their party in a southern city since 1860, when it was held in Baltimore.

On June 24 Franklin D. Roosevelt—as he had in 1924—again nominated Alfred E. Smith, "the Happy Warrior." Roosevelt had recovered sufficiently from his bout with polio to stand with crutches on the stage. He spoke about Smith and party unity, and completed his speech with a call for a Democratic victory. He told all Democrats that "to stand upon the ramparts and die for our principles is heroic. To sally forth to battle and win for our principles is something more than heroic. We offer one who has the will to win—who not only deserves success but commands it. Victory is his habit—the happy warrior, Alfred E. Smith." Roosevelt's speech obviously was persuasive: Smith received 724 ⅔ votes—just 10 short of the nomination. Before results were tallied officially, Ohio's Atlee Pomerene made the nomination conclusive when he announced that Ohio would also vote for Smith.

With Smith's nomination accomplished, the party bosses then began a search for a southern running mate who would "balance" the ticket. After some discussion and the mention of several men as possible candidates, someone suggested Senator Joseph T. Robinson of Arkansas. Robinson received the nomination on the first ballot. He was the first southerner to be on a presidential ticket since the Civil War.

φ φ φ φ

With a few days in between national party conventions, Will Rogers flew to Tulsa, Oklahoma, where he was met by oilman friend Waite Phillips. He visited his old home place, talked with his sister Sallie McSpadden and with Pawnee Bill (Major Gordon Lillie). He also spent one night at his old home ranch near Oologah. He ordered a private plane from Muskogee to pick him up and take him to Texas, but heavy rains had swollen the creeks near where he was staying and he had to cross the streams in a lumber wagon, then carry his bags and wade through mud to get to the field where the plane and pilot waited. Before going on to Houston, he stopped over in Fort Worth one night. Among those waiting to greet him when he stepped out of the plane were H. L. Mencken; Paul Patterson, publisher of the Balti more Sun; H. M. Hyde, political writer; and Fort Worth publishe Amon Carter.

The weather had been hot in Kansas City, but it was even hotte and more humid in late June when the Democrats convened in Hous ton. The press had a choice spot on an elevated platform where the had some breeze through latticed windows. A reporter from the *Deni son* (Texas) *Herald* said Will Rogers sat in front of him, "with rim med spectacles and only one prong to keep them in place; and how he does it when he grimaces is one of the puzzles presented." Neai Rogers were other "notables"—Mark Sullivan of New York, Benari McFadden, the millionaire publisher and physical culturist, and Menc ken. In a newspaper column on June 26, O. O. McIntyre wrote:

> Will Rogers' seat is next to mine and if there was ever a fibberty gibbety guy he is it. His jaws snap 100 times a minute and when he is not wriggling his feet he is shifting from one hip to another or rolling a lead pencil between his palms. I wasn't there a half hour before he had worked me into a spell of the jerks. By night I expect I'll be picking imaginary things off myself. "If you can't sit still, go on home," I finally told him.

As usual, Rogers made as much news as he reported. On June 27 he spoke to a breakfast meeting of Democratic women where Mrs. Woodrow Wilson was a special guest. The *New York Tribune* (June 28) called Rogers "the playboy of the breakfast table," and said Mrs. Wilson "led the laughter this morning when Will Rogers toyed with many topics charged with dynamite." Rogers pleaded with the women to laugh with their opponents as well as at them and had a kind word to say about all the leading candidates for the nomination.

"They're all good fellows," Will assured them. Kidding about his friend Al Smith and charges that he would let the Pope control the White House, Rogers said the Pope had such a big house and "grounds as big as all Texas," that it would take him at least four years to pack up and get ready to move. Referring to Republican Senator Moses who "out in Kansas City just last week began talking about burying Smith," Rogers said, "I just thought he didn't know what he was stirring up, because if he ever starts matching words with Al Smith he'll wish Pharoah's daughter had never lifted him out of the bullrushes." Concerning the same appearance, the *New York Times* (28 June) said Will referred to the keynote speech by Claude Bowers and said that "he hadn't known the Republicans could be called so many things in one evening."

Will might have saved the fifty dollars he spent on the brown suit in Kansas City if he had known what would happen in Houston. A company in New Orleans, as an advertising gimmick, gave a seersucker "wash" suit to all three presidential candidates, including Rogers who represented the "Bunkless Party." Pictures made of Rogers in Houston show him wearing the suit.

Will Durant in a column that appeared in the *Richmond-Times Dispatch* (28 June) said: "There is Will Rogers, the most sensibl man on the floor, laughing at everybody, and yet seeing the human worth in all . . . " The *Review of* Decatur, Illinois (30 June) called Will "a national institution" and said he "poked fun at both the Republican and Democratic conventions, but no dispatches from the conventions have been read with more interest than those sent by Rogers. Few if any correspondents have cut as deeply into the real facts as has Rogers . . . . His jibes and jolts are taken as humor, but they have a way of staying with you."

(Texts for the following articles are based on the *New York Times* unless otherwise noted. Variations are from the *Tulsa Daily World* TDW.—The Editors)

New York Times, June 25, 1928

Article #1 Democratic Convention

AS WILL ROGERS SEES HOUSTON PROBLEMS[1]

Plenty of Chance for Comedy Whatever the Democrats May Decide to Do; A Wet Head and Dry Tail is the Prospect for the Ticket, the Republicans Having Pre-empted the Only Possible Straddle.

By Will Rogers

Special to the New York Times

HOUSTON, Tex, June 24.–Everything is as quiet, restful and beautiful, you wouldn't think there was a Democrat in a thousand miles. Been here three days, havent heard a cheer, a band, an argument, or even an echo.

I wouldn't stay for the thing, but I know that a Democrat is just like a baby, if it's hollering and making a lot of noise, there is nothing serious the matter with it; but if it's quiet and still and don't pay much attention to anything, why that's when it's really dangerous.

The Kansas City convention took the life out of this one in more ways than one. You know you wouldn't feel so good either if some one had just announced to you ten days ago that it was Tunney and Dempsey that you were to meet in the finals.[2]

But there is bound to be some comedy coming, and here is the reason: Since prohibition was unearthed nine years ago, there has only been one argument invented that a politician when he is cornered can duck behind, and that is the old applesauce one: "I am for law enforcement." It don't mean anything, never meant anything, and never will mean anything.

"It would take practically a lunatic to announce: "I am against law enforcement."

Democrats Left in Open

Now the Republicans held their convention first, and naturally they grabbed this lone tree to hide behind. Now that leaves the Democrats out in the open. If they say anything about prohibition, they either got to say, "It ought to be modified," or "It shouldn't be modified." They can't duck behind the old alabi tree, "I am for law enforcement," for there is only room for one in back,[3] and a Republican is already hiding there.

If I had been the Democrats, I would have held my convention first, so I could have grabbed that alabi first, if I had had to held it three years ago.

Now, naturally, the logical thing to do if it was a legitimate business would be to nominate with Smith another wet as Vice President, and also put into the platform a plank on modification and have the whole prohibition thing out, on a straight-out issue, and let the voters settle it once and for all.

BUT politics is not a "legitimate" business, and they won't do it that way. Why? Because they don't know if there is more wet votes, or dry votes. So they are afraid to take a chance.

The Only Straddle Pre-empted

So they will try to "straddle the same way the Republicans did. BUT, as there has only been one "straddle" invented in nine years (and the Republicans appropriated that), why it's going to be pretty hard for these boys to think up a substitute in just this one week.

So anything that is done will have an awful good chance of having some comedy attached.

For there is only THREE other things to do, and here they are:

Nominate with Smith a dry Vice President. Well there is a sure fire laugh, for you then have an animal with a WET head and a DRY tail.

Now you may salve the drys with a dry Vice President. But up to now no one has ever paid enough attention to one to know if he is pickled or petrified.

The next thing they can do is nominate for Vice President a man that no one knows whether he is wet or dry. In other words, a man that has remained of so little interest to the country that no one has ever taken the trouble to find out.

The third plan is to nominate anybody, either wet or dry, as Vice President and then put in the platform a strictly dry plank.

That brings more laughs. Smith, running on a dry platform. That's like turning a whale loose in Death Valley.

Simple Problems Faced by the Boys

So all the boys are up against here is just these few simple problems.

"We want Smith, for he is the only man we got a chance with."

"We wish he was dry instead of wet. But, as he is not, we got to make the most of it. We got to dress him up so he will look wet in the cities and dry in the country."

"We got to hold our wets. But for God's sake don't turn loose of the drys."

It's like I remember Coolidge said one time, "I am for labor, but not against capital."

They got to promise the women something pretty dry or they will go to Hoover.

So, boy, these babies are studying.[3]

Tammany Hall and these cities are their meal ticket, but the women and the W. C. T. U.[4] are their clothing and lodging.

So if these boys are not shouting and singing down here, it's because they not only have a convention on their hands, but a problem.

There is bound to be some laughs, and they will be serious and unintentional, which are the best laughs in the world.

New York Times, June 26, 1928

Article #2 Democratic Convention

HEAT AND CROWDS IMPRESS ROGERS[5]

Wise-Cracks From a Veteran Observer on Many Points in the Convention: What Women Want There: And How Rogers Met their Demand—The State of Prohibition and of Vice Presidential Booms.

By Will Rogers

Special to the New York Times

HOUSTON, June 25.—She is beginning to look like a convention. If all the Democrats here voted the same ticket, why any candidate could be elected.

Everybody has on a linen or palm beach suit, not white, but it was once. If perspiration was a marketable commodity, the party could pay off the national deficit.

The Rice Hotel lobby is so packed I have reached up and mopped three other perspiring brows before I could find my own. There is a nice cool breeze blowing outside down here all the time, but nobody will go outside.

It looks like all a convention is, is just to sweat on each other. The lobby is so crowded that part of the New York delegation can't say a word.

And badges. If all the badges were laid end to end, they would reach to the White House.

Activities of the Notables.

Was up in Barney Baruch's room last night. He was busy unpacking his blank checks, getting ready for the deficit. Admiral Dr. Grayson was with him. We talked till daylight of the times when Presidents were Presidents.

Was at lunch with Mrs. Woodrow Wilson at Jesse Jones's roof home, on top of one of his cloud-ticklers. Wonderful place. The only home I have seen to beat it was Waite Phillip's Buckingham Palace in Tulsa, Okla. Mrs. Wilson looks wonderful and is as pleasant and charming as ever.[6]

Had a long chat with young Governor Dan Moody. Dan is for Smith, if Smith will promise to make the party quit drinking and carousing.[7]

Chatted with my old friend, Uncle Josephus Daniels. Uncle Joe would like to have the party eliminate gin and bitters.[8]

Pat Harrison is for harmony, and he don't look natural running on that platform.

There is a fine rodeo show on here, and when I just can't stand looking more delegates in the face, I go out and look at the calves and bucking horses, and you know it's kind of a relief.

Women Drys and Righters.

The women drys here have a regular hall where they go and pray that no wet shall enter the Kingdom of Heaven. They forget that when women enter politics their prayers don't mean any more to the Lord. They are just classed with lepers.

A band of women hailed me yesterday and wanted me to write something about helping them get "equal rights." So I told them I thought myself that they had too many, and it was mighty nice of them to want to split some of them with the men.

The Vice Presidential candidates today were as follows: From 9 to 12 was Cordell Hull of Tennessee. Then from 12 to 3, Jesse Jones, the Tex Rickard of promoting political combats. At 3 o'clock the heat in the lobby had changed the candidate to Governor Donahey of Ohio, a Democrat who thrives on Republican votes and whose record equals Smith's.[9] And then when I wrote[10] my old fighting friend, Joe Robinson, is the logical nominee.[11]

The whole talk down here is wet and dry; the delegates just can't wait till the next bottle is opened to discuss it. Prohibition is running about a quart to the argument here now.

The South say they are dry and by golly if the bootleggers don't rush on some more mighty quick they will be.

Tammany's Hard Role.

Tammany delegates were coached and instructed not to drink while here, and they are the lonesomest looking gang you ever saw. They all say, "Why pick on us to be the only sober ones here?"

Tomorrow it starts—the biggest show in the world. Houston is doing its part nobly. The actors have had four years to think up new things to call the Republicans, and it will be worth the money, for

Democrats are the only race that can have arguments, even when they agree.

New York Times, June 27, 1928

Article #3 Democratic Convention

WILL ROGERS'S IDEA OF THE NEW BIG SHOW[12]

Good Time Had by All in the Afternoon With Prayer and Song—No Speeches; Later Bowers Got Going: Mr. Rogers Finds Him 'Some Denouncer'—If He was a Republican He'd Be Ashamed to Collect Votes.

By Will Rogers

Special to the New York Times

HOUSTON, June 26.—The show was called to order at 12:20, Jefferson time.

It took Clem Shaver twenty minutes of steady hammering to get order enough for them to listen to a prayer.[13] They didn't want to listen to a prayer. It was an argument that they wanted to listen to.

That was where he made his mistake. If I were Chairman of a Democratic convention, when I wanted it quiet I would announce "Just one moment, hyenas, if you will be quiet, we will start a debate, and it has the possibilities of ending in a fight."

That will shut 'em up in a minute.

The meeting didn't hold long. It was the shortest Democratic gathering on record. Some man prayed. I didn't get his name or political faith. But from his earnestness, I should say he was a Democrat. He not only asked for guidance, but he wisely insinuated for votes.

He read his prayer, ending with the Lord's Prayer. He read that too. The reason he read that, he may have had a different version of it for this occasion.

I am going to keep going to these conventions till I find a preacher that can pray from memory and practice. These that I have seen all act like it was their maiden prayers.

The Lady Who Sang

Well, after he had finished asking for guidance and material support in November, why a lady sang, and How!

Say, she was good. The only thing stopped her was a man made a motion to adjourn. She had on an awful pretty big picture hat. I imagine from the way she was dressed she kinder figured that she might be called on.

She opened up with the "Star Spangled Banner." She had a dandy voice and she knew the song, she didn't read it. People applauded her for knowing the words and before you knew it she just started right in singing another, ad lib, too. It was "America." She did that because a lot of people don't know which is our national air.[14] "America" or "The Star Spangled Banner." So, being a good Democrat, she just took no chances on the party losing through not singing the right song, so she sang 'em both and good, too. Well, when the audience realized that she knew all these old folk songs, they applauded and by Golly she knocked 'em off "Dixie."

Well "Dixie" in Texas, is just as sure fire as a flask.

H. L. Mencken,[15] the undesirable element of literature, was sitting by me and he suggested she follow it with "Marching Through Georgia." I knocked him under the press table, before Captain Hickman,[16] my Texas Ranger friend,[17] could get out his gun to totally dispose of him.

So it's as I say, we didn't have a thing at this convention but singing and praying.[18] It was more like a revival than a convention. There was no speeches made and a good time was had by all.

It's a wonderful hall and everybody hopes it was not built in vain. It seats enough people to elect Jim Ferguson for President if they all voted alike.[19]

Claude Bowers the New Denouncer.

But the big event was tonight. You know I have been telling you all the time about this fellow. Claude Bowers,[20] ever since last Spring when he made a bunch of hungry Democrats quit eating and applaud at the Jackson Day dinner.[21] He is kinder one of my proteges. Well, brother, I don't have to tell you. You had a radio.[22] You must have heard it. If you didn't, you missed the treat of a lifetime.

I thought Jim Reed could denounce. Why, Jim's denouncing would be taken as compliments after this baby got through.[23]

And Hamilton, what a sucker he made out of Hamilton! Why, if I was Andy Mellon I wouldn't even want to be known as the best treasurer since Alexander Hamilton.

And say, didn't he give Andy a dig, too? Why, he had no respect for men in high places at all.

Why, here at one time some of them said I had shown disrespect for our Government by just imitating some of them, while here this little fellow gets up there, and what he calls them! And he wasn't joking about 'em like I was. He was on the level.

It wasn't a keynote speech. It was a "lock and key" speech, and after he had finished, why, the whole Republican Party should have been put under lock and key.

It must be true, or they could sue him. Course, him just being an editorial writer, he hasn't got anything. But Barney Baruch and Jesse Jones and Kenny and Norman Mack,[24] and them, they have got a little left over from the Democratic Administration, and they put this fellow up to saying it.

Why, if I was a Republican I would be ashamed to go to the polls and collect my votes after that.

New York Times, June 28, 1928.

Article #4 Democratic Convention

WILL ROGERS ADORNS WOMEN'S BREAKFAST[25]

The Only Male Party Invited, He Says, and Us Women Sure Had Some Fun, Great Need of Country Is More Elevators, If Houston is Typical—How to Enlist Both the Wets and the Drys.

By Will Rogers

Special to the New York Times

HOUSTON, Texas, June 27.—This morning they got me out of bed early to attend a big breakfast given to over a thousand political women who have left their husbands, bed and board,[26] and are assisting in America's champion pastime.

I was the only alleged man at the breakfast. Just think of that, the only male party invited to attend the principal social function of the female contingent.

Well, the old "sheik" (I mean sheep) of Claremore, Okla., sure did look his best in the only "seersucker" suit I had worn since a baby. These women are a great audience, when you get 'em off to themselves and speak to 'em in their native tongue.

Us women sure had some fun. Mrs. Dan Moody, the charming wife of Texas's Governor, was on my right and Mrs. Emily Blair (whom the affair was really given for) was right by me, and I had the surest fire finish in the world.[27] I introduced Mrs. Woodrow Wilson, who made an awful nice and appropriate speech.

I really had what would be called the keynote speech among us women.

The breakfast was billed for 9 o'clock on the roof of the Rice Hotel, and on account of the elevators we all arrived for a lovely luncheon. Everybody talks about "what the country needs." What this country needs is more elevators.

If you get a place in one you don't like to give it up, so you just keep it, and half of Texas is just riding up and down.

Note on Smith Family Weddings

Met Mrs. Al Smith and her lovely family over at the hall this morning. We recalled old times when I used to visit their box at the late Democratic upheaval in New York. She looks mighty fine. I told her every time I pick up a paper that another son or daughter had just married and that I was beginning to have apprehension as to how long that could last.

Sam Blythe, who sits by me in the convention, and the best political writer that ever lied for a candidate, told me that out of fifty years' going to conventions this was the prettiest and best hall he ever saw. Odd McIntyre was here with us. He was sitting with Sam and I, but he had to go back to New York to wash the dog.[28]

As to the Tents of Israel.

Last night Claude Bowers ended up his wonderful speech with the following: "The battle hour has struck. Then to your tents, O Israel." Now what do you suppose that Israel was put in there for. The only thing I never saw was one living in a tent. When he mentioned farm relief, the District of Columbia and the Virgin Island banners were carried around for twenty minutes.

Joe Robinson disposed of the prohibition problem this morning easier than any one I had ever heard. He said: "There are wets and drys both in the Democratic Party. I don't think we should do anything to lose the drys' support and I think we should keep the goodwill of the wets."

Joe really solved it, but I would like to see him nominated. He is from my wife's State and it would mean a lot to her. We know the Robinsons and they are fine folks. And Joe not only would make a fine Vice President but would be able to step in in case of a national calamity–God forbid that such should happen! but Joe is really competent to care for such.

Real Memorized Prayer at Last.

Well, I have finished my mission at conventions. Finally a preacher prayed last night from memory and not from manuscript and, a funny thing, it was my old friend, Dr. Jacobs of Houston,[29] and he is a cattleman in the week days. He raises Brahma cattle and Presbyterians.[30]

If it wasn't for paying our respects[31] and a few more days' hotel bills to Houston, why, the thing is over.

So, voters, get in the middle of the road. Don't sell your vote too cheap. For this is one campaign where the Democrats will have as much money as the Republicans. Smith has as much backing as Hoover, so hold out for the highest bidder.

Tammany Hall has got more money than the Engineers' Club.

"Unbutton your purse, O Israel."

New York Times, June 29, 1928.

Article #5 Democratic Convention

WILL ROGERS LOOKS OVER THE NOMINEES[32]

Finds Letters of Introduction Needed for Some of Them and Duly Supplied. Republicans are Kind to Women, Children and Dumb Animals, Like 'Al'—and Why!—A Note on the Platform

By Will Rogers

Special to the New York Times

HOUSTON, Texas, June 28.—If you think the Democratic Party is not a large party, you just sit day after day and count the men in it that are nominated. There was candidates' names presented down here that the newspaper men had to go back to the old United States census reports to find any mention of them.

Most of the speeches were not nominations, they were letters of introductions.

I knew Kansas would furnish the comedy. What Georgia was to the Republican Convention, why Kansas was to the Democrats. Some fellow talked for two hours, nobody knew who he was. You couldn't tell who he was talking for or against, and when he finally finished and mentioned his man we were more in the dark than before.

If I had been him out of respect for my candidate after I finished my speech, I wouldn't have mentioned who it was. No one would ever suspected and perhaps a good man's name would have been saved.

Tom Taggart of Indiana had his usual trading material nominated.

Senator George rallied the drys about him last night, but when they left the hall and the Smith delegates got their corkscrews working, George was left stranded on a pile of empties higher than the convention hall.[33]

A Jim Reed Disappointment.

Everybody was disappointed that Jim Reed didn't nominate himself, and after Jim heard the man that did it, I imagine he wished he had. Jim Reed could have taken that convention crowd and had 'em hollering their badges off.

Franklin Roosevelt, a fine and wonderful man, who has devoted his life to nominating Al Smith, did his act from memory. Franklin Roosevelt could have gotton far in the Democratic Party himself, but he has this act all perfected and don't like to go to the trouble of learning something else. So he just seems satisfied going through life nominating Al Smith.

It was a fine speech. It always has been. But it's always been ahead of its time. Now he has 'em believing it.

The only part I didn't agree with is where he said that Al was "good to women, and children and dumb animals," and he insinuated that the Republican President and nominee were not. Now Franklin, you are wrong about the Republicans and the dumb animals. They just thrive on dumb animals. They are like Lincoln with the poor. They must love 'em, for they have so many of them in the party, and I even believe that the Republicans like children, not perhaps as children, but they are the material of which voters are made in a few years. Also, I believe the Republicans would be kind to 'em, just so they would grow into manhood quicker.[34]

Governor Ritchie, who jumped when he saw the horse first get scared, and not after the runaway had gotten dangerous, made his usual to the point, and forceful speech, according to his own farsightness. It was just on the verge of a Cabinet speech.

Jeffersonian Principles

I have heard so much at this convention about "getting back to the old Jeffersonian principles" that being an amateur, I am in doubt as to why they *left them* in the first place.

All you hear about here is the amount of graft and corruption, but each man wants to put his nominee where it is going on. Why if these offices are as bad as they say they are, I wouldn't want a decent friend of mine to even want to go in them.

They are stalling with the platform, and when it is ready there is not a wire walker in America that can stand on it.

But say, the jokes are all on the convention, and no one can find one on the town. I haven't heard one speck of criticism of the way the whole thing has been handled. It's been simply marvelous. The whole State has done its part. Beautiful hall, hospitality and how, and the weather has always been a cool breeze, and nights you sleep good when you get a chance. Old Texas has done herself proud, and if they don't get a winner out of it, it won't be the fault of hers.

It's got to a point here now where State delegations will caucus on a half quart.

So, hurrah for Texas, and Houston. Viva Señor Smith!

New York Times, June 30, 1928

Article #6 Democratic Convention

MR. ROGERS SUMS UP / BOTH CONVENTIONS

Likes the Latest Nominee — / Finds Him a Real-Two-Fisted, / He Candidate.

WOMEN AS BAD AS USUAL[35]

For Himself He Has Heard All the / Speeches, Seen All the Badges He / Wants, and is Off for an Air Ride.

By WILL ROGERS.

Special to The New York Times.

HOUSTON, June 29.—Well boys, she blowed up about noon today in a blaze of Harmony.

Joe Robinson of Arkansaw got the nomination, with more Democrats agreeing than had ever agreed on one thing in the history of the party.

They got a great fellow in Joe. He is a real two-fisted he-candidate. He comes from the wilds of Arkansaw, where they are hard to tame. I have had one in my house for twenty years and there is just no managing 'em.

As usual, the nominating speeches brought out names that sounded like a new immigration list. The old soverign State of Oklahoma upheld her reputation for not even comedy last night.

Everybody was in a hurry and sweating, and all the States were voting on the Smith nomination when it got to them. Course they didn't agree,[36] and the whole 15,000 people had to stop for half an hour while they called all their names, and instead of sending twenty there was forty come with half a vote each. You would think that if a delegation stayed here a week they would know how to announce their vote.

But Mississippi saved Oklahoma's record, for when it got to them they acted a bigger fool.

To my friend, Governor Ritchie, goes the record of stealing second with the bases loaded, for the first time in any convention. You could pretty near tell that Ritchie was a wet without him announcing it.

This morning somebody in nominating their candidate told about them having been in Alaska, Germany, England, Russia, Cuba and South America. I couldn't think of any American that had been all these places but Herbert Hoover, but it wasn't. It was General Allen.[37]

Mrs. Joe Robinson went over when Joe was nominated, to the box of Mrs. Alfred E. Smith and told her that at all public receptions that she would be glad to take care of the overflow at her house.

Women seconded, and nominated, as often as they got the chance, and they were just as bad as usual. Senator Gore[38] of Oklahoma made the best speech during the entire convention in seconding Jim Reed's nomination.

Jim Reed, bless his old fighting heart, took the floor at 12 o'clock last night and didn't "turn the rascals out" till 1:30.[39] Had a chat with Mrs. Charles Dana Gibson, Lady Astor's sister.[40] She was on the New York delegation. They are natural politicians, that gang.

The platform I will discuss later. A man read it last night, perhaps the last man that will ever read it.

Well, it's been a great time. These Democrats are a great bunch. Just as happy as if they were working. Houston, the police, the people, everything, was great, and so was Kansas City. I tell you it was two fine conventions.

But I have looked at enough badges[41] and heard enough speeches that if I ever hear another man say, "The grand old Republican Party" or, "Back to the Jeffersonian principles," I will go to the gallows with a clear conscience. I just want to go back home and go to sleep for a month.

All the speakers said "we are making history." Well, I don't want to be disrespectful to either party, but I am just tired of seeing history being made.[42] I have got to go home and take care of my own campaign.

Good-bye, Houston, take care of yourself. But don't ever bid for another one of these things. You might get it. I got to get back to Beverly Hills and see Mary Pickford's hair cut.[43]

Good night, everybody! I hope the next election is a draw, and they have to run it off. This is Graham McNamee and Captain White[44] signing off, and swearing off from all conventions.

Come on airplane. Let's show these delegates how to travel!

Your's, WILL ROGERS.[45]

REPUBLICAN CONVENTION OF 1932

President Herbert C. Hoover's administration began on a note of optimism. During the prosperous first six months of his term in office, the "Great Engineer" enjoyed a considerable popularity. Most Americans—including Will Rogers—believed that a man was in office who had risen above politics. By June 14, 1932, the picture had changed considerably. A depression had plummeted the American economy into a chasm from which there seemed no exit. While President Hoover initiated some government recovery programs, his inability to respond dramatically to the new conditions gradually lost him the support of the nation. Republicans and Democrats alike realized that the Republican era was coming to a tragic close.

Although most Republicans believed that Hoover was the only acceptable candidate, a few party leaders thought it would be advisable to bring Calvin Coolidge out of retirement or find some other candidate. The rather sizable opposition to Hoover was reflected in the half-hearted candidacy of former Senator Joseph I. France of Maryland who entered and won some primaries. Many important Republican leaders such as Senators Borah and LaFollette refused to take a stand for or against Hoover. As the issue of who would represent the party at the polls in the fall was resolved before the convention, all the delegates had to do was to select a vice president and decide the party's position on prohibition.

Republicans were undecided about the liquor issue, and this confusion threatened the convention. Supporters of a "wet" party plank staged a six-mile-long parade, a circus, and a yacht show to convince people to agree with their ideas.

There were party members who desired to drop Hoover; some of them wanted Curtis, for he had been an acceptable vice president, and others supported former Deputy Chief of Staff Major General James A. Harbord of New York, Hanford MacNider of Iowa, national commander of the American Legion, or perhaps Alvin T. Fuller of Massachusetts. But no one really had a chance for the nomination except President Hoover. When the convention began James R. Garfield presented a platform to the delegates which loosely stated that the prerogatives of the federal government should remain supreme, but that individual states might decide their policies through popular referendum.

Joseph Scott of California nominated President Hoover on the third day of the convention. Hoover was nominated quickly thereafter by 1126½ votes. And, although thirteen candidates received votes on the first ballot for vice-presidential nomination, Curtis again was selected. Few Republicans were optimistic about their chances for victory in the coming election.

φ φ φ φ

In the four years between the conventions of 1928 and 1932, Will Rogers had done more things, gone more places, and touched more lives than most people do in a busy lifetime. His first "talking" picture in 1929 led to his steady rise at the box office and by 1933 he would be one of the most popular stars in the country. He also was in great demand as a radio performer, and could get as much as $10,000 for a single thirty-minute performance. Readership of his newspaper columns had grown, and his income increased accordingly. In mid-November of 1931 he began an around-the-world trip, returning in February of 1932, from which he wrote feature articles for *Saturday Evening Post*. He added to his land holdings, buying beach-front acreages on the coast near his ranch. Everything he did seemed to succeed.

Meanwhile, the tempo of America had slowed down to a crawl. Following the stock market crash of 1929, depression swept over the country with panic and despair, touching nearly every household in some way and bringing tragedy to millions. If Hoover had seemed a "shoo-in" in 1928, his chances grew smaller by the day as the depression deepened. Yet Will Rogers found many kind things to say about the incumbent. Hoover personally asked the humorist to "help restore confidence," and Will did his optimistic best in his newspaper columns and radio broadcasts. He may not have been one of Hoover's biggest boosters, but he respected the office, realized the dilemma, and truly liked Hoover as an individual. He did what he could to get people to coöperate with the government's efforts to stop the downturn in the economy, to think and act positively instead of giving up in despair.

In a radio speech April 20, 1930, he reminded his listeners that it was Hoover who had practically "won the war"—World War I—with his food programs. He mentioned that Hoover was an orphan, that he had a "wonderful character" and had worked his way through school, become a successful engineer and held responsible jobs all over the world. He recalled to their memories that Hoover was not really a politician—that he had been drafted for the nomination in 1928 and that the whole nation by its votes had said, "He is the kind of fellow we want."

"When Mr. Coolidge was in and just let everything go, that was wonderful," Will told his radio audience. "Nobody ever asked Coolidge to fix a thing. We just let everything go and everybody grabbed off what he could and all, never fixed anything." But with Hoover in office, people expected him to be able to "fix" everything from farm relief and prohibition to prosperity.

In January of 1931, exasperated at the government's inability or unwillingness to act in getting food for the hungry, especially in the states where drought had added to their woes, Rogers made a flying tour through Arkansas, Texas and Oklahoma, sometimes making several appearances a day; he raised approximately $225,000 for relief. But he had met with Hoover and John Barton Payne of the Red Cross in Washington before he began— still trying to work with the President and not against him. Although he may not have agreed with Hoover on many things, true to form, Will Rogers could never kick a man when he was down. And Hoover was down by convention time, 1932.

(Texts for the following articles are based on the *New York Times* unless otherwise noted. Variations are from the *Tulsa Daily World TDW.*—The Editors)

New York Times, June 13, 1932

Article #1 Republican Convention

WILL ROGERS FINDS CHICAGO HIGHLY EXCITED / OVER BASEBALL TEAM AND CAPONE'S BIRTHDAY

By WILL ROGERS.[1]

Special to THE NEW YORK TIMES.

CHICAGO, June 12.—It's a beautiful Sunday afternoon here. Just the idea of Chicago having a Sunday strikes the rest of the country strange, don't it?

Well you never saw as much excitement in your life. The whole town is all het up. You wouldn't think Republicans could generate any enthusiasm, but they did, and so did the Democrats. It must have been a great game; it went thirteen innings, and Chicago won it. Beat Boston 5 to 3, and the game wasn't even held here, it was in Boston. But the Cubs were fighting for the lead.[2]

I started rushing around the various hotels this afternoon and would ask, "Well, what do you hear? Are they going to nominate Coolidge or Hoover?" And the fellow would answer, "Guy Bush has held 'em to three hits, and it looks like he will win."[3]

Into the Congress Hotel I rushed (that's where they take in just Congressmen. The other hotels won't let a Congressman put up with them). Well, I saw a group and said, "Well, boys, she starts Tuesday? Are you straddling or going wet?"

"If they can beat Boston, they are a cinch for the pennant."

Well, I couldn't find out a thing about politics, and I guess that's just about the way the whole country looks at it. Nobody here knows they are holding a convention. There is lots of flags out, but Tuesday is Al Capone's birthday, so who knows?[4]

Nicholas Murray Butler, the man that converted John D. Rockefeller Jr., is here. He don't care so much about Rockefeller going wet; what he is after is a donation for Columbia University.[5]

Ogden Mills, Secretary of the late United States Treasury, arrived early. He had to borrow money from France to get here on.[6]

With Congress still in session and no Congressmen and Senators here, it's like going to Sister Aimee's temple without her being there.[7]

The whole town is on edge, just waiting for the Democrats to come. You know at a big dinner when you sit down there is nothing on the table but little individual dishes of nuts. Well, that's what this Republican convention is before a big dinner; it's just the "nerts."

New York Times, Tuesday, June 14, 1932

Article #2 Republican Convention.

WILL ROGERS UNCOVERS 'SCANDAL' IN POSSIBLE DROPPING OF CURTIS

Finds Republicans Looking for Vote-Getter in Second Place Such as Charley Chaplin or Amelia Earhart—Badges and Drinks So Plentiful Delegates Don't Know What to Do With the Former.[8]

By Will Rogers

Special to the New York Times

CHICAGO, June 13.—Well, got some scandal for you today, for it wouldn't be a Republican convention without some sort of undercover "finagling." They are out now to throw poor old Injun Charley Curtis off and get another Vice President.

Now, they are trying to do this at the last minute. They wouldn't tell him a few months before and let him run and get his seat back in the Senate. They wait till now to root him out. Their alibi is that he is too old in case something happened to the President. Well, they knew a few months ago how old he would be about now. Anyhow, how can you tell when a Vice President makes good and when he don't. They have never given one anything to do yet to find out.

What they are after, only they haven't got the decency to come right out and say it is:

"We are in the hole and we got to try and dig up somebody that will help us swing some votes. It's not your age, Charley; its not your party loyalty. You got to be the goat, not us. So any one we can think of that can carry the most votes we are going to nominate 'em, be it Charley Chaplin or Amelia Earhart. You been a good Injun, but its votes not sentiment we are after this year. So long, Charley, take care of yourself."

The Vice Presidential candidates, in case they throw out Curtis, is Charley Dawes, Pat Hurley and Hanford MacNider.[9]

My candidate for President on both parties blew in here today, John D. Rockefeller Jr. He and I may huddle on plans.

The[10] convention (so the advance literature says) opens tomorrow, and tomorrow the House of Representatives votes on the soldiers' bonus. Only way they can make this meeting worth while is to put in a radio loud-speaker and let us get the speeches from Washington on the bonus, then they can pack Convention Hall here.

Being at this show listening to a "keynote" speech, while those in Washington is going on, is like listening to a Chautauqua lecture when you could have gone to the Ziegfeld Follies.

If the House votes the soldiers the bonus tomorrow we are arranging a window for the Secretary of the Treasury to jump out of.[11]

Mr. Dickinson of Iowa is the "keynoter" and he has the toughest job of any of them ever.[12] If he points to accomplishments he is sunk, and if he views with alarm, he is sunk, so we are liable to get two solid hours on the weather.

The wet lobbyists have taken the whole convention. They give you a badge and a drink. Lots of us don't know what to do with all the badges.[13]

Lots of beautiful ladies lobbying for the wets. If a man will just act doubtful he can get a lot of attention.

The alternates are camped on the edge of town and are being cared for by the Salvation Army. They say they are going to stay till they get badges as big as the ones the delegates has.[14]

Charley Dawes is the most popular man in town. He still has a bank that's open.

All you can hear is, "When does the Democrats come?" Chicago is trying to sublet this convention to Cicero, Illinois.[15]

New York Times, Wednesday, June 15, 1932

Article # 3 Republican Convention

CONVENTION 'A FLOP' TO WILL ROGERS; KEYNOTE SPEECH TOO MUCH FOR CABINET[16]

Stimson, Mills and Hurley Walk Out and Brown Sleeps Through It, Comedian Reports—Those Who Could Hear Anyway Beat Others in Leaving When Loud Speakers Fail.

By Will Rogers

Special to the New York Times

CHICAGO, June 14.—In the theatrical business when a thing don't go, or it is a flop, we say that "it laid an egg." Well, the Republican convention "laid an egg" here today. The house wasn't near sold out. The loud-speaking system didn't work and half of 'em couldn't hear the "keynote" speech. They got mad and got to leaving, but not as quick as those that was sitting near and could hear it.

Poor Senator Dickinson did the best he could with the material he had to work with. Like all political speeches, any humor in it was unconscious. At the finish he said, "We have never been a party of critics and complainers."

Well, for two hours, he had been telling us nothing only what the Democrats hadn't done to restore prosperity, or had done to prevent it.

Here is how the speech was received by the Cabinet. My press seat was near an exit, just ideal. When he got to the diplomatic relations, Secretary Stimson went by.[17] I hailed him and asked him why he was walking out. He said "He is breaking my heart."

Mills Hopes for "Balance."

Then he got to the budget, and rushing by comes Ogden Mills. Ogden says, "I hope he can balance it; I can't."

When he got to the disarmament part, by comes Assistant Secretary Jahncke of the navy. He says, "You can sure disarm oratorically anyhow."[18]

Pat Hurley was really the first to walk out on him. Pat left on the opening paragraph, which was "Threescore and twelve years ago, our nation was saved by the Republican party."

Well, Pat's got too much humor for that. So we went out and got a hot dog and had our picture taken with Bill Skelly, another Oklahoman.[19]

Postmaster General Brown was sitting where he couldn't get out, so he went to sleep.[20] Secretary Wilbur—I afterwards went around and called on him in his box. He and his wife and I talked about our boys at Stanford. Asked him why he stuck. He said, "Oh, it's not so bad here; I can't hear a word." Pretty wise crack for a Stanford man, for it's never stood out for its humor.[21]

Found "Alice" and had a big chat with her during the speech. (That's when everybody did their visiting—it was like an intermission). Alice was looking fine, only she had the whooping cough and caught it from her little daughter, Paulina Longworth. She was trying her best to give it to all the standpat Republicans she could, and I was cheering her on.[22]

Invocation Suddenly Remembered.

The show run for about an hour. Then somebody happened to tell Simeon Fess that an invocation had not been delivered and that, if the Republicans hoped to corral any of the church vote, they had better have a little prayer. So they prayed just ahead of Dickinson's speech, but it didn't seem to have any effect on the Lord or Dickinson either, for the Lord just let it go on, and so did Dickinson. So the prayer was a total loss. But the Bishop had a mighty fine voice and, being a real Hoover disciple, he read his prayer.

The Mayor of Chicago welcomed the delegates and tried to sell 'em a lot, and said everybody would have protection while here. It was after he finished that they thought of the prayer. But the Mayor did a good job.[23]

Silas Strawn thanked somebody for bringing the convention here, but he didn't get a hand from any one from Chicago.[24]

Tonight they are offering $1,000 for the author of the speech, dead or alive. Dickinson swears he didn't write it, that it was slipped under his door at night, and that he had to deliver it.

Louis B. Mayer, a power in our movies and a power in California

Republicanism, came along, and I chatted with him during the speech. I accused him of stealing it out of Metro-Goldwyn-Mayer's scenario department that had been sent in as a comedy. Louie said he didn't, but that he would buy it and take it back.[25]

Floyd Gibbons and I fought the Chinese war over again and wished we was back where something really happens.[26] Congressman Tilson of Connecticut earned himself undying fame by asking 'em to please adjourn.[27] What in the world they can possibly do tomorrow, only a clairvoyant can tell. This convention should have been put on between sessions of the Democrats.[28]

Curtis to Be Tomahawked.

Regarding the Vice Presidency, it's just like I told you yesterday. Poor Charley is to be tomahawked in the back. Three months ago they asked him to sit tight with 'em another term, but just like they took the country from the Indians they won't let this old "Injun" even have a seat.

Charley Dawes will be your Vice President. Now Charley Dawes's own kin folks don't think any more of him than I do. I am, and always have been, crazy about Dawes. He is able, fearless, and don't give a damn for any of 'em.[29] And, incidentally, he has had nothing to do with this ambushing of poor "Lo." It's just an old Republican custom. They needed some votes and Dawes can get 'em more than anybody else. So he will be drafted for the job.

So Dawes starts his career all over again, goes to the Vice Presidency, then from there to the Ambassadorship of Great Britain, then again in the Fall of 1937 he will be back home to head[30] the "Reconstruction Finance Corporation," to assist the same banks he assisted this year.

So it's Hoover and Dawes.

On prohibition it will be a "straddle," resubmitting to the voters. That's a direct straddle, for it's saying,[31] "We can't make up our minds what to do, so you see if you can make up yours."[32]

New York Times, June 16, 1932

Article # 4 Republican Convention

WILL ROGERS SEES SYNTHETIC PARADE; FINDS SHOW 'HITTING ON ABOUT HALF'

"Jimmy" Rolph Just Wanted a Drink, Comedian Says, So Delegates Fell in Line, Not Knowing Whether They Marched for Hoover or Sister Aimee.[33]

by Will Rogers

CHICAGO, June 15.—Well, they met again today. There was no way of preventing it. They all had their tickets and their badges and the chairs was there, so they figured they had just as well use all of 'em. Yes sir, everything was there but the performers.

The curtain went up. Then a man announced that the show would go on at 9 o'clock tonight. Course they filled in with a few little acts, and a "sham" parade. You've heard of sham battle where they imitate a battle. Well, this was a parade where they imitated a parade.

Bert Snell—an old friend of mine,[34] by the way, that I used to know and meet in Longworth's office when I hung out there—well, Bert went home last night after the keynote speech and he got to thinking of a lot of things that Dickinson hadn't called the Democrats yesterday.

Nobody else could but Bert did. He has known 'em longer than most of us.

And so today, during a lull when the Ohio pall-bearers wasn't singing the blues, why Bert jumped to the microphone and he showed those eleven hundred Republican postmasters seated as delegates that Judas Iscariot was the first Democratic floor leader and Al Capone was one of the last.

Then he said that while our Savior had rescued the world in Biblical times from the Democrats, masquerading as the Medes and Persians, that Herbert Hoover was the modern Savior. In fact he kinder give the engineer the edge over the carpenter.

Well, it was while he was speaking that the delegates got the idea of this "sham" parade. Jimmy Rolph (our Jimmy from California) who is not only a good Mayor and a good Governor but a darn good comedian. Well, Jimmy sits right down in front of the speakers. Every time he gets tired and wants to stretch, why he waits till they make what might be humorously construed as a "point."[35]

He has a big California bear flag and he gets up and waves it. (Now they think he is on the level with this. They don't know that he is just kidding.) So he gets up and starts shaking his flag. And everybody else that is tired gets up and joins him. It's an old trick of his, but these rubes back here don't know it.

Well, he wanted a drink so he started marching toward the door. All the others got to following him with their banners.

Nobody knew if they was marching for Hoover, Sister Aimee or Jimmy Walker.[36] So what was perhaps the greatest "synthetic" parade that any convention ever had was started by Governor Jimmy Rolph wanting a drink.

Alice had given about half the convention the whooping cough and was laid up with it herself today. So that means from a feminine angle the show was hitting on just about half.

The social end of the Republican party gave Pat Hurley a big fine banquet last night. I was invited (by Pat), but forgot to bring the old blue serge with me so couldn't even get in the hotel, much less the hall. He made a fine speech in which Mr. Hoover didn't get any the worst of it.[37]

Brisbane made one of his noted wisecracks about me in the papers this morning and had the creditors swooping down on me.[38]

They tried to sell seats to this thing for $22 apiece. These Republicans just won't admit there is depression. You couldn't get $22 a seat to see Senator Fess tango with Texas Guinan.[39]

They are trading box seats at this show for standing room at the Democrats.[40]

This afternoon I got to wondering if they really had given Mr. Curtis any notice, so I put in a call for him at the Senate, feeling that he would tell me about it, and we had a long chat and he did.

And sure enough, they hadn't. He said that all the time they had assured him that he was the man. He said if they had told him he would have run for his Senate seat. Then he give me the lowdown on the real objection. It's not age. Some of 'em want a real wet. They want a dry head, and a wet tail to the ticket. He said he understood that Mr. Dawes was out, and that from his latest talk with Chicago, that he was still the candidate.

Then I called up General Dawes in Washington. He was at the Willard Hotel and we had a mighty pleasant chat.[41] Didn't cuss, just asked me if I had read his statement. Said he had nothing new to add to it. I told him they needed him mighty bad, not only on this job, but pretty near any job we have to do in this country. I told him that if it was on account of his private business, to not let that stop him, that no Vice President had ever exactly been overworked, that there is no better time to concentrate on something important than when some Senator is speaking for two days on nothing at all.

Now, maybe I convinced him, mayby I didn't, but I got my own idea.[42]

New York Times, June 17, 1932

Article #5 Republican Convention

WILL ROGERS DECIDES CONVENTION IS DESTINED FOR HISTORY OR ASHCAN[43]

Democracy and Free Speech Got a Set-Back When the Machine Bundled Up Former Senator France and Threw Him Into Alley, Says Humorist.

By Will Rogers

Special to the New York Times

CHICAGO, Ill., June 16.—Well, the old Republican convention of 1932 went into either history or the ashcan at three thirty this afternoon.

Our Joe Scott from California, an orator from a crop of orators, nominated Mr. Hoover. And Joe nominated him, he didn't just put his name up; he said something. He is the triple-tongued elocution hound of our own Hollywood. Joe not only nominated Hoover but invited everybody to the Olympic Games, not even Democrats barred.[44]

Joe took up the hardships of maternity in the early days when mothers had no drug stores and a scarcity of clergymen, and showed that under the guidance of Herbert Hoover that all those little difficulties had been rectified. He insinuated that under Democrat Federal control motherhood would again become a burden. But our Joe did a good job.[45]

And say, I saved my "Injun" Charley Curtis for vice presidency. The rascals was just ready to stab him when we caught 'em.

So it's the same old vaudeville team of Hoover and Curtis.

They nominated Hoover, but after a tough fight.

Curtis Beat 3 Good Men.

Curtis beat three good men, all of 'em. McNider is especially a promising young fellow, but he's got plenty of time.[46]

Democracy and the right of free speech that you hear so much about had a setback there today. Ex-Senator France[47] wanted to withdraw his own name and propose the name of Calvin Coolidge for President. Well, that machine just bundled him right up and threw him into the alley.[48]

That was the real sensation of the convention. The only way you could have got Calvin Coolidge's name before that convention would have been to have it come in under an assumed name.

During all the ravings of the accomplishments of the Republican party not one mention was ever made of Coolidge,[49] so when Snell and his strong-arm men stopped France and bodily threw him off, there is no possible Cabinet job can ever be too high for them.[50]

12,000 Democrats in Galleries

Last night was a real session. It sounded like something, but that's because there was twelve thousand Democrats in the galleries. Eighteen[51] thousand out of nineteen thousand yelled for repeal last night, but the one thousand had a vote.[52] So there wasn't a vote in a carload.

From now on you will just hear two kinds of arguments over prohibition, one fellow denouncing the Hoover plank and the other fellow trying to explain it.

The resolutions committee just got a dictionary apiece and found all the possible phrases and words that didn't mean anything, then got 'em together and called it a resolution. It's dry in the morning and becomes wetter as afternoon wears on.

It offers no solution or no drinks. But it will prolong the argument. The press boys accused me of writing Joe Scott's speech.

H. L. Mencken was backing the Presidential candidacy of Senator France. If he had been elected, The American Mercury would have replaced the Congressional Record.

A lady with orchids on her bosom made a plea for the return of prosperity.

Like a Country Picnic

Didn't get to see my old friends, the Ohio Glee Club, before they left. They was good singers and fine fellows and, while they dressed like pall-bearers, they livened up a mighty dull wake at times.

But, take it all in all, it wan't a bad convention. And they are kind'er like a country picnic—you meet a lot of old friends from everywhere and see all the newspaper boys again. Of course there has just got to be so much "hooey" and "boloney" at those things, no matter what party is producing the show. But you do have to hand it to the Republicans. They come here to do something and they did it. They may not be spectacular, but they get results.

Now for Chicago. She did herself proud, and all the boasted drinking didn't show up. I don't think it was morals that prevented it, I think it was the hard times. But it was very well behaved.

The police were courteous and fine. The hotels gave very reasonable and splendid service. So Chicago made a good record and proved it's been mighty badly maligned in the past. Now she is over and don't you darn Democrats go underrating these two boys they got up.

You better pick your best, and then may the best team win—that is, the best for the country, be it Democratic or Republican, for a guiding hand in any business now needs encouragement and especially in guiding the biggest business in the world. Lord, what a tough time to have a country on your hands![53]

See you at the Democrats, where they will let anybody nominate everybody.[54]

DEMOCRATIC CONVENTION OF 1932

The Democrats who assembled in Chicago at the end of June, 1932, were in high spirits. They knew they would be nominating the next president of the United States. There were several candidates for the nomination, but the frontrunner was New York governor Franklin D. Roosevelt. He had been elected governor in 1928, re-elected in 1932, and obviously was the strongest party candidate. But there were others who wanted the presidency and there were still others who for personal reasons wanted to place their candidate in office.

On New Year's day of 1932, with the support of William Randolph Hearst, a sixty-one-year old Texan, "Cactus Jack" Garner formally entered the race. John Nance Garner was the powerful speaker of the house of representatives, and with Hearst's financial and newspaper support the Texan seemed a strong candidate. While Garner once allegedly remarked that the latch on the executive office door looked like "the handle on a casket," he did not stop the movement for his candidacy, and soon William McAdoo had delegate votes for Garner in California, while Tom Connally and Sam Rayburn of Texas lined up their state.

Texans early attempted to bring Oklahoma into Garner's camp, but the Sooner state had its own candidate in Governor William H. "Alfalfa Bill" Murray. Murray maintained a folksy demeanor and appealed to many proverty stricken westerners with his slogan "Bread, Butter, Bacon and Beans." Other colorful candidates aspired to the nomination. Senator J. Hamilton Lewis of Illinois appealed to many people. "Ham" Lewis was a showman and his taste in clothing earned him great criticism. He was credited with introducing spats in this country, and Speaker Reed once had referred to him as "that garrulous rainbow." With his whiskers painted pink and wearing a wig, he had almost everyone constantly laughing at him. Governor Albert C. Ritchie of Maryland was a favorite son candidate.

There were those candidates whose presence was less noticeable, but who remained as threats to Roosevelt. Newton D. Baker really did not want the nomination, but was definitely available. He had the support of Robert Woodruff, the Coca-Cola magnate, while Senator Carter Glass, dramatist Robert Sherwood, Adolph Berle, Mark Sullivan, and even to some extent Walter Lippmann also supported Baker as the best compromise candidate. Finally, Alfred E. Smith, former presidential candidate and governor of New York, was a possible nominee. Although he had remained out of politics after 1928, Smith was still in communication with the party leaders and ready to accept a draft for the nomination. National Party Chairman John Raskob had constant contact with Smith and knew the former governor's attitude.

Roosevelt was the only candidate with potentially enough support to win the needed 770 votes. He entered all state primaries except those where he would offend favorite son candidates—he wanted to avoid alienating anyone. On March 6 the first primary was held in

New Hampshire and Alfred Smith was considered the favorite. Roosevelt, with the support of the state organization, won by a satisfactory margin. Then in the North Dakota primary, a farm state where "Alfalfa Bill" Murray the progressive Oklahoman enjoyed popularity, Roosevelt won handily. In Georgia Roosevelt beat Garner by a considerable margin. Although he lost some primaries, Roosevelt had 417 votes pledged and claimed an additional 129 votes before the convention opened.

Roosevelt's managers established convention headquarters in the Congress Hotel, and there put up a delegate map for all to see their candidate's popularity. In Louis Howe's room was a special set of telephones and equipment allowing any delegate to sit down and converse with Roosevelt in Albany, New York. This apparatus was deemed necessary because Roosevelt was not in Chicago as were several other major candidates. Of the other hopefuls only Garner remained out of town. He was in Washington, and Sam Rayburn represented him at the convention. Garner told Rayburn and Bascom Timmons, an old Texas friend, that he did not want his name before the convention if it would deadlock the meeting. Newton D. Baker was not a declared candidate, but he had representatives in Chicago at the convention headquarters in the Congress Hotel while he remained in Cleveland. Baker's supporters included John W. Davis, Judge Samuel Seabury, John Steward Bryan, editor of the *Richmond News-Leader,* and Wendell Wilkie, then a young lawyer.

There were 1154 votes at the convention, and Roosevelt controlled more than any other candidate; yet the presidential hopeful had too few votes to win the nomination. On the night of the third day of the convention the platform committee submitted its work to the delegates. A. Mitchell Palmer and Cordell Hull had designed the platform and had not called for repeal of prohibition. Smith forces insisted on this addition, and Roosevelt acquiesced. A bank deposit guarantee plank was suggested, but the delegates did not want it included. "Alfalfa Bill" Murray suggested several planks including immediate payment of soldiers' bonus money as well as giving the states power to tax interstate commerce. He thought that to solve the depression the government should just print more money, thereby resolving all problems with currency. He also asked for a draft law in time of war and asked the government to declare a moratorium on foreclosure of mortgages. Murray's ideas were too radical. The accepted party plank was not significantly different from those offered in previous conventions; it called for a balanced budget, sound currency, and other measures to change the conditions of the depression. It was not very revolutionary, and it proved that the Democrats had few ideas how to resolve the depression. Repeal of prohibition was the most enthusiastically received part of the platform.

On the day for nominations Governor Ely of Massachusetts delivered an excellent speech placing Al Smith's name before the convention. Roosevelt was nominated by John E. Mack in a boring unimpressive presentation; Senator Tom Connally of Texas nominated Garner with a speech that was a tribute to the "great state of Texas." The first ballot ended as most delegations not previously committed to

Garner or Roosevelt voted for favorite son candidates. A more significant second ballot began at 5:15 a.m., and such Roosevelt supporters as Joseph P. Kennedy pressured Garner supporters to switch to their candidate. Kennedy told William R. Hearst that if Roosevelt did not win then Newton D. Baker might, and a Baker victory frightened the isolationist California publisher. Roosevelt managers offered "Cactus Jack" the vice presidency. They even offered to appoint McAdoo secretary of state if he would swing the California delegation. The results of the second ballot announced at 8:05 a.m. showed that Roosevelt had gained only 11½ votes. Tom Pendergast of Missouri had given his votes to Roosevelt, and it was expected that Roosevelt would get all the Missouri votes except that of Mrs. Donnelly who was engaged to James Reed. On this second ballot Smith dropped to 194¼, while Garner received 90¼. Governor Murray's votes from Oklahoma were given to Will Rogers.

While the third ballot was being taken Arthur Mullen again approached Tom Connally to see if Garner would accept the vice presidency; the Texan said he believed Garner would do so. An adjournment was planned after this vote, but the convention was detained when North Carolina reported 25.04 votes for Roosevelt and .96 for Byrd. After a rather long and complicated explanation of the mathematics involved, the vote was allowed to stand as reported. Thus on the third ballot Roosevelt received 682.79, Smith 190¼, and Garner 101¼. Oklahoma switched its votes from Will Rogers to Roosevelt.

During the adjournment the Roosevelt managers determined that the only way to win was to rope the Texas delegation. Then some rather coincidental occurences brought a distinct change at the convention. George Rothwell Brown, a Hearst associate in Washington, talked with Garner at 11:00 a.m. and immediately thereafter announced that the Texan had decided to accept the vice presidential nomination. And by an unsual circle of communications, Arthur Mullen relayed Garner's decision to Senator Connally. However, Mullen might have been involved in some chicanery, for neither Farley, Rayburn nor Howe, had heard about the decision. Obviously Mullen was mistaken when he claimed that Garner had announced his decision before noon on Friday. However, all of this presumptive communication was unimportant, for by 3:00 p.m. that afternoon Garner had made up his mind to accept the second place on the ballot. Also during this period Farley had talked again with the California delegation, first offering to place McAdoo on the ticket as vice president, and then Garner.

Congressman Sam Rayburn obtained the Texas votes for Roosevelt in spite of Amon Carter's insistance on Garner. The California delegation too was set to announce for Roosevelt. However, when the balloting began, the plan almost collapsed because McAdoo was absent from the stadium. He had run out of gas on the way to the stadium, ridden part of the way on a police motorcycle, and ultimately arrived by taxi just in time to cast California's votes for Roosevelt. Although out of breath from the hair-raising motorcycle ride, McAdoo loudly announced California's 44 votes for Franklin Delano Roosevelt. Thereafter Illinois, Maryland, and Texas quickly joined the Roosevelt bandwagon. Garner was placed on the ticket as Roosevelt's running mate the next day.

Roosevelt flew in from Albany to address the convention. He promised that he would try to do something to alleviate the suffering caused by the depression, and, he said: "I pledge you—I pledge myself to a new deal for the American people. Let us all here assembled constitute ourselves prophets of a new order of competence and of courage. This is more than a political campaign; it is a call to arms. Give me your help, not to win votes alone, but to win in this crusade to restore America to its own people."

ψ ψ ψ ψ

Because of Rogers' ability to act when everyone else seemed paralyzed, as well as his common sense approach to government, editorial writers again tried to promote him for the presidency. A writer for a newspaper in Winston-Salem, North Carolina, said Rogers appeared "in imminent danger of being nominated for the presidency by either or both political parties!"

"Never in all American history has such a man projected his shadow ahead of him in public life," the article continued; "never has America produced such a wit who essayed to express his impressions of things in an affected 'half-wit' fashion and secured such expressions of genius." Stressing that Rogers had more practical knowledge than any other man of his time, the editor nevertheless feared such a move: "It would mean his finish. He is too fine a man to be maligned as all presidents are. He is too valuable a man as a free public oracle." When Amon Carter introduced Rogers to the American Newspaper Publishers Association, Carter said he would nominate him "right now!" But the furor for him became even louder as the Democratic convention got underway in Chicago.

Rogers had taken time in between the Chicago conventions to fly down to Oklahoma, a trip that took four hours, to visit friends and relatives and enjoy " a whale of a good meal of cornbread and beans" and spend the night at the ranch near Oologah; then he flew to Fort Worth and on back to California for a week. On Saturday night, June 25, he spoke to editors from all over the country at a park in Beverly Hills. Taking a plane back to Chicago, he arrived Sunday morning after "flying all night." The first thing he did was huddle with each of the candidates for nomination, including an hour's session with William Murray, governor of Oklahoma. Though he might seem to be just visiting around, Rogers always did his "homework" and knew what was happening behind the scenes as well as on the floor of the convention.

It was hot in the stadium—so hot that delegates as well as men of the press took off their coats and loosened their ties. As Damon Runyon said in his column, it was "hotter than a Kansas cornfield in Midsummer." Restless as usual, Rogers moved about, visiting with the candidates, the delegates, and the women at the convention. Other writers might report party positions on broad, national topics, but he sought to give his readers a sense of actually being at the stadium, living in the crowded hotels and walking the packed streets of Chicago. He stressed the discomfort of the heat, the problems of getting a decent room—or any room at all. While such details added no intellectual substance to his reports, they gave readers a sense of being there and portrayed the convention as something more than an extended binge of drinking and vote buying.

By including women in his reports, showing the presence of wives and families, Rogers humanized his writing. Another common touch was added when he reported his supposed interviews with candidates—making up the conversations he reported, yet stating "truths" just the same. But his biggest problem was getting away from the fans who tried to stop him everywhere he went. Finally, on Wednesday Will Rogers took the rostrum and spoke for nearly an hour. The *Chicago American* said he was literally dragged to the platform during the recess and the Democrats "went stark raving mad in a delirium of joy when the Oklahoman, who is one of the brilliant feature writers covering the convention . . . was escorted to the platform." The crowd of 20,000 gave him the wildest ovation heard so far. Continuing, the article quoted Rogers as saying, "I'm not a delegate, I have no political affiliation in this convention, no one paid my way here. So if I'm rotten I won't owe you anything. I'm going to stand here and act a fool until the Democratic party agrees on prohibition. I'll be here from now on. As soon as they can get enough of the platform committee sober enough they will turn in a platform."

Rogers kidded and said nice things about each of the candidates; he called Jack Garner "an old Texas prairie dog," but said he loved him; he said the country would be in good hands if Ritchie were elected, and then he became serious:

> Now, you rascals, I want you to promise me one thing. No matter who is nominated, and of course some of you are going home disappointed that it was not your man, no matter who is nominated, don't go home and act like Democrats. Go home and act like he was the man you came to see nominated. Don't say he is the weakest man you could have nominated; don't say he can't win. You don't know what he can do, or how weak he is until next November. I don't see how he could ever be weak enough not to win. If he lives until November he's in.

An article in a Chicago paper by Elmer Davis told of an imaginary conversation with "Mr. Gloom" who said he was for Will Rogers, first, last, and all the time. "He's the only man who has yet addressed this convention who, when he showed signs of stopping, was greeted with shouts of 'No, no, go on!' Any man who could have such an effect on these hot and hungry delegates would sweep the country. It's a blame good thing for Roosevelt and Ritchie and the rest of them that the convention was technically in recess at the time. If some fellow'd got up and nominated Rogers right then, he'd have got two-thirds of the vote as quick as a secretary could have called the roll . . . "

Heywood Broun wrote of the same talk: "I think it is a little ironical that the same convention which thinks Will Rogers is a clown accepts Huey Long as a statesman." Writing about the "Roosevelt-Garner party" *Editor and Publisher* magazine said Will Rogers had more fun than anybody at the convention. Referring to the twenty-two votes that went to Rogers from the Oklahoma delegation, the report continued:

> If the mob had had its way the comedian would have made most of the speeches and doubtless would have been the nominee. He was fast asleep, head thrown back and resting on another reporter's typewriter, when Alfalfa Bill Murray threw his 22 votes to 'that sterling citizen, that wise philosopher, that great heart, that favorite son of Oklahoma, Will Rogers.' A tornado of approval swept the Stadium, but Rogers would have slept right through this moment of glory had not colleagues of the press punched him in the ribs. He came out of the trance dazed but smiling, and let out a long, loud laugh when he learned what had happened. The crowd was yelling for a speech, but Rogers ducked his head. Earlier in the evening a gallery god, with a fog horn voice, got a big laugh from the comedian. A platform orator was about to second the nomination of Garner and had described that statesman's qualifications for the high office in glowing terms. Gradually he led up to the name of this 'beloved citizen, this faithful servant of the people, this tower of strength in time of need," when the gallery god roared 'Mickey Mouse.' Rogers doubled up like a jack-knife.

In the *Chicago Tribune,* writer Edgar Brown called Will's nomination "a master stroke, albeit a sort of a delayed pass." He said the dead-serious candidates tried to laugh it off, but, "It caused no end of worriment, for who can say what a Democratic convention will do in the dizzy dawn of the morning. . . "These were votes Roosevelt would have given his eyeteeth for at that moment," Brown said. "But shucks, says Will, what's a few votes more or less? He's the unofficial President already."

This was Will Rogers last convention, but he was immensely popular and received accolades from the delegates, the gallery and his fellow scribes.

(Texts for the following articles are based on the *New York Times* unless otherwise noted. Variations are from the *Tulsa Daily World TDW.*—The Editors)

New York Times, Monday, June 27, 1932

Article #1 Democratic Convention

EVERYBODY PLANS TO STOP EVERYBODY, WILL ROGERS OBSERVES IN CHICAGO[1]

He Finds the Air Charged With Democracy and Much Lightning—Hears the Keynote Rehearsed at Breakfast and It Sounds Good With Food.

By Will Rogers

Special to the New York Times

CHICAGO, June 26.—Flew all night by plane from California and arrived here this morning in air charged with true democracy and the good feeling of every candidate for his own delegates.

If this convention stopped right now two days before it starts, it's been a better convention than the Republican one.

In fact if it did stop right now and they blindfolded some child and had her pick a name from the hat as candidate they would go home in better humor than they are liable to.

The plan is to "stop" Roosevelt, then everybody "stop" each other. At a time when the Democrats should be "starting" they are "stopping." They are trying to change the "two-thirds rule."[2] Can't change it, the hotel men are against it.[3]

Ham Lewis,[4] the Illinois Senator, parted his red whiskers yesterday and fifty-eight delegates jumped out. He said to 'em, "Boys, I can't feed you any longer, go out and get the best offer you can."

Now there is fifty-eight delegates thrown on the mercy of a broke convention. I went to my man, Bill Murray, and said to him, "Bill we can buy these Illinois delegates cheap. They are just home talent and belong around here and won't cost us much."[5]

Bill says, "Buy 'em hell! Let's sell 'em ours."

New York, on account of the depression and looking for an offer, sent their delegation uninstructed.

Had breakfast with Senator Barkley of Kentucky, the keynote speaker. He rehearsed his speech all through it. I told him it sounded good to me, but I was eating, and that if he served the delegates a meal with it it would be the most relished political speech ever delivered.[6]

But it was a good speech, a Kentuckian can't make a bad speech. He's got the three elements of the ideal orator: As a Senator he has had the practice, as a Kentuckian he will be fortified with the proper nourishment, and as a Democrat he will have the ideal cause.

Every candidate is confident, for Democrats always do the unexpected. The Democrats can develop more hope and less votes than anybody. The difference in the two parties is, the Democrat feels that some day he will be President, while the Republican knows that he will be postmaster.

But anyhow, win, lose or draw, he always gives us a show, and he feels that this year 'lightin' will strike him," and the way it's cracking outside now as I write this, it probably will.[7]

Had a private chat today with every candidate. Al, always frank, said, "I am not only trying to stop Roosevelt, I am like the rest of 'em—trying to stop everybody but myself."

Ritchie said, "Well, Will, I stand for what the people seem to want, if I can just get some delegates to stand for me."

Garner's men feel that if nominations should ever accidentally get to be a question of ability, they have a splendid chance.[8]

Talked with Governor Byrd of Virginia, a very high-class man, which is practically his only handicap.[9]

Bill Murray and I huddled in a room for an hour and decided that if they don't compromise on him, we are going to give Oklahoma back to the Indians.

Jim Reed, bless his old fighting heart, has got Missouri with him. When you can serve your State forty years, and still have 'em with you, that's not a bad obituary for one tombstone.

Speaking of obituaries, such things have no place in Democracy's 1932 plans, but yesterday a true democrat, not politically, but religiously, died. A New York priest, Father Duffy, by long odds the most beloved man in New York City. I am of his faith, you are of his faith, for his faith was humanity. When you can make New York miss you you must have been a man, and that's what it will do for Father Duffy.[10]

New York Times, January 28, 1932

Article #2 Democratic Convention

WILL ROGERS SAYS PARTY ACTS LIKE A BUNCH OF REPUBLICANS[11]

Here 1,100 Democrats Meet, but There Is Not a Fight, Not a Hiss, He Laments, Ashamed, and Calls for Action—Barkley's "Note" Was All Right, Though.

By Will Rogers.

Special to the New York Times

CHICAGO, June 27.—No convention today. The Democrats met, talked, agreed and adjourned. So the day was a total loss. The convention officially opens tomorrow.

It wasn't even a rehearsal today. Nobody fought, nobody even split the party.

Well, if you ever saw a disgusted bunch of people leaving a hall, it was all of us today.

Here people had traveled hundreds of miles, joined delegations, some come as spectators and paid fancy prices to see what? To see 1,100 delegates sit there and act like a lot of Republicans.

Why, there wasn't an argument in a carload.

Cheered everything; hissed nothing,—why it made me almost ashamed I was a Democrat!

Here we have written about it, advertised it as a combat, a gigantic struggle of candidates, and conflicting platforms, and then everybody goes out kissing each other. Shades of Thomas Jefferson, shadows of Andy Jackson, and outlines of William Jennings Bryan. Are you going to degenerate[12] into a party of agreement, and mutual admiration? Is it the influence of the female delegates that have ruined the reputation of the old "hell raising, rip snorting" convention?[13] And made you spineless, in fact effeminate. Shame on you.

Now don't let's have another session like that one. Wake up tomorrow and atone for today. Show 'em you are not a lot of "back-slapping" Republicans and agreeing with each other; get in there and fight.

A Plea for Combat

If a speaker says something, no matter if it's right or wrong, disagree with him, chuck him out. That's what's always made our conventions stand out. Why two more sessions like this one today and you will have no more people listening to you over the radio than the Republicans did. Be Democrats, fight, fight, and don't put on another synthetic thing like that today.[14]

Raskob, the receiver of the Democratic party, opened the convention and General Motors dropped 5 points.[15]

The talking started at 12 o'clock and everybody didn't become entirely exhausted till almost 4.

Raskob spoke of his "great interest" in the Democratic party. Interest nothing, he will do well to even get 50 per cent of his principal back that he has put in. He said it had been an "experience and a lesson to him."

The Democrats showed the touch with the common people by having Miss Evangeline Booth[16] of the Salvation Army ask the Lord to bless 'em around early November.

When she took the stand to deliver her invocation a lot of delegates just out of force of habit started to go up and get their rations. It was a fitting tribute to the head of this great charity organization to have picked her, for the Democrats are much nearer the Salvation Army than the Republicans. And evidently being a Democrat, Miss Booth prayed very long and very earnestly. She didn't read her prayer, which was an improvement over all the men preachers.

The Democrats always sing "The Star-Spangled Banner." The Republicans never sing (till after election). The lady singer knew both verses, and I was just starting to write about her, complimenting her, when I found she had notes made and was reading from them.

Next came Mayor Cermak of Chicago. He beat 'em all to the name of Thomas Jefferson. (It's always a race with the Democrats to see which speaker can mention Jefferson first.) Well, Cermak drew the first blood of the Democratic National Convention by grabbing Jefferson early.

It was awful timely the way he dragged him in. He said "Chicago and Thomas Jefferson had much in common; they both loved liberty."

The Mayor said, "The next President has not been named yet." Did he mean that there is no name that Herbert Hoover hasn't yet been called? But the Mayor made a good speech.

Now comes California. Isadore Dockweiler read Thomas Jefferson's first inaugural address. It wasn't so long. That ought to have been a tip right there to the other speakers if they were true disciples of Jefferson.[17]

Now comes Senator Barkley with the keynote. What do you mean "note?" This was no note. This was in three volumes. Barkley leaves from here to go to the Olympic Games to run in the marathon. He will win it, too, for that race only lasts three or four hours.

But it had to be a long speech, for when you start enumerating the things that the Republicans have got away with in the last twelve years you have cut yourself out a job.

He touched on the highlights of their devilment. He did not have time to go into detail. This is one keynote speech you can forgive the length, for when you jot down our ills you got to have a lot of paper. He had it all over the Republican keynoter, for this fellow was reading facts while the other fellow had to read alibis.

Barkley did a fine job of delivery, and, too, he was on his feet at the finish.[18]

New York Times, June 29, 1932

Article #3 Democratic Convention

ROGERS IS PROUD OF CONVENTION FIGHT; SEES PARTY GETTING BACK TO NORMAL[19]

Whole Day "Wasted" on Question of Seating "Porcupine" Long—Mr. Rogers Plans to Nominate Coolidge, Who May Be a Democrat for All Anybody Ever Heard Him Say.

Special to the New York Times

By Will Rogers

CHICAGO, June 28.—Ah! They was Democrats today, and we was all proud of 'em. They fought, they fit, they split, and adjourned in a dandy wave of dissension.

That's the old Democratic spirit. A whole day wasted and nothing done. I tell you they are getting back to normal.

A whole day fighting over what? A President? No. A platform? No. Well, then, what did they take up eleven hundred delegates' and twelve thousand spectators' time for? Why, to see whether Huey Long, the Louisiana porcupine, was to sit on the floor or in the gallery.[20] Well, the porcupine sticks right on the floor. And, the other four hours was fighting over who would be chairman of a convention that's already a week old.

John W. Davis, a man that knows what it is to be a Democrat, made the best speech so far; he was speaking for Shouse or Walsh. He seemed to want to have the two of 'em alternate, one act one week, and the other the next.

He seemed to have no resentment over Walsh, for what Walsh got him into in 1924 at Madison Square. Davis must be broad-minded. And he has got humor too. It took a defeat to make a good comedian out of him.

Iowa couldn't vote till they phoned to their kinfolks in Southern California. Iowa kept fighting over how to vote on Huey Long, all the time the thing was over, and whether they voted or killed each other didn't make any difference to the vote.

Holding up a big convention waiting to pick a chairman is like holding up a world series game waiting to pick out what prominent citizen will throw out the first ball.[21]

I bet this convention cured Senator Dill from ever trying to make two speeches on the same subject. They gave him seven and a half minutes to listen to his boos and hisses.[22]

To Huey Long goes the credit of being the first to split the party and get 'em acting like Democrats. I'll bet when judgment day comes things will go along unusually quiet till all at once there will be the blamedest fight and it will be over what to do with Huey. By golly, he made a good speech today. He won his own game.

Mr. Barkley, today's toastmaster, said "We will be entertained by a song," by somebody. Well, I had never heard that announcement at a convention before, and as I had just been talking to Irving Berlin,[23] the best songwriter in the world, why I just figured that this was one of his new ones he was having put over. But the minute it started I knew it wasn't. It was a kind of a "pep" song.

Went around to kinder get the feminine angle today. Had a fine old-time chat with Mrs. Woodrow Wilson, who looks lovely. Then, of course, I found Alice, who after all is about as much Democrat as she is Republican. In fact, she is wise to both sides. Seemed like old Houston and Madison Square times to visit Mrs. Al Smith, always smiling, always pleasant.

Then Mrs. McAdoo who has been in the midst of stirring times, even in her short span of life. And Mrs. Ed Hutton[24] of New York, wife of the man that runs those little innocent blackboards with numbers on 'em that keep getting littler.

As you go into the Stadium there is a board with all the names of the States and how much they have contributed to the campaign; looks exactly like a stock market board. I thought at first the Democrats were maybe on the "curb." I knew they couldn't make the big board.

Who do I run into looking at the board to see if he would get any of his money back but my best friend, Barney Baruch. He is going to have some news for me tonight. He is one of the men that meet in the little room where the candidates ARE nominated. No candidate will accept the Vice Presidency. By Saturday all of 'em will be grabbing at it.

The best candidate the Democratic party can nominate you don't hear anything of. It's Owen D. Young, the most able man in both parties.[25]

They wouldn't let 'em nominate Calvin Coolidge at the Republican convention, so I am going to try and do it here. He might be a Democrat. Nobody ever did hear him say.[26]

You can't beat the old Democrats for comedy.

Time means no more to them than to a Mexican "burro."

Tomorrow we will spend the day fighting over who will be permanent ticket taker. Who will be nominated? Say, if it's taken all Spring and this far into Summer to pick just a chairman, why it looks like Roosevelt's youngest son will be nominated, as he will be the only living descendant.

The Democrats are the only known race of people that give a dinner and then won't decide who will be toastmaster till they all get to the dinner and fight over it.

No job is ever too small for them to split over. But you would a loved 'em today. They was real Democrats.[27]

New York Times, June 30, 1932.

Article #4 Democratic Convention

WILL ROGERS NAMES AMOS AND ANDY AS WINNERS IN STOP-EVERYTHING RACE[28]

He gives Them the Nominations in First "Serious Seance" at Chicago—Yet No End Is in Sight Because "A Democrat Is Born but Never Adjourns."

By Will Rogers

Special to the New York Times

CHICAGO, June 29.—Amos and Andy[29] won the nomination at ten minutes to two this afternoon.[30]

By nominating them that takes care of the President and Vice President's office both. Brother Crawford, a fellow-member of the great fraternity, the Mystic Nights of the Sea, nominated them, the Kingfish and "Lightnin" seconded.

Eddie Dowling,[31] a very popular New Yorker, replaced Senator Walsh of Montana as chairman of the convention.

It was the first serious meeting that's been held by the Democrats during this whole "seance."

The resolutions committee were trying to draw up the platform. They didn't start till 10 o'clock. How they were expected to agree on prohibition in two hours when they hadn't been able to in twelve years was a mystery to everybody but the Democrats.

This whole convention has been "Stop Roosevelt," "Stop Smith," "Stop a dry plank,"[32] "Stop a too-wet plank." Everything has been stop something, so today they just stopped the convention.

Nobody was asked to vote on anything today, so there was no fights. Half the Iowa delegation was still in the hospital from trying to count their own votes yesterday. Huey Long, the Louisiana porcupine, is still the hero of the whole convention.

This is the third day of the convention. This is the day the Republicans adjourned. Adjourned! Why, the Democrats haven't done anything but meet and pray yet. How can you tell when a Democratic convention is adjourned and when it's not?

A Democrat never adjourns. He is born, becomes of voting age and starts right in arguing over something, and his first political adjournment is his date with the undertaker.

Politics is business with the Democrat. He don't work at it, but he tells what he would do if he was working at it.

If they don't hurry up and start voting on a President why some of these delegates will become so hungry they will vote for the first man with a ham sandwich.

Ham Lewis's Illinois delegates are begging him to take 'em back. They haven't been able to make any better connections.

The delegates in these big hotels are beginning to move from the dining room into the coffee shop.

The telephone bills from here to Governor Roosevelt will cost more than the Democrats will make out of it if they are elected.

I am still trying to get the floor to nominate Coolidge. Democrats did better with him than anybody we ever had in.

I tried to get the platform committee to just send in the first plank in the platform. That would have kept 'em fighting for the rest of the day.

But everybody was in good spirits today. They have learned where all the places are now, and everybody feels at home.

The life of the party is Amon G. Carter and his Forth Worth (Texas) Garner band.[33]

Met Melvin Traylor[34] for the first time yesterday. He is a very able fellow that is thought very highly of by lots of good Democrats.[35]

Went down to his bank today and had a long chat with Charley Dawes. He has had to neglect his own business in the past to help look after ours. But he is back home now, and that will add needed confidence to the financial structure of this great mid-West city. He's a fine citizen, is Charley Dawes.

Chicago is on her very good behavior. There hasn't been a soul shot. No devilment of any kind.

It's been a fine convention, nobody nominated, nothing done.[36] But what difference does it make? After all, we are just Democrats.[37]

New York Times, July 1, 1932.

Article #5 Democratic Convention

WILL ROGERS NOW DESIRES TO KNOW WHO'LL BE ABLE TO BUY THAT BEER[38]

It Will Take Money, He Says, and People Will Get Fooled if They Expect Repeal to Solve All the Nation's Ills—He Makes Peace With Mrs. Sabin and Her Fellow-Workers.

By Will Rogers

Special to the New York Times

CHICAGO, June 30.—Why in the world didn't they have that fellow Ely, Governor of Massachusetts, not only nominate Al Smith but nominate all of 'em. He was good. Chairman Walsh tried to stop him and give a Gunboat Smith decision, but the audience wouldn't let him.[39]

Bless old Texas and California, they marched with their heart in it for Jack Garner. There was none of the synthetic stuff with them. Senator Connally made a good nominating speech for Garner, too.[40]

You remember away back in the early part of 1928? I had a piece in *The Saturday Evening Post* asking Smith not to run that year; that things wasn't right; that anti-prohibition was growing but not enough.

A Writer Who Was Right.

I told him that it was a Republican year and no Democrat could be elected; that prohibition feeling would be strong enough in 1932 to put him over. Well, you will pardon me for bringing that up now, but I just can't help it. Us folks that write are right so little of the time that we have to brag on these very rare occasions.

Well, if he had done that we would all have been home two days ago. They would have nominated him on the first half-ballot this year and the Democrats would have "walked in" to the White House. What reminded me of this was last night Al spoke himself of being four years ahead of his time.

Well, been having a lot of fun here with what I jokingly call "my old wet sister friends," Mrs. Sabin[41] and her gang. We got all our difficulties thrashed out and I am still sticking to my two original statements that they "hopped" on me about.

I said society women taking up nickels on the street in New York wouldn't help their cause with the farmer or ranchwoman and it didn't. And then I said the wrong people was for it in order to get it through. Well, what I mean by the "right" people was folks like John D. Rockefeller Jr. There is one individual that turned the tide more than New York's "400" or Chicago's "75."

Then last night when these delegates switched over, that's what I meant by the "right people," for their vote put it in the platform, and that's the bunch of people switching over that could do the trick. The others had been wet all the time but couldn't get it put over so they must have been the wrong people to put it over.

A Bow to the Ladies

But these ladies did do some fine work, conscientious work, lots of 'em without the thought of the personal publicity connected with it, and they deserve to reap all the glory of the winner.

Did the Democrats go wet?[42] No, they just layed right down and wallowed in it. They left all their clothes on the bank and dived in without even a bathing suit. They are wetter than an organdie dress at a rainy day picnic.

The plank was made from cork, nailed together with a sponge.[43]

Now here is a funny thing about this whole convention. There just wasn't a thing that the people would listen to only prohibition. Any kind of economic reform plank or amendment met with "Boo!"

Now somebody is going to get fooled on this thing. As bad as the Eighteenth Amendment needed something done to it, it can't remedy all our ills. It if brings in all the tax money it's supposed to, where is that money coming from to be spent for it?

Now, He Wants the Price

I wish the convention, when they saw they had the beer, would have listened to some other speaker that might have had a plank to present to show 'em where to get some bread with the beer. Some of these not-too-far-away days we are going to realize that our troubles are so much deeper than beer that we will wish we had listened to something else, after we had the beer.

But we got one advantage anyhow, we can drown our troubles legally.

But wait a minute! Just how much fun is it going to be to drink now when we ain't breaking any law? They have taken all the fun out of drinking. What's some other amendment we can break in its place?

New York Times, July 2, 1932.

Article #6 Democratic Convention

WILL ROGERS 'ROBBED' OF 22 VOTES, SO HE ENTERS EX-CANDIDATE CLASS[44]

Oklahoma, Put to Sleep by Nominating Speeches, Awakens in Time to Parade With Borrowed Emblems in the Bedlam for Governor Murray.

By Will Rogers

Special to the New York Times

CHICAGO, July 1.—Politics ain't on the level. I was only in 'em for an hour but in that short space of time somebody stole 22 votes from me. I was sitting there in the press stand asleep and wasn't bothering a soul when they woke me up and said Oklahoma had started me on the way to the White House with 22 votes.[45]

I thought to myself, well, there is no use going there this late in the morning, so I dropped off to sleep again, and that's when somebody touched me for my whole roll, took the whole 22 votes, didn't even leave me a vote to get breakfast on.

Course I realize now that I should have stayed awake and protected my interest, but it was the only time I had ever entered national politics and I didn't look for the boys to nick me so quick. Course I should have had a manager but the whole thing come on me so sudden and I was so sleepy. I had been taking opiates all night. No man can listen to thirty-five nominating speeches and hold his head up. And I am sure some of these that did the nominating can never hold theirs up again.

Could Have Got Job With Votes

Now I don't want you to think that I am belittling the importance of those 22 votes. They was worth something there at that time. Not in money, mind you, for there is not $2.80 in the whole convention. But they buy 'em with promises of offices.

I expect at that minute Roosevelt's bunch would have given me

Secretary of State for that 22. And I could have sold Al Smith for maybe Mayor of New York.

Ritchie would have given me the whole State of Maryland with the Vice Presidency thrown in just for amusement sake.

Why, I could have taken those votes and run Andy Mellon out of the embassy in England with 'em. I could have got that job with only ten of the votes.

And what do I do—go to sleep and wake up without even the support of the Virgin Islands. They not only took my votes but they got my hat and my typewriter. I not only lost my 22 delegates but I woke up without even as much as an alternate.

Now what am I? Just another ex-Democratic Presidential candidate. There's thousands of 'em. Well, the whole thing has been a terrible lesson to me and nothing to do but start in and live it down.[46]

Parades for Murray

Did you ever parade at 6 o'clock in the morning? Course not, nobody ever did but the Democrats. I have been in circus parades and Wild West parades, but I had never entered a political parade. I had laughed at many a one, but had never become looney enough to participate.

But this morning as dawn was breaking over the machine gun nests of Chicago and you could just see the early peep of light down early rising gangsters' rifle barrels, one of Oklahoma's ex-Governors arose and started to put in nomination a fellow-Governor. His melodious voice aroused me from my slumbers. It was a friend, Henry Johnston,[47] nominating my old friend Bill Murray. When he finished the Heavens broke loose, noise accompanied by bedlam, and what dashes into the arena, not as you would expect at that hour of the morning, a milk wagon, but a band of beautiful little girls, all dressed in kilts, and thank goodness, not playing bagpipes but musical instruments.

They had come all the way from Oklahoma City to help "our Bill" Murray's parade. Was I going to get in it? If I could get woke up I was. I had no hat.

Handed Hat and Cane

Brisbane had been sleeping on mine during the nominating speeches. So Amon G. Carter, Texas's sole surviving dirt farmer (whose farm is on the principal street of Dallas), acted as my unmounted outrider. He handed me a straw hat with the word "Texas" on the band, and for no reason at all (like Democrats do everything) somebody handed me a cane.

I waved it till I almost hit Mrs. Woodrow Wilson in the eye.

Along the route of march we picked up a couple of girls who had been stranded by some earlier demonstration. They evidently was just "thumbing" their way around the hall. I was against taking them on. But Amon thought perhaps they were maybe F. F. V.'s from the old Commonwealth of Virginia and were trying to make their way back to Governor Byrd's headquarters in the Culpeper corner of the hall.

Recognizes Left-Over Republicans

Then as if by magic the rising sun started creeping in through the stained glass windows of this great cathedral of liberty and justice, and I got the first real look at our traveling companions. The heels of their shoes were much run down, which we knew at a glance was the badge of the Republican party. And then we realized that they were left-overs from the late Hoover uprising in the same hall a few weeks ago.

Some kindly soul that had temporarily escaped depression handed me a box of popcorn, so I had rations through the biggest part of the pilgrimage. The hall runs about three miles to the lap.

The journey got us no votes, but like all these half-witted convention parades, it kept anyone else from getting any votes, or rest either, until every marcher has become thoroughly disgusted with himself.

I am glad Chicago's children didn't come by on their way to school this morning and see how this wonderful system of choosing our country's leaders was conducted. They would never again have asked, "What's the matter with the country?"

(Will Rogers actually wrote several telegrams and a few regular weekly articles during the time he covered most of the political conventions. These telegrams and articles will be included in forthcoming volumes specifically designed for his regular columns. The actual convention articles are reasonably complete except for 1932. After Rogers left the convention, he journeyed to Claremore, Oklahoma to visit friends and relatives. While there he sent two daily telegrams which essentially concluded reports on the Democratic Convention. We have chosen to include these two in this volume; these also will be included in future volumes of the daily telegrams.—The Editors)

New York Times, July 4, 1932

MR. ROGERS, DOWN IN OKLAHOMA, STILL HEARS DEMOCRATIC NOISES

To the Editor of The New York Times:

CLAREMORE, Okla., July 3.—Flew down here to recuperate from one straight month of speeches. Heard a mule braying a while ago at the farm and for a minute I couldn't tell who he was nominating.

Roosevelt made a good speech yesterday and he gave aviation the biggest boost it ever had. Took his family and flew out there. That will stop these big shots from thinking their lives are too important to the country to take a chance on flying.

But it was a good thing the convention broke up. Times was hard. Some of the delegates had started eating their alternates. Cannibalism was about to be added to the other Democratic accomplishments.

Keep the following records straight. It was California that sold out and not Texas. Texas was for sticking even after California had quit 'em.

I have one thing to be thankful for. I am the only defeated candidate that didn't have a band on my hands to ship back home.

Could an artist paint a more pitiful picture than a poor defeated candidate waking up the morning after the vote and seeing thirty-five horn tooters that had, on account of the humane laws, to be delivered back home? It's enough to discourage candidates but it never does. Four years later they are back again, same ones.

Yours,
WILL ROGERS.

New York Times, July 5, 1932

MR. ROGERS RECALLS THE VICTORY OF THE RURAL BOYS AT CHICAGO

To the Editor of The New York Times:

NOWATA, Okla., July 4.—The Democratic Convention was a victory of the country boys over the city slickers.

New York and Chicago come there thinking that on account of being uninstructed Tammany was no more for Smith than Smith is for Tammany.

Well, they thought they would be in a position to stop Roosevelt, sell out to the highest bidder and go home driving the band wagon.

Great idea! All that went wrong with it was that the old orange squeezers from California thought of it first, sold out and was on their way West with the loot before New York and Chicago jiggilos could get their cards marked.

It was a lesson in rural politics.

Yours,
WILL ROGERS

NOTES

REPUBLICAN CONVENTION OF 1920

1 Title Variation: THE CONVENTION WILL BE IN ORDER / WILL ROGERS HAS THE FLOOR / by Will Rogers / Unbranded Oklahoma Cowboy and Famous Movie Star, *OKN*.

2 Chauncey Mitchell Depew (1834-1928). U.S. senator (1899-1911); president of New York Central Railroad (1885-1899). Known mainly as an after-dinner speaker, and spoke at the unveiling of the Statue of Liberty; delegate to every Republican national convention from 1888 to 1924. He addressed the convention of 1920 at the request of the delegates.

3 Prohibition had been in force since January, 1920. Rogers had written about the "noble experiment" in 1919 in *The Cowboy Philosopher on Prohibition.*

4 Prior to the Republican convention at Chicago there were at least nine candidates campaigning to obtain the Republican nomination for president. (See Introduction).

5 Francisco (Pancho) Villa (1877-1923). Mexican revolutionary figure who had raided Columbus, New Mexico, in 1916. When U.S. army troops chased Villa into Mexico, the Mexican president ordered the troops out of the country. Villa was assassinated in 1923.

6 After widespread publicity criticizing the extravagant and improper use of money by Republican candidates for the presidential nomination, Republican Senator William E. Borah on March 16, 1920, introduced in the Senate a resolution which called for the investigation of the campaign expenditures of all aspirants for the nomination.

The Democratic campaign textbook for 1920 accused the Republicans of spending $2,672,162 as opposed to the Democrats $105,382. The following figures were cited:

Republicans		*Democrats*	
Wood	$1,598,709	Palmer	$50,682
Lowden	414,948	Cox	20,000
Johnson	200,000	Gerard	14,000
Hoover	172,895	Edwards	12,900
Harding	107,709	Owen	4,000
Poindexter	71,000	Hitchcock	8,800
Coolidge	68,000	McAdoo	none
Butler	34,730		
Sutherland	4,173		

7 Title Variation: WILL ROGERS SAYS / by Will Rogers / Famous Oklahoma Cowboy, Humorist and Motion Picture Star. *OKN*.

8 John D. Rockefeller (1839-1937). Founder of Standard Oil Co. and at one point considered the wealthiest man in the world. Known as a great philanthropist having given away an estimated $530,000,000 to various educational, scientific and religious institutions. Rogers referred to Rockefeller often in his articles. One of the philanthropist's characteristics was giving away shiney new dimes. Rogers once beat him to the draw and gave Rockefeller a dime.

9 Frank Orren Lowden (1861-1943). Lawyer; governor of Illinois (1917-1921). In 1920 Lowden was a leading candidate for the presidential nomination, but his Pullman connection (he had married George Pullman's elder daughter in 1896) and high style of living militated against his gaining the support of many laborers and small farmers.

10 This line was omitted from *OKN*.

11 Early in 1920 a congressional investigation into military aircraft expenditures beginning in 1917 was conducted. The money Rogers referred to was an estimate of the amount suggested to the general staff and congress as the total amount needed for a war aircraft program. Congress actually appropriated $640 million for the program. The hearings about these expenditures were recorded in ten thousand printed pages; it was a major news item of the day.

12 This line was omitted from *OKN*.

13 Hiram Warren Johnson (1866-1945). Governor of California (1911-1917).

U.S. senator (1917-1945). In 1920 the Hearst newspaper chain supported him for the presidential nomination; he won the California Republican primary and enough support in other states to poll 133 votes and win third place on the first four ballots at the Republican national convention. Johnson was approached to be second man on the Harding ticket, but he refused.

[14] Leonard Wood (1860-1927). Army general; governor of Mindanao. At the beginning of the convention of 1920 Wood had the largest following of delegates; he led the balloting during first ballots, but his supporters were outmaneuvered and sufficiently disorganized to allow Harding to win.

[15] This line was omitted from *OKN*.

[16] This line was omitted from *OKN*.

[17] Eamon DeValera (1882-1975). Irish statesman born in New York. Led the unsuccessful Easter Rebellion in Ireland in 1916; British court sentenced him to death, but changed to life imprisonment because of his American citizenship. Released in 1917, he was later elected to the British Parliament. The Sinn Fein convention in 1917 elected him "President of the Irish Republic," a paper organization. He was again sent to prison in 1918 and escaped to U.S. in 1919 still as President of Irish Republic. Later served as Prime Minister of Ireland (1937-1948; 1951-1954; and 1957-1959). He attended the Republican convention of 1920. (This line containing DeValera was omitted from *OKN.)*

[18] Title Variation: WILL ROGERS SAYS: / By Will Rogers / Famous Oklahoma Cowboy Wit and Motion Picture Star. *OKN*.

[19] This line was omitted from *OKN*.

[20] This line was omitted from *OKN*.

[21] Frank Knox (1874-1944). Leader at the Republican national convention of 1920. A member of Leonard Wood's unsuccessful campaign team; he offered the seconding speech for Wood. He was a journalist and vice-presidential candidate on the Republican ticket of 1936 with Alfred Landon. Knox became secretary of the navy under President Franklin D. Roosevelt.

[22] Boies Penrose (1860-1921). U.S. senator (1897-1921); Republican boss of Pennsylvania. Penrose did not attend the convention of 1920, but was aware of the proceedings as a consequence of telephone conversations. He exerted strong political influence on Republicans. Spencer Penrose, his brother, later built the Will Rogers Shrine of the Sun in Colorado.

[23] George Herman "Babe" Ruth (1895-1948). Popular baseball player who was playing for New York in 1920. He was voted the American League's most valuable player in 1923 and established the home-run record of 60 in one season which stood until Henry Aaron broke the record during 1974.

[24] William Cameron Sproul (1870-1928). Governor of Pennsylvania (1919-1923). During the convention of 1920, he received the unanimous vote for the presidential nomination from his state and those of a few other states through seven ballots. Penrose supported Sproul for the presidential nomination.

[25] The following two quotes were found in the *OKN*, but were ommitted from the NEA tear sheet:

> De Valera says he wishes they could raise as much money for presidential candidates in Ireland as they do here.
>
> Wood started in with two or three hundred delegates but by the time the convention starts he will be lucky if they do not take his army commission.

[26] Title Variation: WILL ROGERS SAYS / By Will Rogers / Famous Oklahoma Cowboy Humorist and Motion Picture Star. *OKN*.

[27] Hog Island (Pennsylvania). U.S. ships were built and launched at Hog Island during World War I.

[28] Boies Penrose and Philander Chase Knox were Republican senators from Pennsylvania supporting Charles Evans Hughes (1862-1948); Hughes had been the Republican candidate against Woodrow Wilson in 1916. The election had been undecided for three days before Wilson finally was declared the victor.

[29] William Edgar Borah (1865-1940). Republican U.S. senator from Idaho (1907-1940). In the 1920's Borah was a powerful force in foreign affairs; he initiated the Washington Conference of 1921, and was chairman of the senate committee on foreign relations from 1924. He was a widely known isolationist, for he had opposed vehemently the League of Nations.

[30] Title Variation: WILL ROGERS AND PENROSE HOLD THE CONVENTION / By Will Rogers / Famous Oklahoma Cowboy Humorist and Motion Picture Star. *OKN*.

[31] Title Variation: Famous Oklahoma Cowboy Humorist and Motion Picture Star. *OKN*.

[32] "Dardanella." Popular song of 1919 by Felix Bernard, Johnny Black, and Fred Fisher.

[33] William Hays (1879-1954). As chairman of the Republican national committee (1918-1921), Hays presided temporarily as chairman of the convention; postmaster general (1921-1922); president of Motion Pictures Producers / Distributors of America (1922-1945).

[34] Henry Cabot Lodge (1850-1924). U.S. representative from Massachusetts (1887-1893); U. S. senator (1893-1924). His leadership in the fight against the League of Nations propelled him to prominence as a party leader. Lodge was temporary chairman of the convention of 1920; his address attacked the League of Nations, the Democratic party, and Woodrow Wilson.

(Thomas) Woodrow Wilson (1856-1924). Democratic president (1913-1921). Advocated the entry of the U. S. into the League of Nations and refused to compromise with senators who wanted revisions. At the Republican convention of 1920 Wilson was a natural target.

[35] The peace delegation to Versailles included only one Republican member, Henry White. Wilson's refusal to include any congressmen and only one relatively unknown Republican member prompted resistance to Wilson's policies. Rogers wrote his impressions of the Versailles settlement in his book, *The Cowboy Philosopher on the Peace Conference* (1919).

[36] William Jennings Bryan (1860-1925). Bryan was the Democratic candidate for president in 1896, 1900, and 1908. Supported Wilson and was an influential party leader. Served as Wilson's secretary of state (1913-1915); he resigned over Wilson's *Lusitania* note. Was noted speaker on Chautauqua circuit and later participated in the trial of John Scopes.

[37] Title Variation: WILL ROGERS SAYS / By Will Rogers / Famous Oklahoma Cowboy, Humorist and Motion Picture Star. *OKN*.

[38] Chautauqua. A summer entertainment program lasting from three to five days, held in a large tent; programs were given in the afternoon and evenings. Many artists appeared on these cultural programs for small towns; William Jennings Bryan toured the Chautauqua circuit for years.

[39] This line was omitted from *OKN*.

[40] William Randolph Hearst (1863-1951). Newspaper publisher who supported the nomination of Hiram Johnson of California in 1920. Hearst owned papers in the West and East, and had run unsuccessfully for mayor of New York City in 1906 and 1909.

[41] Title Variation: WILL ROGERS SAYS / By Will Rogers / Famous Oklahoma Cowboy, Humorist, and Motion Picture Star. *OKN*.

[42] Cardinal James Gibbons (1834-1921). Archbishop of Baltimore offered the invocation at the convention.

[43] The Republican platform straddled the League of Nations issue. Elihu Root, William Howard Taft, and Charles Evans Hughes supported the League; yet some party leaders strongly opposed it. Harding refused to take a stand on the issue, and therefore avoided considerable conflict.

[44] I asked Boies: "Why *don't* you people nominate Admiral Sims for vice-president and get the Democrats to nominate Secretary Daniels?" NEA.

[45] William Sowden Sims (1858-1936). American naval officer who commanded American naval operations in European waters during W.W.I.

Josephus Daniels (1862-1948). Secretary of the navy (1913-1921).

In 1920 Admiral Sims submitted a report to the senate naval affairs subcommittee accusing the U. S. department of the navy of mis-managing naval operations during the war. The subsequent hearings revealed bitter hostilities between Admiral Sims and Secretary of the Navy Daniels.

[46] Title Variation: WILL ROGERS SAYS / By Will Rogers / Famous Oklahoma Cowboy Humorist and Motion Picture Star. *OKN*.

[47] General Leonard Wood and Frank O. Lowden were the leading delegates during the first day's balloting. The convention adjourned after the fourth ballot and the next day on the tenth ballot, Senator Warren G. Harding of Ohio received the Republican endorsement for president.

[48] "They cheered him for 42 minutes." *OKN*.

[49] Henry J. Allen (1868-1950). Republican governor of Kansas (1919-1923). U. S. senator (1929-1930); completed the term of Charles Curtis when Curtis was

elected vice president with Hoover. Nominated Leonard Wood for president at the Republican convention of 1920.

William Gibbs McAdoo (1863-1941). Secretary of treasury (1913-1918). R. R. executive before days as a public servant, but as secretary of treasury he served also as director of the railroads when under government control. Rogers referred to the fact that although a brigadier general, Wood was not sent overseas as a military leader during World War I.

50 Charles Stetson Wheeler of California placed Johnson's name in the running for president and Representative Thomas D. Schall of Minnesota, who was blind, made one of the seconding speeches. The speeches were limited in length, but Schall was voted permission to continue praise of his nominee beyond the appointed time.

51 Cornelius (Connie Mack) McGillicudy (1862-1956). Baseball catcher who became manager of Philadelphia Athletics in 1901; he served in that position until 1950. During the early 1920's Mack was rebuilding his team and was suffering a poor record.

DEMOCRATIC CONVENTION OF 1920

1 Title Variation: Famous Oklahoma Cowboy, Humorist, and Motion Picture Star. *OKN.*

2 Warren G. Harding (1865-1923). Received the Republican nomination for president on the tenth ballot in 1920. On the initial ballot he had received only 65½ votes. He defeated Democrat James M. Cox; he served three years and died while in office before all of the scandals of his administration were exposed.

3 Wilson, while touring the country supporting the League of Nations, had collapsed from exhaustion. He recovered slowly and was unaware of some aspects of politics. During his illness Mrs. Wilson and Admiral Grayson supposedly exercised the prerogatives of government.

4 Edward Mandell House (1858-1938). Served as President Wilson's adviser during his administrations. After Wilson's illness he no longer conferred with House.

5 Will Rogers performed before President Wilson five different times. In Roger's book, *The Illiterate Digest,* he described the first such performance.

6 Cary Travers Grayson (1878-1938). Naval physician who attended President Wilson. Grayson had great authority after Wilson was stricken, for he decided what and how much information about the daily operations of government the president should be given.

7 Joseph P. Tumulty (1879-1954). Secretary to Woodrow Wilson while governor of New Jersey, and remained with Wilson until 1921. When Wilson was stricken Tumulty suggested that Dr. Grayson declare the president incapaciated, allowing Vice President Marshall to assume the duties of chief executive. This created a conflict, and after Wilson's recovery the president was less favorable toward Tumulty.

8 James Alexander Reed (1860-1944). U. S. senator from Missouri (1911-1929). Reed bitterly opposed the Versailles Peace Treaty and Covenant of League of Nations thereby aggravating a dichotomy in the Democratic party. The Missouri state Democratic convention denied him a delegate's seat at the convention of 1920, and the credentials committee refused to seat him. When Cox refused to endorse Reed's anti-League position, the senator declined to endorse the national ticket.

9 McAdoo had hesitated about seeking the nomination fearing he would alienate his father-in-law, President Wilson.

10 Alexander Mitchell Palmer (1872-1936). Attorney general (1919-1921) who was noted for his onslaught on alleged domestic radicalism during the "Red Scare." He was a leading contender for the Democratic nomination during this convention.

James Middleton Cox (1870-1957). Journalist and political leader from Ohio. U. S. representative (1909-1913); governor (1913-1915; 1917-1921); Democratic candidate for president in 1920; he was nominated on the fourth ballot. He selected Franklin D. Roosevelt as running mate, but lost to Harding in a Republican landslide.

[11] Title Variation: "DON'T MAKE ME LAUGH, THE BOY WILL WALK IN" / By Will Rogers / Famous Oklahoma Cowboy and Motion Picture Star. *OKN.*

[12] Homer Stille Cummings (1870-1956). Served as chairman for the national committee (1919-1920), and temporary chairman of the Democratic convention of 1920. He offered the keynote address at San Francisco which was a recital of achievements of the Democratic administration and a denunciation of the Republicans. Cummings was also mayor of Stamford, Connecticut (1900-1902; 1904-1906) and U. S. attorney general (1933-1939).

[13] I said: *OKN.*

[14] Tammany Hall. Headquarters of the New York County Democratic Committee and of the Society of Tammany, or Columbian Order. Tammany Hall was organized in 1789, and incorporated as a charitable organization in 1805. William M. ("Boss") Tweed became leader in 1860, and under his leadership Tammany was raised to state power in 1868 with the election of Tweed's candidate for governor. After electing another governor in 1910, Tammany ruled the state until 1932, with the exception of six years. Franklin D. Roosevelt's attempts to control the organization in 1932 failed, and he therefore reduced it to the status of a county organization.

[15] Title Variation: Famous Oklahoma Cowboy and Motion Picture Star. *OKN.*

[16] Robert Latham Owen (1856-1947). U. S. senator from Oklahoma (1907-1925). Owen was of Cherokee ancestory; he supported and initiated Indian legislation in the senate. Owen was a leading advocate of U. S. entrance into the League of Nations. D. Hayden Linebough of Oklahoma placed Owen's name in nomination at the convention of 1920. He was the first man nominated for the presidency at the convention.

[17] Irvin Shrewsbury Cobb (1876-1944). Journalist, humorist, and dramatic writer who wrote the book *Judge Priest* which later provided the basic story for a movie in which Rogers starred. On the twenty-third ballot, Cobb received one-half vote from Kentucky for president.

[18] James W. Gerard (1867-1951). U. S. ambassador to Germany (1913-1917); he later wrote a book entitled *My Four Years in Germany;* greatly in demand as a public speaker after his return to the U. S. in 1917 (W. W. I.); teamed with Herbert Hoover in providing relief for Belgium and France. He centered on the South Dakota primary and U. S. G. Cherry of South Dakota placed his name in nomination at the convention. When James Cox was selected, Gerard supported him. In every subsequent campaign Gerard served as either chairman of the finance committee, treasurer or honorary treasurer of the Democratic national committee.

[19] The Ziegfeld Follies was organized by Florenz Ziegfeld who began his career as a promoter of musical features for the Chicago World's Fair, 1893. His music revue the *Follies,* noted for lavish settings and attractive chorus girls, was introduced to the United States in 1907 and was highly successful for the next twenty years. Will Rogers, with W. C. Fields, Eddie Cantor and hundreds of other entertainers, performed for Ziegfeld for several years. Rogers actually worked for Ziegfeld intermittently from 1915-1925.

[20] Bryan had been secretary of state in Wilson's cabinet until 1915 when he resigned because he believed the president's note to Germany about the sinking of the *Lusitania* would lead the U. S. into war.

[21] The president said: "I would but, Will, he won't work—I tried him once." *OKN.*

[22] I said: "Well, everything is going all O. K. out at the weegee seance, isn't it?" *OKN.*

[23] He said: "Yes, but I am afraid when they get to voting that some candidate with a couple of quarts of Old Crow will stampede the convention." *OKN.*

[24] Title Variation: WILSON TELLS WILL ROGERS THE LATEST FROM FRISCO / By Will Rogers / Famous Oklahoma Cowboy Wit and Movie Star. *OKN.*

[25] Bainbridge Colby (1869-1950). Secretary of State (1920-1921); Wilson's law partner (1921-1923). One of the founders of the Progressive party; ran for senator on that ticket in 1914, 1916. Attended the Democratic convention of

1920, and participated in the debate on the formation of the platform, and on the resolutions committee.

[26] Carter Glass (1858-1946). U. S. representative (1902-1919); U. S. senator (1920-1946). Member of the national Democratic committee (1916-1928); chairman of the committee on resolutions at the convention.

[27] The following quote was included in *OKN,* but was omitted from the *NEA* tear sheet:

I said: "Mr. President they say Burleson left here two weeks ago on a fast mail train and hasn't arrived there yet."

[28] Daniels was a delegate from North Carolina during the Democratic convention of 1920.

[29] Thomas Riley Marshall (1854-1925). Governor of Indiana (1909-1913); vice president of U. S. (1913-1921). Rogers referred to the fact that the vice president had little power or influence. Marshall was very popular with the American public, but he had few responsibilities in government.

[30] Ireland had attempted to gain its independence from Great Britain during W. W. I. and the struggle for an independent Ireland continued in 1920.

[31] In 1920 Alvaro Obregon became president of Mexico. American investors in Mexican oil and land worried that the new president would assert that subsoil rights belonged to the Mexican nation. Americans wanted their Mexican property rights protected, but Obregon refused. The controversy between foreign investors and the Mexican government continued throughout the 1920's.

REPUBLICAN CONVENTION OF 1924

[1] Title Variation: COULD NOMINATE COOLIDGE WITH ONE POSTCARD / COUNTRY KNOWS WHAT DELEGATES GO TO CONVENTION TO FIND OUT / WILL HAS CANDIDATE / TAKES HAYS AND VALENTINO TO CLEVELAND TO USE IN CASE OF DEADLOCK. *TDW.*

[2] Calvin Coolidge (1872-1933). Coolidge had been elected as Harding's vice president in 1920. Coolidge was colorless and inactive; when he became president after Harding's death, he remained rather lackluster. Coolidge thought very highly of Will Rogers and they were on very good terms.

[3] Harry Lauder (1870-1950). Popular Scottish singer who was knighted for entertaining troops during World War I.

[4] Senator Henry Cabot Lodge was an influential party member who usually participated in party decision-making. Lodge also had supported Irving L. Lenroot for vice president in 1920.

[5] Rudolph Valentino (1895-1926). Popular movie star of the 1920's. He starred in such famous silent movies as *The Shiek,* and was the romantic star of the era.

[6] Frank Lowden, former governor of Illinois, was suggested for the vice presidency; he led through two ballots and withdrew his name on the third ballot; finally Charles Dawes was elected as Coolidge's running mate.

[7] Title Variation: DULL TIME BEING HAD BY ALL AT CLEVELAND 'CHAUTAUQUA'. *TDW.*

[8] William Ashley "Billy" Sunday (1862-1935). Popular evangelist who reached the height of his career in 1920's.

[9] As Coolidge was the only serious contender for the Republican presidential nomination, the decision of who would be Coolidge's running mate was the only excitement. (See introduction).

[10] William McKinley (1843-1901). Republican president of the United States (1897-1901); defeated W. J. Bryan twice for president but was assassinated in 1901; his vice president, Theodore Roosevelt, became president.

[11] Fanny Brice (1891-1951). Comedienne and Ziegfeld Follies star best known for playing the role "Baby Snooks." *Funny Girl,* a musical comedy of 1964, was based on her life.

[12] Frank Waterman Stearns (1856-1939). Dry goods merchant who supported Calvin Coolidge's election as governor of Massachusetts and later as vice president. At Harding's death, Coolidge gave a permanent suite in the White House to Stearns and his wife. Stearns held no public office, but perhaps was Coolidge's closest friend.

[13] Title Variation: FIRST CONVENTION THRILL EXPERIENCED BY ROGERS IS MEETING BILL BRYAN / BUT EVERYBODY THOUGHT THE COWBOY HUMORIST WAS A PLAIN-CLOTHESMAN SENT ALONG TO GUARD W. J. FROM THE REPUBLICANS AT "CONSCRIPTION" GATHERING. *TDW*

[14] We were the only two aliens in the entire hall, he, solitary democrat, bull moose, both of us entered not to jeer but to be instructed. *TDW*

[15] William Jennings Bryan covered the Republican convention of 1924 for the same newspaper syndicate as Will Rogers. Rogers and Bryan sat together in the press stand and had lunch together one day. They also met at the Democratic convention that same year.

[16] Samuel George Blythe (1868-1947). Political writer for the New York *World* (1900-1907); he joined the staff of the *Saturday Evening Post* writing a weekly feature on national politics and biographical sketches of people prominent in politics.

[17] Theodore E. Burton (1851-1929). Served as temporary chairman to the Republican convention of 1924, and gave keynote speech the first day. U. S. representative from Ohio (1889-1891; 1895-1909; 1921-1929); U. S. senator (1909-1915).

[18] On the second day of the convention the La Follette Progressive delegates presented the platform, but the convention voted to adopt the majority report. Robert M. La Follette (1855-1925) U. S. senator from Wisconsin (1906-1925). La Follette became the Progressive party candidate in this election.

[19] Title Variation: WILL ROGERS STARTS LATE BOOM FOR HIS FILM BOSS, WILL HAYS; HAS ABOUT ENOUGH OF BRYAN. *TDW*

[20] Joseph Morris Weber (1867-1942) and Lewis Maurice Fields (1867-1941). Burlesque comedians and theatrical producers. Weber and Fields were at the zenith of their career (1877-1904), when they appeared in their own theater in burlesques of popular productions.

[21] You remember one of them used to get just as many laughs as the other and he is taking the comedy. *TDW*

[22] Frank Wheeler Mondell (1860-1939). U. S. representative from Wyoming (1895-1897; 1899-1923); served as permanent chairman of the Republican convention of 1924. Gave address glorifying Republicans and notified Coolidge of his nomination. He was influential in the Harding administration but after losing the senate race in 1922, he refused Harding's offers to appoint him ambassador to Japan or governor of Puerto Rico.

[23] Now he knows that is a lot of applesauce, for a chairman at one of these conventions is nothing more than an auctioneer with a hammer, receiving and taking the delegates yeas and noes. *TDW*

[24] He copied the best gag Burton had yesterday and tried it right back on the same audience today, and it went almost as big as it did yesterday. *TDW*

[25] Occasionally an editor corrected typos and grammar; for example, *NYT* read "came".

[26] Title Variation: ROGERS WRITES CONFESSION, ADMITS HE LEFT CLEVELAND TO AVOID BEING NOMINATED / Cowboy Humorist Expects to Be Remembered by Historians as "the First Man to Leave Convention in 1924;" / Gives World Scoop on Coolidge Nomination. *TDW*

[27] *TDW* inserted the following statement as the opening sentence: Cleveland, I am gone.

[28] Alvin C. York (1887-1964). World War I hero who was credited with single-handedly capturing an entire German machine gun battalion. He was given the Congressional Medal of Honor, and later was the subject of the movie, *Sergeant York*.

[29] John Joseph Pershing (1860-1948). Army chief of staff (1921-1924); commander of the American Expeditionary Force to Europe during World War I; was given the rank General of the Armies in 1919 by Congress; George Washington was the only other person to have held that title.

[30] William McAdoo served as secretary of the treasury, and director of the railroads, during the war. Rogers referred to "Gone West," which during the war was a euphemism for a soldier's death in France. Rogers may have been mixing metaphors here—he often did so.

[31] The statement Rogers referred to was made by William T. Sherman and it was "War is Hell."

DEMOCRATIC CONVENTION OF 1924

[1] Title Variation: TWO BIG SHOWS READY TO OPEN / Follies Will Not Lose Patronage to Democratic Meeting / MEN NOT ATTRACTIVE / Convention Delegates Stand Poor Second to Girls of Music Show. *TDW*

[2] The Democratic convention was held in Madison Square Garden, while the *Follies* were staged at Amsterdam Theater.

[3] Alfred Emanuel Smith (1873-1944). Governor of New York (1919-1921; 1923-1928); sought his party's presidential nomination in 1920, 1924, and finally became the nominee in 1928. His Catholicism and adamant opposition to prohibition dampened his political success.

Oscar Wilder Underwood (1862-1929). U. S. representative from Alabama (1895-1896; 1897-1915); U. S. senator (1915-1927); Democratic floor leader (1911-1915). Underwood had been a leading presidential candidate in the nominating convention of 1912, and finally was nominated in 1924.

Samuel M. Ralston (1857-1925). U. S. senator from Indiana (1923-1925); governor of Indiana (1913-1917). Ralston was a dark horse candidate in the convention of 1924, and twice during the deadlock between McAdoo and Smith, party leaders asked him to resolve the impass; he steadfastly refused to run.

[4] Ann Pennington (1892-1971). Dancer for the Ziegfeld Follies who won fame as the dancer with the "dimpled knees."

[5] There are some people so old fashioned that they still listen to a riddle. *TDW*

[6] Imogene Wilson (1902-1948). Ziegfeld Follies chorus girl whose romance with Ziegfeld comic Frank Tinney became a front page sensation in 1924, he was charged with felonious assault. The incident ruined his career, but Wilson became famous.

[7] Evelyn Law and Martha Lauber. Chorus girls in the Ziegfeld Follies. Rogers referred to the spectacular costumes used in his shows .

[8] Now these politicans suits are all made in the Chautauquas. *TDW*

[9] Byron Patton Harrison (1881-1941). U. S. representative from Mississippi (1911-1919); U. S. senator (1919-1941). Selected as temporary chairman of convention of 1924 and delivered the keynote address.

[10] Title Variation: SOONERS 'LOST,' ROGERS BELIEVES / Says Delegation Started Out to Parade New York, End to End / WILL IS 'ALL EXCITED' / But He's Afraid They'll Spoil the Convention Yet by Nominating Someone. *TDW*

[11] This line was omitted from *TDW*.

[12] Eleanor Randolph Wilson McAdoo (1890-1967). Youngest daughter of Woodrow Wilson. Married McAdoo in a White House ceremony in 1914. He was secretary of the treasury and 50 years old, she was 24. The marriage ended 20 years later in divorce.

[13] Tuesday is what they call credential day. *TDW*

[14] Title Variation: ROGERS AMUSED BY CORDELL HULL / Chairman Announced That Cardinal Gibbons Would Deliver Invocation / FOLLIES NOW OPENED / That Explains Why There Was No Session Held by Democrats Tuesday Night. *TDW*

[15] Well, the democratic scandals got started Tuesday. *TDW*

[16] Cordell Hull (1871-1955). U. S. representative from Tennessee (1907-1921; 1923-1931); U. S. senator (1931-1933); U. S. secretary of state (1933-1944); awarded the Nobel Peace Prize in 1945. Chairman of the Democratic national committee in 1924 and spoke to the delegates at the beginning of the convention.

Patrick Joseph Hayes (1867-1938). Catholic priest who was installed as archbishop of New York in 1919, and cardinal in 1924.

[17] Anna Case (1889-?). Opera soprano who sang with the Metropolitan Opera until 1915, when she became a concert performer; toured the U. S. and Europe in 1925. In 1929 she married and retired from the stage.

[18] After they had all finished Chairman Hull announced that Miss Anna Case of Metropolitan would sing it. *TDW*

[19] This sentence was omitted from *TDW*.

[20] John F. Hylan (1868-1936). Mayor of New York City (1918-1925).

[21] The following paragraph was included in the *TDW* article, but was omitted from *NYT*.

> Thursday night there was no session on account of the opening of the Follies. If in my act I should mention the name of George Washington I hope the audience don't start marching and singing "Hail, Hail, the Gang's All Here." *TDW*

[22] I suppose Hull will have Ben Franklin lead us in prayer Wednesday. *TDW*

[23] Title Variation: ROGERS IN RACE FOR V. P. HONORS / Cowboy Humorist Lists an Imposing Array of Qualifications for Job / ONLY ONE AFTER POST / It's Bad Enough, He Declares, to Be Nominated on 'That Ticket' for President. *TDW*

[24] Mrs. Belle Moskowitz was the publicist editor for presidential aspirant New York Governor Alfred E. Smith in 1924, but Mrs. Moskowitz's influence extended beyond simply editing Smith's speeches; she also helped shape policy decisions. Undoubtedly, Rogers framed his "Moskowitz" with the lady in mind.

[25] Charles Dawes, the Republican vice president, had received publicity over an incident with the press, where he allegedly resorted in anger to profanity. Dawes was changing trains at Grand Central Station in New York when asked to appear before a couple of movie cameras that had been set up. He expressed in explicit language no desire to be "in the movies."

[26] Ben Turpin (1869-1940). Slap-stick comedian best known for his crossed-eyes and large toothbrush mustache. Turpin worked for Mack Sennett and his Keystone Studio.

Louis (Bull) Montana (1888-1950). Professional wrestler but best remembered as a fierce faced character actor.

Isidore (Izzy) Einstein (1880-1938) and Moe Smith (1887-1960). Famous federal prohibition agent team known for their disguises and ingenuity in arresting speakeasy operators. Both men were dismissed from the department in 1925 for political reasons.

John Callaway (Jack) Walton (1881-1949). Mayor of Oklahoma City (1919-1923); governor in 1923, but was impeached in the same year.

Ringgold (Ring) Lardner (1885-1933). Journalist for the *Chicago Tribune* and contributor to the *Saturday Evening Post*. Also wrote sketches and lyrics for the Ziegfeld Follies.

Arthur (Bugs) Baer (1886-1969). Columnist for Hearst's paper who got his nickname from a cartoon he drew of a baseball-bodied insect called "Bugs." Baer's second wife was a former Ziegfeld girl.

Reuben (Rube) Lucius Goldberg (1883-1970). American cartoonist who created the comic strips "Boob McNutt" and "LaLa Palooza." Won a Pulitzer Prize in 1948.

Frank McKinney (Kin) Hubbard (1868-1930). Humorist and caricaturist. Employed by the *Indianapolis News*, but his "Abe Martin Sayings" was widely syndicated.

[27] Title Variation: ROGERS CLAIMS ONLY EIGHT OF POSSIBLE 200 WERE NOMINATED / When Smith Was Nominated You Would Have Thought Somebody Had Thrown a Wildcat in Your Face. *TDW*

[28] Well, of all bunk I ever saw collected in one building it was in there today. *TDW*

[29] But when he did get to the end and named Al you would have thought somebody had thrown a wild cat in your face the galleries went so wild. *TDW*

[30] Franklin Delano Roosevelt (1882-1945). Placed Al Smith's name in nomination and would do so again in 1928. Roosevelt worked as Smith's floor leader at the convention of 1924, but could not break the deadlock between McAdoo and Smith. Roosevelt was a member of New York state senate (1910-1913); assistant secretary of the navy (1913-1920). He also had been the vice-presidential candidate on the Democratic ticket in 1920. After Roosevelt's nomination speech, the delegates showed their enthusiasm for Smith by demonstrating for almost an hour. When eventually quieted, the delegates heard Anna Case sing the national anthem.

[31] Catherine A. (Mrs. Alfred) Dunn Smith (1878-1944). Wife of Al Smith and mother of five. Mrs. Smith was described as a deeply religious woman and a devoted mother and wife.

[32] Mrs. Smith is a charming, plain everyday woman, and I watched and studied these two probably next first ladies of the land. *TDW*

[33] Bernard M. Baruch (1870-1965). Successful businessman who officially advised several presidents. As chairman of the war industries board during World War I, he received no salary for this work. Baruch had two daughters and a son, and was a close personal friend of President Wilson's, and therefore a supporter of McAdoo.

[34] Francis Duffy (1871-1932). Father Duffy served as chaplain of the "Fighting Sixty-ninth" or the "Fighting Irish" on the Mexican border and later in France during W. W. I. Father Duffy was obviously a leader of men, and General Douglas MacArthur suggested he would be an excellent battlefield commander.

[35] Albert Cabell Ritchie (1867-1936). Governor of Maryland elected to four terms (1920-1935). Placed into nomination by Howard Bruce of Maryland, and at the conclusion of the nominating speech the governor's supporters held a thirty minute demonstration.

[36] Only Maryland and Delaware were in on this demonstration, but if they had as many votes as they have noise he would be our next leader. *TDW*

[37] Jonathan McMillan Davis (1871-1943). Governor of Kansas (1923-1925). Nominated for president by W. A. Ayers of Kansas, and received votes on fifty-five ballots; he was also in the balloting for vice president in 1924.

[38] A. M. Cummings of Michigan nominated Woodbridge N. Ferris (1853-1928) who had been governor of Michigan (1913-1916); U. S. senator (1923-1928), and a potential candidate for the presidential nomination. He received votes on the first eight ballots. Ferris was at the time of his nomination a U. S. senator and not a governor of the state.

Henry Ford (1863-1947). Founder of Ford Motor Company was once considered a possible presidential candidate, and although he enjoyed the support of the Hearst newspaper chain, he was never considered seriously.

[39] Michael Lambert Igoe (1885-1967). Illinois delegate to the convention who seconded the speech nominating Smith. Will Rogers was relatively accurate, for there were several seconding speeches made for Smith. Igoe was a member of the Illinois state house of representatives (1913-1930) and U. S. representative (1935).

William Hale Thompson (1867-1944). Mayor of Chicago (1915-1923; 1927-1931). Rogers was being humorous in this remark, for Thompson was a staunch Republican.

[40] A delegate from Indiana nominated Ralston.

[41] Rogers referred to M. F. Healy of Iowa who seconded Smith's nomination; although the speech was not eighty minutes long as Rogers said, it did entail a history of the 30 year's war and a tribute to the gallant Rainbow Division from Iowa.

[42] Lewis G. Stevenson of Illinois nominated David Franklin Houston (1866-1940) who was secretary of agriculture and treasurer during the Wilson administration. Michael L. Igoe of that state seconded Smith's nomination, and James A. Meeks of Illinois seconded W. G. McAdoo.

[43] Oh, yes, a woman from Oregon seconded McAdoo for the 90th time. *TDW*

[44] This line was omitted from *TDW*.

[45] Mrs. Alexander Thompson of Oregon made a seconding speech for W. G. McAdoo.

[46] Title Variation: WILL ROGERS APPEARS FOR POOR DELEGATES WHO MUST 'TAKE IT' / Punishment of Continuous Speech-Making of Same Speech Terrific, Cowboy Says. *TDW*

[47] These men do this for fabulous prizes. *TDW*

[48] The thirty-sixth annual international bicycle race was held in Madison Square Garden March 3-9, 1924. Fifteen teams from various nations participated in the race; an Italian-Belgian team won the event. Will Rogers fired the starter's gun.

[49] Mutt and Jeff. Popular comic strip by Bud Fisher.

[50] There were twenty candidates from which the delegates had to choose on the first ballot. Three entire days were spent nominating and seconding all the candidates.

[51] To show you that I must not be alone in my judgment, today there were several speakers who were never allowed to finish. *TDW*

[52] Today they tried a lot of women and outside of one from Pennsylvania the first one that spoke, why, they were just as bad as the men. *TDW*

[53] William M. Maloney of Montana did make the shortest seconding speech

at the convention. Mr. Maloney stated: "Fellow delegates: My voice is hoarse; I cannot speak. I come up here at this time to second the nomination of Al Smith."

[54] I just thought today when you had to hear all this unnecessary shouting about each man, . . . *TDW*

[55] I did want to run for vice president but I have changed since today. I want to go down and take my rope and when the speaker has said enough, I rope him and drag him back to his delegation. *TDW*

[56] Title Variation: DOESN'T TAKE MUCH STRATEGY TO BE QUIET AT THIS CONVENTION / There Are Twelve Thousand Civilians and at Least a Hundred Thousand Cops in and Around the Convention Building. TDW

[57] When you straddle a gag it takes a long time to explain it. *TDW*

[58] He kept on telling the audience that he had not been to bed until three o'clock any morning, and that Saturday morning. . . *TDW*

[59] . . . and at six o'clock Saturday morning, some one happened to think of the democratic party. *TDW*

[60] On the fifth day of the convention Homer Cummings, as chairman of the committee on platform and resolutions, made a speech much as Rogers reported, and he requested that the convention recess until 3:00 in the afternoon. When the convention reassembled at 4:00 that afternoon the report of the platform and resolutions committee was read and debated until 2:00 a.m.

[61] William David Upshaw (1866-1952). U. S. representative from Georgia (1919-1927). Upshaw was an extremely religious man and believed in the total abstinence of alcoholic beverages for all government officials as an example for American youth. He left the Democratic party over the liquor issue, and was nominated by the Prohibition party for president in 1932.

[62] Thomas Taggart (1856-1929). U. S. senator (1916); delegate to all Democratic national conventions (1900-1924); powerful in Indiana Democratic politics.

George E. Brennan (1865-1928). Democratic national committeeman from Illinois at the convention of 1924.

Norman E. Mack (1858-1932). National committeeman from New York to the Democratic national convention of 1924.

[63] Title Variation: SPLIT DELEGATE GETS HIS GOAT / Will Rogers Figuring Yet on How N. Carolina Voted on Klan / HOW HE'D GET VOTES / Lone Case of Gin More Influential Than the Oratory of Pat Harrison. *TDW*

[64] This will go down in democratic political history as one of the memorable days of their party. *TDW*

[65] On the vote on the minority report of the platform committee on an amendment to the religious liberty plank (Ku Klux Klan) North Carolina voted 3 17/20 aye and 20 3/20 no—these fractions caused some concern about how to report the votes; ultimately they stood as cast.

[66] They must use some other tool than a hundred. *TDW*

[67] Singer Midgets. Vaudeville act consisting of thirty-three people, animals and animal trainers. Under contract with the Loew circuit.

[68] . . . and along comes 490 to sleep in them, chaperoned by 480 alternates? *TDW*

[69] . . . who forgot his speech and hence was the best thing there, . . . *TDW*

[70] Cameron A. Morrison (1869-1953). Governor of North Carolina (1921-1925); member of Democratic national committee (1928); U. S. senator (1930-1932); U. S. representative (1943-1945).

[71] Newton Diehl Baker (1871-1937). Secretary of war (1916-1921). Baker read the minority report offering an amendment to the League of Nations plank; he elegantly and impassionately defended the amendment, but it was defeated.

[72] McAdoo had been secretary of the treasury and director-general of the railroads; he resigned in 1919.

[73] Bryan made a great speech, but he didn't sway any of New York's vote. *TDW*

[74] I can walk into that convention Monday with one lone case of gin. . . *TDW*

[75] Pennsylvania Brown might have been a delegate to the convention, or perhaps just someone mentioned briefly in the newspapers of the day for any number of reasons. Her name does not appear in the convention minutes.

[76] Key Pittman (1872-1940). U. S. senator from Nevada (1912-1940). Secretary of the platform committee, and supported the majority report on the League of Nations plank thus refuting Baker's stand.

[77] Monday they start balloting. . . *TDW*

[78] Title Variation: VOTES HIGHER PRICED THAN THEY USED TO BE / Now It Takes 'a Case' Whereas a Delegate Could Be Induced In the Old Days for A Few Beers, Will Rogers Says. *TDW*

[79] Monday it was the audience. *TDW*

[80] On account of this rule they had to adjourn Monday afternoon: . . . *TDW*

[81] Monday night delegates were probably invited to dinners at the Ritz, who up to now have watched their hats in Childs. *TDW*

[82] Favorite son governors who have been holding their states to them finally told them: . . . *TDW*

[83] Personally if I was governor I would hold my delegation until at least Tuesday. Why, they will get twice as much for them as they would Monday night. *TDW*

[84] The government has an income tax man watching all transactions, so in selling you have got to figure on a tax. *TDW*

[85] Politicians who can buy votes. . . *TDW*

[86] . . . so they won't be able to vote Tuesday . . . *TDW*

[87] Title Variation: ROGERS HAS SCHEME TO SEND 3 LEADERS ALL TO WHITE HOUSE / Let McAdoo, Smith and Davis Divide It Into Three Eight-Hour Shifts, His Suggestion to Settle Deadlock. *TDW*.

[88] John William Davis (1873-1955). U. S. representative from West Virginia (1911-1913); solicitor general (1913-1918); ambassador to Britain (1918-1921). Davis became the Democratic nominee after McAdoo and Smith became hopelessly deadlocked; Davis had never received more than 66 votes on the first 87 ballots, on the 13th day on the 88th ballot he fell to 59½ votes, but on each successive ballot gathered momentum. On the 103rd ballot he was elected.

[89] Samuel Gompers (1850-1924). President of the A. F. of L. (1886-1894, 1896-1924). Gompers stressed practical reforms on wages and hours; he opposed radical labor reform action. Rogers is here specifically referring to Gompers' fight for the eight-hour work day.

[90] Alice Roosevelt Longworth (1884-). Daughter of Theodore Roosevelt; wife of Speaker of the House Nicholas Longworth and famous Washington hostess; known for her influence and bluntness in politics.

[91] Princess Elizabeth Bibesco (1897-1945). Daughter of England's first Earl of Oxford and Margaret Tennant, noted author and wife of Prince Antoine Bibesco, a Rumanian diplomat. In 1914 the princess almost created an incident when she wrote a letter for the *New Republic* supporting the nomination of Davis; her husband was Rumanian minister to the U. S., and the U. S. state department was prepared to ask for his removal if an outcry arose.

[92] Willard Saulsbury (1861-1927). U. S. senator from Delaware (1913-1919); member of the Democratic national committee (1908-1920). His name was placed in nomination by Thomas F. Bayard of Delaware. Saulsbury was given the six Delaware votes through 100 ballots, but on the next tally Delaware voted for Davis.

[93] . . . the big break of this voting will come when Senator Saulsbury's six votes are released. *TDW*

[94] I noticed Tuesday . . .*TDW*

[95] Smith is going out to try and pick up a lap tonight on the field. *TDW*

[96] James M. Cox of Ohio had been the Democratic candidate for president in 1920, but lost the election to Harding.

[97] Sallie Turner. Missouri delegate from Kansas City. The Missourians were continually asking for a recount of their delegation. Not only Missouri, but many states followed this time consuming policy.

[98] This whole thing is just being dragged along to educate the westerners and the southerners up to eat hot dogs. *TDW*

[99] Title Variation: ROGERS HAS SCHEME TO BREAK DEADLOCK: NOMINATES HIS MAN / Broadcasts Nominating Speech to be Printed by Press as Soon as Received—No Release Dates on His Speeches. *TDW*

[100] Robert La Follette. Progressive Republican senator who on occasion entered the ranks of the Progressive party as one of its candidates.

[101] Title Variation: WILL ROGERS FAVORS DEFAULTING ELECTION: HE MADE A BAD DEAL / Is 'Covering' Convention for One Price, but Next Time He'll Know Enough to Get Paid by the Month, He Says.

[102] . . . but right here they are sitting and sleeping every day in New York's

municipal swimming hole.

[103] George L. (Tex) Rickard (1871-1929). Prize fight promoter who acquired the old Madison Square Garden in 1920, and within a few years built the new Madison Square Garden from the boxing receipts.

[104] In years to come children will ask their parents, . . . and the parent will say, . . . *TDW*

[105] Underwood was a Democratic presidential candidate in 1912 and 1924. At the convention of 1928. Forney Johnston of Alabama placed Underwood's name in nomination; Alabama cast all 24 of its votes for Underwood through 103 ballots; when John W. Davis seemed to be the majority candidate, the state changed its entire vote in order to support the winner.

[106] . . . another week for Bryan to make another speech. *TDW*

[107] Friday is the Fourth of July, . . . *TDW*

[108] Someone prayed again Thursday at the opening. *TDW*

[109] . . . with a bright red one, is all that kept the Oklahoma men. . . *TDW*

[110] Title Variation: DEMOCRATS HOLD BIG BIRTHDAY CELEBRATION FOR CALVIN COOLIDGE / Rogers Says a Man Must Be Pretty Good for the Opposite Party to Hold a Demonstration All Day Long in His Favor. *TDW*

[111] The biggest celebration ever had . . . was held in Madison Square Garden Friday . . . *TDW*

[112] Augustus Thomas (1857-1934). American dramatist and delegate from New York read the Declaration of Independence to the delegates on July 4.

[113] J. P. Morgan (1837-1913). Wealthy financier who controlled one of the most influential banking houses in the world. An avid art collector.

[114] Thomas Walsh (1859-1933). U. S. senator from Montana (1913-1933). Served as chairman of the Democratic convention of 1924.

[115] . . . it would have been denounced as a senatorial oligarchy and a tool of the interests, written for the sole protection of predatory wealth. *TDW*

[116] Newton D. Baker was nominated for president, but never gained enough votes to be a threat.

[117] . . . as they see who will hang out the next best offer. *TDW*

[118] . . . he never did want to run and never intended to. *TDW*

[119] Taggart was Ralston's floor leader, and was more enthused about Ralston's candidacy than Ralston. After 64 ballots Taggart read the telegram from Ralston withdrawing his name "for the sake of party harmony."

[120] James Cox (1870-1957). Ex-governor of Ohio had been the Democratic candidate for president in 1920. Ohio had been casting all 48 votes for Cox until the completion of 65 ballots, whereupon he withdrew. Here Rogers differed from the official convention minutes, for it was a Henry Goeke of Ohio who actually presented the telegram, not Edmund Moore; the latter was Ohio's national committeeman. After Cox had withdrawn, Ohio cast its 48 votes for Newton Baker.

[121] I'm sending a telegram Friday night . . . as they told me Friday. . . *TDW*

[122] Bryan didn't speak Friday. *TDW*

[123] Title Variation: ROGERS LIKE OTHERS, HE'LL NOT WITHDRAW FROM GARDEN'S RACE / Having Polled Two One-Half Votes for Nomination for President, He'll Attempt to Build Up His Strength Again. *TDW*

[124] On ballot 68 Arizona cast one vote for Will Rogers. This was a popular decision, and led the delegates to ask that Rogers address the convention. He did not address this convention, but did write a platform to run on. On the next ballot Rogers lost Arizona's support.

[125] So my strength dropped back right to where I was when the convention started. *TDW*

[126] I went down Saturday. . . *TDW*

[127] Thomas Walsh had served as chairman of the committee investigating the Teapot Dome scandal.

[128] A. H. Ferguson of Oklahoma introduced a resolution to move the convention to Kansas City, and an extended debate ensued.

[129] They voted Saturday on taking the convention to Kansas City, but rejected its coming there by 1,010 to 88. *TDW*

[130] I had three offers Saturday. . . *TDW*

[131] Title Variation: DEMOCRAT POWWOW IS GETTING TWICE AS FUNNY, ROGERS SAYS / Oklahoma-California Cowboy Says He Is Sitting Pretty if They Eliminate From the Top Down. *TDW*

132 So they adjourned and Saturday night they were to hold another miniature one . . . *TDW*

133 After seventy ballots Edward Fresdorf of Michigan introduced a resolution requesting that Smith and McAdoo withdraw their names because they were deadlocked, and give their support to another candidate to restore the harmony of the party.

134 Now this is none of my make-up. *TDW*

135 Heywood Campbell Broun (1888-1939). Newspaper columnist for the *New York World* (1921-1928), and the Scripps-Howard newspapers (1928-1939).

136 Today is Sunday. *TDW*

137 Title Variation: ROGERS CLAIMS SAME THING HAS BEEN DONE OVER AND OVER AGAIN / Can't You Imagine Charley Murphey Turning Over in His Grave? He Would Have Had Delegates Home a Long Time Ago. *TDW*

138 The additional democratic convention is now called to order. *TDW*

139 Delegate from Oklahoma: Mr. Chairman—. *TDW*

140 . . . as long as there is a possible chance of any man getting a post office. *TDW*

141 Clerk: McAdoo 418 and three-eighths; . . . *TDW*

142 Charles Murphy (1858-1924). American politician who headed Tammany Hall (1902-1924). Murphy died in April 1924, only a couple of months before the convention.

143 William Joel Stone (1848-1918). Governor of Missouri (1893-1897); U. S. senator (1903-1918). Controlled Democratic party in Missouri and was nicknamed "Gum-Shoe Bill" because of his ability to avoid charges of political corruption.

Roger C. Sullivan (1861-1920). Democratic political "boss" in Illinois; dominant figure in state politics for a quarter of a century; he became a national force due to the publicity of attacks William Jennings Bryan made against him.

144 Title Variation: ROGERS, AGED, INFIRM, SENDS HIS SON WILL TO 'DO' CONVENTION / Rogers Boys, Will's Will Provides, Must Take Up His Life Work When Cowboy Dies—Covering Democratic Convention. *ADW*

145 . . . and "unit". . . *TDW*

146 Now, Mr. editorman, . . . *TDW*

147 Mamma got out dad's old press badge . . . *TDW*

148 Jackie Coogan (1914-). Child star who began his career at sixteen months. He performed in vaudeville and later appeared as a child star in movies. He was ten when Will Rogers wrote this article.

149 . . . and one and sixty-five fiftieths . . . *TDW*

150 David Ladd Rockwell (1877-?). Ohio banker who was a member of the Democratic central or executive committees for almost twenty years; active in promoting the candidacy of William McAdoo in 1924.

J. Bruce Kremer (1878-1940). Chairman of the Montana delegation to the Democratic national convention of 1924.

151 . . . take this story and Wednesday . . . *TDW*

152 . . . when I come him feel good. (Apparently, the *TDW* left out a line of print).

153 Title Variation: INFLUENCE OF BRYAN MADE DAVIS NOMINEE, WILL ROGERS CLAIMS / The Commoner Spoke Against Virginian and Wrote Against Him, So That Made It Almost a Cinch, Cowboy Humorist Says. *TDW*

154 I couldn't make the grade physically. I haven't had any sleep. . . *TDW*

155 . . . or either party in faith . . . *TDW*

156 If I could have gotten Bryan . . . *TDW*

157 But I can't afford that. *TDW*

158 Charles W. Bryan was selected for vice president by the Democratic convention of 1924.

REPUBLICAN CONVENTION OF 1928

1 Title Variation: ROGERS DROPS IN ON 'DOGS IN REPUBLICAN MANGER'. *TDW*

2 Herbert Clark Hoover (1874-1964). President (1929-1933); mining engineer, U. S. food administrator during World War I; established American Relief Administration; secretary of commerce under both Harding and Coolidge. During his campaign he made only seven speeches, and emphasized prosperity, farm relief,

and the protective tariff. He approved of prohibition and called it a "noble experiment."

[3] Andrew William Mellon (1855-1937). Conservative Republican financier; secretary of the treasury (1921-1932).

[4] Grace (Goodhue) Coolidge (1879-1957). Rogers once referred to the president's wife as "Public Female Favorite No. 1." She was a gracious and popular first lady—more personable than Coolidge, and increased the number of entertainers invited to the White House. In 1926 Rogers had spent a night in the White House with the Coolidges.

[5] Title Variation: 'CAL HASN'T SAID ANYTHING ABOUT MOVING, ROGERS FINDS. *TDW*

[6] *TDW* omitted the words: I says.

[7] No, none, only . . . *TDW*

[8] William Scott Vare (1867-1934). U. S. representative from Pennsylvania (1923-1927). Vare had replaced Boies Penrose as Republican "boss" of Pennsylvania. Vare and Andrew Mellon were fighting for leadership of the Pennsylvania delegation in 1928. Vare's declaration for Hoover was credited with furnishing the impetus to Hoover's nomination. Vare was elected to the senate in 1926, but he never was seated because of charges of excessive campaign expenditures.

[9] Title Variation: MELLON CAME WITH MONEY, VARE WITH VOTES, SAYS WILL. *TDW*

[10] Simeon Davison Fess (1861-1936). U. S. representative from Ohio (1913-1923); U. S. senator (1923-1935). Fess supported Coolidge for a third term in 1928, although Coolidge stated he would not run. Fess had been defeated in his bid for delegate status at the convention; yet he was temporary chairman and delivered the keynote address.

[11] James Thomas Heflin (1869-1951). U. S. representative from Alabama (1904-1920); U. S. senator (1920-1931). Heflin bolted the Democratic party in 1928 when the convention nominated Smith.

[12] James Watson (1863-1948). U. S. representative from Indiana (1895-1897; 1899-1909); U. S. senator (1916-1933). Leader of Indiana politics and a delegate to the Republican national conventions (1912-1936); chairman of the resolutions committee at the Republican convention in 1920.

[13] Guy Despard Goff (1866-1933). Attorney; held numerous appointments at different times as assistant to the attorney general; Republican U. S. senator from West Virginia (1925-1931).

[14] Charles Curtis (1860-1936). U. S. representative from Kansas (1893-1907). U. S. senator (1907-1913; 1915-1929); vice president (1929-1933). In 1924 he had become the most important member of the Senate when he replaced Henry Cabot Lodge as leader.

[15] Title Variation: ROGERS THINKS LITTLE OF G. O. P. CONVENTION TACTICS. *TDW*

[16] Be a good joke on the senate . . . *TDW*

[17] Title Variation: WILL HAS BUT LITTLE PRAISE FOR CONVENTION SPEAKERS. *TDW*

[18] Jesse Holman Jones (1874-1956). Financier and government official. Jones had virtually built the Houston skyline and was owner of the Houston *Chronicle;* chairman of the finance committee of the Democratic national committee (1924-1928); responsible for bringing the Democratic national convention to Houston (1928).

[19] . . . But not enough guidance to be elected. *TDW*

[20] The following lines were included in the *TDW* article, but omitted from the *NYT:*

> It looks like they have "stopped Hoover." They haven't nominated him. This convention will nominate somebody yet if they ever get around to it. I guess they will nominate Hoover, but not till they have to.

[21] Reed Smoot (1862-1941). U. S. senator from Utah (1903-1933); member of Republican national committee (1912-1920); Chairman of the resolutions committee for the Republican convention in 1928.

[22] He said that we would protect . . . *TDW*

[23] Title Variation: EVEN PREACHERS READ THEIR SPEECHES, ROGERS FOUND. *TDW*

[24] William E. Borah nominated Charles Curtis with a short, well written speech.

25 Borah nominated him with a speech, the shortest, best and most sensible of the entire convention. *TDW*

26 John L. McNab (1873-1950). California delegate who nominated Hoover for president. His speech was too long and turgid, and almost everyone was bored.

DEMOCRATIC CONVENTION OF 1928

1 Title Variation: HOUSTON HAVING ITS CALM BEFORE STORM, SAYS WILL. *TDW*

2 Jack Dempsey (1895-). World's heavyweight boxing champion (1919-1926). James J. (Gene) Tunney (1898-). Boxer who defeated Dempsey (1926); retired undefeated (1928).

3 . . . room for one back there. . . . *TDW*

4 Women's Christian Temperance Union. Founded in 1874 at Cleveland, Ohio, to fight against the saloon as a destroyer of the home and an ally to corrupt politics. This organization was a leader in the prohibition movement.

5 Title Variation: DELEGATES ARE HOT EVEN IF ISSUES ARE NOT, WILL WRITES. *TDW*

6 Waite Phillips (1883-1964). Oklahoma oilman whose mansion is now Philbrook Museum in Tulsa.

Edith (Bolling) Wilson (1872-1961). Edith Wilson was the second wife of Woodrow Wilson. They had been married while he served his first term in the White House. Mrs. Wilson later allegedly exercised the prerogatives of the president while Wilson was stricken with paralysis.

7 Dan Moody (1893-1966). Youngest governor of Texas (1926-1931). Moody was considered as Smith's running mate in the campaign of 1928, but his violent opposition to the repeal of prohibition, which Smith favored, precluded such a ticket.

8 Josephus Daniels as secretary of the navy had prohibited the use of alcoholic beverages on government vessels.

9 Alvin Victor Donahey (1873-1946). Governor of Ohio (1923-1929); U. S. senator (1935-1941).

10 Then as I write this, . . . *TDW*

11 Joseph Taylor Robinson (1872-1937). U. S. representative from Arkansas (1903-1913); U. S. senator (1913-1937). Robinson supported Smith for president in 1928 and argued that no one should be denied the right to seek the presidency because of religious preference. Robinson clashed with Senator Thomas Heflin over this issue, and Robinson carried his fight against bigotry to the Houston convention. Smith was nominated for president and Robinson received the vice-presidential position on the first ballot.

12 Title Variation: DEMOCRATS WANT A FIGHT, NOT PRAYERS, WILL LEARNS. *TDW*

13 Clem L. Shaver (1867-1954). West Virginia politician credited with John W. Davis' nomination in 1924 after Smith and McAdoo deadlocked. Shaver was chairman of the Democratic national committee and presiding officer.

14 . . . America she did, but a lot of people don't know which is the national anthem, . . . *TDW*

15 H. L. Mencken (1880-1956). Author, publisher of *American Mercury;* well known for his acid pen, and often biased criticisms.

16 Captain Tom Hickman, Texas Ranger and nationally known judge of stock shows and rodeos.

17 . . . my Texas rancher friend . . .*TDW*

18 . . . we didn't hurt anybody at this convention but wishing and praying. *TDW*

19 James "Pa" Ferguson (1871-1949). Governor of Texas (1915-1917); impeached for several reasons including meddling directly in the affairs of the University of Texas. He was a controversial governor; his wife later served as governor of Texas.

20 Claude G. Bowers (1878-1958). Author, journalist, and staunch Democrat. Bowers was a noted orator and delivered the keynote addresses at the Democratic national convention of 1920 and 1928, during which he assailed the Republicans.

21 . . . applaud the Jackson Day dinner. *TDW*

[22] You had a race. *TDW*

[23] James Reed of Missouri addressed the convention in 1928 and issued a statement in support of a dry plank. He made a bid for the support of the drys and the presidential nomination. Reed had been outspokenly opposed to President Wilson's support of the League of Nations, and although a Democrat, Reed made speeches in opposition to this Democratic policy.

[24] . . . Jesse Jones and Kennedy, . . .*TDW*

[25] Title Variation: WILL GIVES KEYNOTE TALK AT WOMEN'S BREAKFAST. *TDW*

[26] . . . given to our political women who have left their husbands out of bed and board. . . *TDW*

[27] On June 27, Will Rogers entertained at a breakfast on the roof of the Rice Hotel given in the honor of Mrs. Emily Newell Blair, retiring vice chairman of the Democratic national committee. While Rogers spoke, Mrs. Woodrow Wilson entered the room and the women, ignoring Rogers, rose to applaud the widow of the former president. Rogers interrupted his talk to introduce the famous first lady who made a few remarks and then listened to Rogers' comments. Mrs. Moody had welcomed the ladies on behalf of Texas and the governor.

[28] Oscar Odd McIntyre (1884-1938). Syndicated columnist whose column "New York Day by Day" appeared in over 300 newspapers from 1912-1938. At one point McIntyre was employed as Florenz Ziegfeld's press agent. McIntyre later wrote in his column about his dogs which gathered a large following.

[29] William States Jacobs (1871-1951). Pastor of Houston's First Presbyterian Church (1906-1932), and raised Brahman cattle. Jacobs was a noted radio lecturer and writer about social justice.

[30] He raised Brahma cattle Presbyterians. *TDW*

[31] . . . for paying his respects. . . *TDW*

[32] Title Variation: WILL GETS A BIT FED UP WITH THE WHOLE AFFAIR. *TDW*

[33] Walter Franklin George (1878-1957). U. S. senator from Georgia (1922-1951). George also was nominated for president at the convention of 1928.

[34] Charles M. Howell of Missouri nominated James A. Reed for president. Governor Albert C. Ritchie of Maryland seconded Smith's nomination. Franklin D. Roosevelt had made the nominating speech for Smith in 1924 and 1928.

[35] Title Variation: WILL SAYS ARKANSAWYERS HARD TO TAME—HE KNOWS. *TDW*

[36] Course Oklahoma didn't agree, . . . *TDW*

[37] Henry Tureman Allen (1859-1930). Commander of American occupation forces in Germany (1919-1923); nominated in 1928 for president.

[38] Thomas Pryor Gore (1870-1949). U. S. senator from Oklahoma (1907-1921; 1931-1937). Gore was blind when he served in the senate. He had opposed Smith's nomination in 1924, but supported him in 1928, after he became the Democratic nominee.

[39] Bless his old fighting heart, Jim took the floor at 12 o'clock last night and they didn't "turn the rascal out" till 1:30. *TDW*

[40] Irene Langhorne Gibson (1873-1956). Wife of Charles Dana Gibson, the artist who created the Gibson Girl using his wife as the model. Mrs. Gibson was one of five Langhorne sisters from Virginia; the others included Nancy who married Lord Astor of England and became the first lady to sit in British House of Lords. Mrs. Gibson was involved in politics and served as a delegate to the Democratic national convention in 1928 and 1932. She made a speaking tour of the South for Al Smith.

[41] But, Lord, I have looked at enough badges. . . .*TDW*

[42] *TDW* omitted the lines from "I just want to go back home. . . " to this point.

[43] Mary Pickford (1893-). (Gladys Smith), once married to Douglas Fairbanks, Sr. (1920-1935), was one of the most famous stars in the 1920's. She was known for her blond curls and in June, 1928 she made national news when she cut the curls "secretly".

[44] Graham McNamee (1888-1942). Popular radio announcer who first broadcast the presidential conventions of 1924 and 1928 for the National Broadcasting Company. He also announced sports events and was a narrator for the Universal Newsreels.

Major J. Andrew White, one of the founders of the Columbia Broadcasting

System and served as its first president. White announced many sporting events and covered the national conventions for CBS.

[45] *TDW* omitted: Yours, WILL ROGERS.

REPUBLICAN CONVENTION OF 1932

[1] The *Tulsa Daily World* carried only the daily telegram for June 12, 1932. The *Boston Globe, Los Angeles Times,* and *New York Times* published the convention article. Below is the *TDW* telegram.

Will Rogers Says: - - By Will Himself

CHICAGO, ILL., June 12.—Well, here I am, right at the stage door waiting to see all the actors in the great comedy called "a convention held for no reason at all."

I have the distinction of being the first Democrat white child to arrive at the Republican fiasco.

Breakfast at home Saturday morning, dinner in Kansas City, then into Chicago for breakfast Sunday, but disgraced myself by making the last hop on the train, as there was no regular plane. Guess I am getting old and going back, be taking up golf next.

A newspaper man spoiled my whole convention by asking me if "I was an alternate." Now a delegate is bad enough, but an alternate is just a spare tire for a delegate, an alternate is the lowest form of political life there is. He is the parachute in a plane that never leaves the ground. Yours, WILL ROGERS

[2] The Chicago Cubs played the Boston Braves Sunday, June 12, in Boston; they won the game 5-3 in the thirteenth inning. The win gave the Cubs a game and a half lead over the second place Braves for the National League title. Chicago played in the World Series of 1932, but lost the championship to the New York Yankees.

[3] Guy Terrell Bush (1901-). Baseball pitcher for the Chicago Cubs known as the "Mississippi Mudcat." Bush recorded a 19-11 record in 1932, and was starting pitcher that year in the World Series against the Yankees.

[4] Al Capone (1898-1947). Gangland figure who operated in Chicago during prohibition. In 1931 he had been sentenced to ten years' imprisonment for tax evasion.

[5] Nicholas Murray Butler (1862-1947). Professor of philosophy at Columbia University and later president (1902-1945). Butler was a staunch advocate for repeal of the eighteenth amendment, for he believed that unless the Republicans came out solidly for repeal they could not win the November elections. He lectured and debated with drys over the issue. John D. Rockefeller, Jr. (1874-1960), formerly a strong prohibition advocate, approved and supported Butler's repeal plank.

[6] Ogden Livingston Mills (1884-1937). U. S. representative from New York (1921-1927); under secretary of the treasury (1927-1932) until Andrew Mellon resigned; Mills completed the year as secretary of the treasury. Mills was a respected expert on finance and served on the U.S. House Ways and Means Committee. He served in 1920 as Republican party chairman of the committee on policies and platform.

[7] Aimee Semple McPherson (1890-1944). Evangelist with a great following during the 1920's and 1930's. She was a faith healer, and later constructed a temple in Los Angeles.

[8] Charles Spencer Chaplin (1889-). An English comedian who starred in silent films. The little tramp of Chaplin's silent films is still popular.

Amelia Earhart (1898-1937). First woman to cross the Atlantic in an airplane (1928). She disappeared on a Pacific flight in 1937.

[9] Charles Gates Dawes (1865-1951). Vice president of the United States (1925-1929). Leading financier, lawyer and politician. Originated the Dawes plan for solving the German reparation payment question. Rogers refers to Dawes' much publicized outburst against reporters in New York.

Patrick J. Hurley (1883-1963). Oklahoma Indian who served as secretary of war (1929-1933), and held other diplomatic posts. He was considered a strong vice-presidential possibility if Curtis were not reelected.

Hanford MacNider (1899-1968). Army officer and hero of both World Wars.

There was a strong movement at the convention to oust Charles Curtis as vice president. Republicans wanted to nominate Charles Dawes, but Dawes refused to run thereby crushing the movements. Curtis was renominated, for Hoover supported him.

10 *TDW* began their June 13 article here.

11 This sentence was omitted from *TDW*

12 Lester Jesse Dickinson (1873-1968). U. S. representative (1919-1931); U. S. senator (1931-1937). As temporary chairman of this convention Dickinson's keynote address was presented to an auditorium only partially filled; those in attendance were apathetic except when Hoover's name was mentioned, according to newspaper accounts. The speech was the typical denunciation of the Democratic party and praise of Hoover and his administration. Dickinson was known primarily as an orator and was called "the Demosthenes of the Steppes"; he had been mentioned as Coolidge's vice-presidential possibility in 1924 because of his oratorical ability.

13 The previous two paragraphs were switched in order of appearance in the *TDW:* "Mr. Dickinson . . . do with all the badges."

14 The previous two paragraphs were omitted from the *TDW* article: "Lots of beautiful ladies . . . ones the delegates has."

15 *TDW* was signed: "Yours, WILL ROGERS."

16 Title Variation: WILL ROGERS SAYS: *TDW*

17 Henry Lewis Stimson (1867-1950). Secretary of state in the Hoover administration(1929-1933).

18 Ernest Lee Jahncke (1877-1960). Assistant secretary of navy (1929-1933). Jahncke was the national committeeman from Louisiana at the convention of 1932.

19 William G. Skelly (1878-1957). Founder and president of the Skelly Oil Company. Skelly served as Republican national committeeman from Oklahoma (1924-1940).

20 Walter Folger Brown (1869-1961). U. S. postmaster general (1929-1933).

21 Ray L. Wilbur (1875-1949). Secretary of the navy under Coolidge; appointed secretary of the interior by President Hoover (1929-1933).

22 Paulina Longworth (1925-1957). Daughter of Congressman Nicholas Longworth and Alice Lee (Roosevelt) Longworth, close friends of Will Rogers.

23 Anton Joseph Cermak (1873-1933). Leader of Illinois Cook County Democratic party, and elected mayor of Chicago in 1931. Supported Franklin Roosevelt for president. When an assassin attempted to kill President-elect Roosevelt in 1933, he hit Cermak instead, and the mayor died of the wound.

24 Silas H. Strawn (1866-1946). Chicago lawyer and civic leader.

25 Louis Burt Mayer (1885-1957). Started as movie producer and eventually merged his movie company with others to become Metro-Goldwyn-Mayer Corporation.

26 Floyd Gibbons (1887-1939). Well-known correspondent who first reported Villa's activities in Mexico while traveling with the Mexican; Gibbons later journeyed to France with Pershing; reported the Irish Revolution (1919); Polish Revolution (1926); and the Chinese-Japanese War (1931-32) that Rogers referred to here. Gibbons sailed for the Orient on the same vessel as Rogers on November 21, 1931.

27 John Q. Tilson (1866-1958). U. S. representative from Connecticut (1909-1913; 1915-1932); state representative (1904-1908); served on the Mexican border as a lieutenant colonel of the second infantry, Connecticut National Guard (1916); delegate to this convention having declined running again for re-election.

28 *TDW* omitted all of the article up to this point.

29 . . . and don't give a d--- for any of 'em. *TDW*

30 . . . he will be brought back home . . . *TDW*

31 . . . for 'tis saying: . . . *TDW*

32 The Republican party would not take a definite stand on the prohibition issue; they adopted a wet-dry plank that Hoover accepted.

33 Title Variation: WILL ROGERS SAYS:*TDW*

34 Bertrand Snell (1870-1958). U. S. representative from New York (1915-1939). Served as permanent chairman to Republican national convention in 1932.

35 James Rolph, Jr. (1869-1934). Mayor of San Francisco (1911-1932); governor of California (1931-1934). Well known for being outspoken and gregarious.

36 James John Walker (1881-1946). Colorful mayor of New York City (1926-

1932), was being investigated at the time of the convention of 1932 over charges of negligence of duty, and absence of economic management; he resigned as mayor the same year.

[37] On June 14, Hurley gave a speech before the Women's National Republican Club at the Republican convention. Hurley stated women voters had elected Hoover in 1928.

[38] Arthur Brisbane (1864-1936). Newspaper editor who worked for both Pulitzer and Hearst owned papers. In 1917 he began his editorial column, "Today," which was eventually syndicated to 200 daily and 1200 weekly newspapers. Built Ritz Tower building, and with Hearst, the Ziegfeld Theater.

[39] Mary Louis Cecilia "Texas" Guinan (1884-1933). Actress and night club hostess who became famous as a result of her conflicts with prohibition agents.

[40] *TDW* omitted all of this article from the beginning to this point.

[41] . . . General Dawes in Washington, who was at the Willard hotel . . .*TDW*

[42] *TDW* was signed: "Yours, WILL ROGERS."

[43] Title Variation: WILL ROGERS SAYS: *TDW*

[44] Joseph L. Scott (1868-1958). Lawyer and delegate from California who renominated Hoover for president.

The Olympic Stadium in Los Angeles, California, was the site of the Olympic games of 1932, beginning on July 30.

[45] *TDW* omitted the two previous paragraphs from their article: "Our Joe Scott . . . did a good job."

[46] This sentence is found elsewhere in the *TDW* article.

[47] Joseph Irwin France (1873-1939). U. S. senator from Maryland (1917-1923). France twice offered himself to the Republican party as presidential candidate; in 1920 and 1932. In 1932 at the Republican convention he mounted the platform in an attempt to stampede the meeting to Calvin Coolidge. Ruling him out of order, Chairman Snell called the police and had France ejected.

[48] This paragraph, including the word variation, was placed differently in the *TDW* article: . . . Former Senator France . . .

[49] This paragraph is also reordered in *TDW:* . . . way you could have got Calvin Coolidge . . .

[50] This paragraph is found at the end of the *TDW* article.

[51] These two sentences were placed in different order in the *TDW* article. There is also a word variation as listed: . . . because there were 12,000. . .

[52] These two sentences also were placed differently in the *TDW* article.

[53] *TDW* omitted all of this part of the article: "From now on . . . on your hands!"

[54] *TDW* was signed: "Yours, WILL ROGERS."

DEMOCRATIC CONVENTION OF 1932

[1] Title Variation: WILL ROGERS SAYS: *TDW*

[2] At this point, the *NYT* omits 2 sentences that the *TDW* included—as follows: "It takes two-thirds to change it. If two-thirds of the Democrats agreed they wouldn't be Democrats." *TDW*

[3] There was a resolution introduced at the convention to change the rule from ⅔ to a simple majority vote for nominating the presidential candidate. (See introduction for this resolution and its consequences.)

[4] James Hamilton Lewis (1863-1939). Unsuccessful candidate for the Democratic nomination for vice president (1896, 1900). Representative from Washington (1897-1899). Moved to Illinois in 1903, and was elected U. S. senator (1913-1919; 1931-1939).

[5] William "Alfalfa Bill" Murray (1869-1956). Governor of Oklahoma (1931-1935); delegate to the Democratic national convention of 1908, 1912, 1916, and 1932.

[6] Alben William Barkley (1877-1956). U. S. representative (1913-1927); U. S. senator (1927-1949); vice president (1949-1953). He made the keynote address at the convention in which he blamed Republicans for the nation's ills.

[7] *TDW* omitted the preceding seven paragraphs from "Ham Lewis the Illinois Senator . . . " to " . . . it probably will."

[8] John Nance Garner (1868-1967). U. S. representative from Texas (1903-

1933); speaker of the house and vice president (1933-1941). Garner was definitely a potential presidential nominee at the convention of 1932.

[9] Harry Flood Byrd (1887-1966). Governor of Virginia (1926-1930); Democratic national committeeman (1928-1940); U. S. senator (1933-1965).

[10] *TDW* article was signed: Yours, WILL ROGERS.

[11] Title Variation: WILL ROGERS SAYS: *TDW*

[12] Are we going to degenerate . . . *TDW*

[13] . . . rip-snorting" Democratic convention? *TDW*

[14] *TDW* ended here with: Yours, WILL ROGERS.

[15] John J. Raskob (1879-1950). Chairman of Democratic national committee (1928).

[16] Evangeline Cory Booth (1865-1950). Leader of the Salvation Army in the U. S. for thirty years. She strongly supported prohibition and later was an ardent leader opposing its repeal.

[17] Isidore B. Dockweiler (1867-1947). Member of the Democratic national committee (1916-1932).

[18] Rogers accurately related the events of the first day of the Democratic convention. After John J. Raskob, chairman of the Democratic national committee, opened the convention, Evangeline Booth, commander of the Salvation Army in the U.S., offered a prayer. Madame Rose Zulalian of Boston then sang the "Star-Spangled Banner," Mayor Cermak welcomed the delegates; Raskob gave a short speech that included his support of the eighteenth amendment. Isidore Dockweiler of California read Jefferson's first inaugural address; then Barkley, as temporary chairman, gave a long speech praising the Democratic party and denouncing the Republicans and the Republican platform. He especially attacked their plank on prohibition for being unclear.

[19] Title Variation: WILL ROGERS SAYS: THEY FOUGHT, THEY FIT, THEY SPLIT AND ADJOURNED IN A DANDY WAVE OF DISSENSION. *TDW*

[20] Huey Pierce Long (1893-1935). U. S. senator from Louisiana (1931-1935); governor (1928-1931); Democratic national committeeman (1928-1935).

[21] June 28 after the prayer and a solo by Mrs. Howard Austin of Missouri, minority reports were given concerning the seating of delegates from Louisiana, Puerto Rico, and Minnesota—prolonged debate followed over who should be seated. When this question was finally settled, the committee on permanent organization presented two names for permanent chairman, Thomas Walsh or Jouett Shouse. Debate over which would be elected followed, with Walsh winning the majority vote. After Walsh's speech, the convention adjourned for the day.

[22] Clarence Cleveland Dill (1884-?). U. S. representative from Washington (1915-1919); U. S. senator (1923-1935); delegate to the Democratic national conventions in 1920, 1924, and 1932.

[23] Irving Berlin (1888-   ). Famous songwriter who composed lyrics for Ziegfeld Follies and other musicals.

[24] Mrs. Edward (Marjorie Post) Hutton (1887-1973). Marjorie Post was the daughter of Charles Post, founder of Postum Cereal Co. Edward Hutton was founder of the New York Stock Exchange firm of E. F. Hutton. Edward Hutton was Mrs. Post's second of four husbands.

[25] Owen D. Young (1874-1962). Attorney; associated with Charles Dawes as an American representative to the reparations conference (1924); chairman of the conference (1929); assisted in development of Young plan for German reparations.

[26] *TDW* omitted all paragraphs from: "John W. Davis, a man that knows . . . " to ". . . did hear him say."

[27] *TDW* was signed: Yours, WILL ROGERS.

[28] Title Variation: WILL ROGERS SAYS: AMOS AND ANDY WON BOTH NOMINATIONS IN FIRST SERIOUS MEETING OF 'SEANCE'. *TDW*

[29] Amos 'n Andy. Popular radio program that had begun in 1928, and was broadcast five times a week until 1943. Amos was Freeman F. Gosden and Andy was Charles J. Correll. The two actors played every male role in the series including Brother Crawford, henpecked and complaining; Kingfish, the conniver; and Lightin', the slow-mover. All the male characters belonged to a lodge, the Hall of the Mystic Knights of the Sea. Amos 'n Andy was probably the most popular radio show of the 1930's, but after the war, Negroes were offended by the blackface humor and the show ceased.

[30] "Amos and Andy" won the nomination, at the great Democratic national convention in Chicago at 10 minutes to 2 this afternoon. *TDW*

[31] Eddie Dowling (1884-1976). Actor, director, producer, and playwright who also organized and was the first president of the USO shows.

[32] . . . "stop a dry,". . . *TDW*

[33] Amon G. Carter (1879-1955). Publisher of the Fort Worth *Star-Telegram* who was called the one-man chamber of commerce of Fort Worth and West Texas; he also was influential in Dallas, and a long-time friend of the Rogers family.

[34] Melvin Traylor (1878-1934). Chicago banker nominated for president at the convention of 1932.

[35] *TDW* omitted this part of the article, beginning with: "This is the third day of the convention . . ." up to this point.

[36] On June 29, the platform committee asked for a recess so that they could conclude the platform; during the recess informal proceedings were held by Eddie Dowling. Dowling introduced many of the celebrities, the first to speak to the convention was Will Rogers. Others introduced to the convention included Clarence Darrow, Gene Tunney, Senator Thomas Gore of Oklahoma, Rear Admiral Richard Byrd, Claude Bowers, Damon Runyon, Jack Lait, Mrs. Woodrow Wilson, Alice Roosevelt Longworth, and Father Coughlin. Will Rogers introduced Amos 'n Andy. At the evening session the platform was read and minority planks were debated until 1:00 a.m.

[37] *TDW* article ended here with: Yours, WILL ROGERS.

[38] Title Variation: WILL ROGERS SAYS: *TDW*

[39] Joseph Buell Ely (1881-1956). Governor of Massachusetts (1931-1935). Ely nominated Alfred Smith for the presidency at the Democratic convention in 1932.

[40] Thomas T. Connally (1877-1963). U. S. representative from Texas (1917-1929); U. S. senator (1929-1953); delegate to the Democratic national conventions (1920, 1932, 1936, 1940, 1948); state representative (1901-1904).

[41] Pauline (Mrs. Charles) Sabin. National chairman of the Women's Organization for National Prohibition Reform. Mrs. Sabin wrote a letter to the *New York Times* to reply to a Will Rogers article that said the reason prohibition would not be repealed was "because the wrong people want it repealed." Rogers' next article explained the meaning of his "gag." Mrs. Sabin had been New York's first Republican national committeewoman, but bolted the Republican party in 1932 because of the prohibition plank.

[42] *TDW* article began here. It omitted all previous paragraphs in this article.

[43] These 2 paragraphs are the only part of this article used by the *TDW*. The *TDW* concluded their article with the following paragraphs:

> Both conventions, minds and time, have been so taken up with getting the country wet that they forgot to put in a plant to provide the price of this much talked of drink. It's going to be lawful to get a drink but not possible.
>
> Al Smith was by far the sensation of the convention and had by far the best speech.
>
> I just want to know what all these old dry officeholders that went wet overnight are going to tell those Baptist preachers back home. They are going to say: "Father, I can't tell a lie. I saw the votes coming and I had to go after 'em?"
>
> Yours,
> WILL ROGERS.

[44] Title Variation: WILL ROGERS SAYS: SOMEBODY TOUCHED HIM FOR HIS ROLL OF 22 VOTES WHEN HE WENT TO SLEEP. *TDW*

[45] On the fourth day of the convention, June 30, debate on the Democratic platform was concluded. The majority platform was accepted advocating a constitutional amendment to repeal prohibition. The question of prohibition had been the primary reason for debate. After the vote on the platform was taken, nominations for the president began. The convention recessed from 6:00 p.m. until 9:00 because radio was not broadcasting the convention during these hours. The nominations, seconding speeches, and first three ballots all continued until well into the morning.

[46] *TDW* article ended here with: Yours, WILL ROGERS.

[47] Henry S. Johnston (1869-1965). Governor of Oklahoma (1927-1929).

INDEX